NEW TESTAMENT LIES

NEW TESTAMENT LIES

◆

THE GREATEST CHALLENGE TO TRADITIONAL CHRISTIANITY

Daniel T. Unterbrink
Author of
JUDAS THE GALILEAN

iUniverse, Inc.
New York Lincoln Shanghai

NEW TESTAMENT LIES
THE GREATEST CHALLENGE TO TRADITIONAL CHRISTIANITY

Copyright © 2006 by Daniel T. Unterbrink

All rights reserved. No part of this book may be used or reproduced by any means, graphic, electronic, or mechanical, including photocopying, recording, taping or by any information storage retrieval system without the written permission of the publisher except in the case of brief quotations embodied in critical articles and reviews.

iUniverse books may be ordered through booksellers or by contacting:

iUniverse
2021 Pine Lake Road, Suite 100
Lincoln, NE 68512
www.iuniverse.com
1-800-Authors (1-800-288-4677)

ISBN-13: 978-0-595-39855-3 (pbk)
ISBN-13: 978-0-595-84254-4 (ebk)
ISBN-10: 0-595-39855-3 (pbk)
ISBN-10: 0-595-84254-2 (ebk)

Printed in the United States of America

Contents

INTRODUCTION		vii
Chapter 1	IS JESUS DEAD?	1
Chapter 2	JESUS IN HISTORY	8
Chapter 3	PILATE'S REIGN	31
Chapter 4	THE BIRTH NARRATIVES	38
Chapter 5	JOHN THE BAPTIST	49
Chapter 6	ONE TEMPLE CLEANSING OR TWO?	64
Chapter 7	BARABBAS	70
Chapter 8	JUDAS ISCARIOT	76
Chapter 9	YOU WILL INDEED DRINK FROM MY CUP	86
Chapter 10	THEUDAS AND JUDAS THE GALILEAN	92
Chapter 11	HOW MANY GOSPELS?	99
Chapter 12	PAUL AND CAESAR	108
Chapter 13	NOT ONE PERSECUTION, BUT THREE	130
Chapter 14	ACTS—A MISLEADING ACCOUNT	139
Chapter 15	JAMES, THE SADDUC	162
Chapter 16	THE FOURTH PHILOSOPHY	173
Chapter 17	WHAT WOULD JESUS DO?	188

CHAPTER 18 JESUS IS STILL DEAD	199
BIBLIOGRAPHY	209
NOTES	211

INTRODUCTION

Religion is big business, and Christianity leads in the rush for dollars. Consider how many churches pass around the collection plate at every service. Hard earned money is mindlessly passed over to those who preach the gospel, the good news of Jesus Christ. The local church is just one of the many avenues in which believers are encouraged to share their wealth. The message of Jesus routinely invades homes through mediums such as radio and television. The televangelists are itching to separate you from your money, offering prayers and tokens of Jesus' love: prayer beads, prayer towels and any item possibly touched by the hand of God. Book sales reach into the billions; the subjects ranging from the last days to Bible commentaries to everyday living. And the merchandising is endless. Jesus can be found everywhere and promoting all sorts of causes and items. As long as you keep giving, then you can remain a loyal subject to Jesus.

This multi-billion dollar empire is supported by the great minds of our time as well as those who have studied Christianity throughout the ages. Not only do the preachers and priests proclaim Jesus, but the scholars do as well. It is in the interests of those employed by the church to support the church, but does the church control the historians and scholars too? Unfortunately, the invisible hand of the church exerts the greatest pressure upon those who should be objective.

Church scholars and historians are employed by institutions. Many of these institutions are directly controlled by various churches. Consider how many universities are tied to the Catholic, Methodist or Baptist churches. Notre Dame, Boston College, SMU, and the myriad of small colleges with Baptist in the title are just a few examples. Surely, "scholars" from these universities must hold onto traditional beliefs. But what about the state colleges? The separation of church and state must provide the historians cover from the arrows of the fundamentalists. Even this is not true. State universities must be very careful not to offend donors. Historians and religious scholars risk promising careers if they express challenging theories against orthodoxy. Thus, we have historians blindly accepting the church's view of the birth of Jesus, his life and his death. Very few venture outside the rigid parameters of acceptability. That is why it is so hard to find good solid historical analysis of the timeline of Jesus and his church.

A few years ago, a fundamentalist Christian co-worker placed a newspaper article on my desk. The article claimed that the first-century ossuary of James, the brother of Jesus, had been found outside of Jerusalem. The inscription on the ossuary read: "James, son of Joseph, brother of Jesus." To the orthodox Christian, this was confirmation of the Gospel story which linked the three names in the inscription. To me, it seemed too convenient. In my thinking, Joseph was the weak link in the inscription. There was a Jesus and a James, but Joseph may have been more legend than father.

Two great Biblical scholars, Hershel Shanks and Ben Witherington III, wrote a book praising the archeological find, entitled: *The Brother of Jesus*. Positive book reviews came from *Time*, *Newsweek*, *The Wall Street Journal* and John Dominic Crossan. Could this be the Holy Grail of archeology, they all asked? For his part, Mr. Shanks insisted that Christian scholarship was nearly 100 percent sure of the ossuary's authenticity. He blasted critics, often citing their lack of publishing credentials as a way of discrediting them. He denounced Robert Eisenman, author of *James, the Brother of Jesus*, because Eisenman said the inscription was a forgery; it was "too pat." In attacking Eisenman, Mr. Shanks wrote the following:

> The first person to weigh in, almost immediately after the announcement, was an academic well known in the profession for his <u>quixotic views</u> and efforts to garner publicity. He wrote a book contending that the Teacher of Righteousness, mentioned in the Dead Sea Scrolls, was none other than our James, Jesus' brother. <u>It is a one-man theory</u>. (1) (emphasis mine)

In short, anyone outside of the insiders' "club of eternal truth" was not worthy of an opinion concerning the ossuary. Note that Eisenman was attacked for his "quixotic views," and his theory concerning James was not accepted by any other scholar, "a one-man theory." By Mr. Shanks' reasoning, anyone with a view substantially different from the upholders of traditional Christianity, must be dismissed. He refused to even mention the lowly Robert Eisenman by name, but denigrated Eisenman's character and beliefs as a way of exalting himself and his "club of eternal truth."

This same attitude of presumed superior knowledge will be brought out against my book. It is true that my theory is a "one-man theory," but Mr. Shanks' arrogance does not disprove my research. Although I am a lowly Medicare auditor by trade, I am in the habit of finding answers to difficult questions. I challenge him and his "club of eternal truth" to disprove my findings. After all, was not the "club" right concerning the ossuary? Not quite! The ossuary was recently proved a fake. How could the defenders of the truth have all been wrong? This muddy reasoning by the "club" has been defining right and wrong for too long. As you read my book, please be skeptical, but at least be open to my ideas. A closed mind can make colossal errors. Isn't that right, Mr. Shanks?

To understand Jesus, should we go back to Martin Luther, or to Augustine, to Jerome, to the Gospel writers (Matthew, Mark, Luke and John), to Paul the apostle or to the only historian of this period of Jewish history, Josephus? Certainly the closer we get to the time of Jesus, the better chance we have of discovering truth. The earliest documents come from Paul, ranging anywhere from 40-55 AD. Josephus wrote the *Jewish War* in 75 AD and *Antiquities of the Jews* in 93 AD. The Slavonic Josephus is another version of the *War*, comprising most of the Greek version with additional information in some instances and less information in other places. This was written by Josephus, and additions to it are either from the pen of Josephus or from an early Jewish Christian. For example, while Josephus did not write about John the Baptist in the *War*, a wild man who baptized in the Jordan is mentioned three different times in the Slavonic version. However, these notices of John are not orthodox, leading one to believe that they were inserted into the text at a very early date. (Narratives that go against the grain of traditional or orthodox teachings are most likely authentic, while orthodox statements generally reflect the church at a much later time. The mention of Jesus in *Antiquities* is no doubt a later interpolation as that particular passage makes it appear as if Josephus was a practicing Christian; and nothing could be further from the truth!) The Gospels were written some time after Josephus, with Mark the earliest and John the latest. All other documents from later writers are dependent upon these earliest of accounts of Jesus and his time.

In this book, the greatest weight will be given to Paul's writings, the letter of James and to Josephus, including the Slavonic Josephus. Paul's letters are the earliest record we have, but these letters should be assessed very carefully in regards to reliable information. Paul had his own agenda, and this agenda was much different than the Jerusalem apostles, represented by James, John and Peter. Josephus, on the other hand, had his own biases, which must be acknowledged before taking him at his word. He had a disdain for the poor and for those who represented the poor, calling them bandits and thieves. This feeling came from his own upbringing and his personal experiences with the bandit leaders. In any event, Paul, James and Josephus will be the primary sources of information.

The secondary sources will be the Gospels and Acts and other very early writings such as the Pseudoclementine literature. (The Pseudoclementine literature is an alternative to the book of Acts, where Paul was cast as the enemy and not the hero of the story.) The Gospels and Acts must be dealt with carefully because much of the information has been sanitized or changed from the original in order to serve orthodoxy. For example, Paul wrote about the central three apostles, called the Pillar apostles. They were Cephas (Peter), James and John. For Paul, James and John were brothers, related to Jesus. In the Gospels, the central three were also named Peter, James and John. Except here, James and John were brothers, and sons of Zebedee, an unrelated figure to Jesus. Which were the correct central three? Obviously, the Pillar apostles of Paul were the real deal. The Gospels changed the three for some reason. In this book, we will find out exactly why this and many other changes were made.

◆   ◆   ◆

I have entitled this book, *New Testament Lies, The Greatest Challenge to Traditional Christianity*. The New Testament is supposed to be the good book, the book of truth. How on earth can anyone claim that this masterpiece by God is not true? And if it is not true, then how can a false document be used to prove its own invalidity? Truth and lies can be combined in various combinations to produce misleading information. For example, if I tell you that your mother wants to meet you at Starbucks at two o'clock to discuss her recent doctor's appointment, then I have given you four pieces of information: the who, the where, the when and the why. Suppose I knew that your mother wanted to meet you at noon, but knowingly gave the time of two o'clock instead. Would I be lying to you? After all, I did properly relate the who, the where and the why. By misleading you as to the when, you no doubt missed your mother, and probably broke her heart as well. This, indeed, was a calculated lie, insidious as it was wrapped in layers of truth.

This modus operandi is prevalent throughout the Gospels and the book of Acts. For example, in Acts chapter 10, Simon Peter was summoned to Caesarea, where he met the Gentile, Cornelius, and summarily <u>included</u> him within the church. In *Antiquities*, a Simon was summoned to Caesarea to answer to King Agrippa for his teachings of <u>exclusion</u>. The person (Simon), the place (Caesarea) and the time (approximately 43 AD) were all the same. However, the "why" was changed from exclusion to inclusion.

Another example of Acts' working method concerns the imprisonment of James and Simon Peter in chapter 12. In this traditional story, James was put to death by the sword while Simon Peter miraculously escaped. At this same time, according to Josephus, James and Simon, the sons of Judas the Galilean, were imprisoned and then crucified. Although the people were different in the two stories, the same names were used, Simon and James. Both accounts involved imprisonment and death and occurred in the late 40's. Is this story a coincidence in that a Simon and James were the main characters? If this was the only case, then it would be a coincidence. But this same type of history occurs over and over, throughout the book of Acts. In fact, it appears as if the entire history of the early church is complete fiction, based upon real events in the writings of Paul and of Josephus.

But why would the authors of the New Testament write a fictional account of Jesus and the early Jewish church? Did they have something to hide? The answer to this last question is a resounding yes! It is my contention that the true Jesus was the most important historical figure of first-century Israel. To Josephus, Jesus was known as Judas the Galilean.

Josephus provided a wealth of information concerning Judas, a Messiah figure of the day. (This was not Judas Iscariot. That Judas was pure myth and is detailed in Chapter Eight). The famous Judas of first-century Israel was Judas the Galilean. This Judas did the same things that the Gospel Jesus did; he cleansed the Temple, was proclaimed Messiah and founded his own philosophy, termed the Fourth Philosophy. Josephus wrote about Judas, his sons and his grandson. Yet no one knows about him today.

On the other hand, Josephus wrote nothing of the life or movement of Jesus. Only a third or fourth century interpolation exists within his writings. This lone message of Jesus sounds more like a later creed than the skeptical writings of Josephus. This lack of information concerning Jesus is as compelling as the wealth of information concerning Judas. Did Josephus miss out on the greatest story ever told? I do not think he missed one thing.

This book will try to prove the following hypothesis: Jesus was the title for Judas the Galilean. It is my view that Josephus wrote extensively about Jesus but used his known name to outsiders: Judas the Galilean. Jesus was a title for Judas just as Peter (Rock) was a nickname or title for Simon. If this is true, then the whole history of Christianity will be turned upside down.

By using an earlier time frame for Jesus and the early church, the hero of Christianity, Paul, becomes the enemy of the Jewish disciples of Jesus. Since Paul's gospel concerning grace is the centerpiece of traditional Christianity, any attack on Paul is an affront to orthodoxy. Thus, the hypothesis of Jesus being Judas the Galilean is the greatest challenge to traditional Christianity.

◆ ◆ ◆

Organization of this book is by topic. Individuals such as John the Baptist, Judas Iscariot, Barabbas, Pilate, and James, the brother of Jesus, all have separate chapters devoted to them. Events such as the birth narratives and the temple cleansings are also examined. Broad topics, including Paul's gospel message and the history of the Fourth Philosophy, are handled after a firm foundation has been laid. In short, most areas which have baffled scholars throughout the centuries have been addressed. To make these topics understandable, I have included many timelines, which include the traditional history and my revised history, based upon my Judas the Galilean hypothesis.

To avoid confusion, the following terminology must be understood: the term Fourth Philosophy is synonymous with Jewish Christianity and Judas the Galilean with Jesus. Sometimes I will use Judas/Jesus in the text. It must be understood that Jewish Christianity (Fourth Philosophy) was a totally different movement than the Gentile Christianity of Paul. (This Gentile Christianity is the basis of today's traditional or orthodox Christianity.) That is why James and Paul had such different views concerning the interpretation of the Law. James upheld the Law while Paul preached his new gospel of "grace," a doctrine which abandoned the Law. In addition, Paul was also named Saul in Acts and in Josephus. Paul was simply a Christian nickname for Saul.

Since the writings of Josephus are instrumental in deciphering the New Testament, references to his two great works are placed within the text, saving the reader time from constantly flipping back and forth from the Notes. In the text, *Antiquities of the Jews* and *The Jewish War* will be noted as *Ant.* and *War.*

1

IS JESUS DEAD?

As it stands today after two thousand years, Christianity is dependent upon irrational thinking. This irrational mindset not only corrupts the clergy but scholars as well. In no other historical endeavor does the scholar put aside the rational in order to follow the unlikeliest scenario. Traditional Christianity or Pauline Christianity was founded among people without first-hand information concerning Jesus, and today's religious establishment is dependent upon this shaky foundation for the current belief system about Jesus and his church.

The traditional view of Christianity, held by Catholics, Protestants and Fundamentalists, goes something like this. Jesus was born somewhere between 4 BC and 6 AD, lived thirty-three years and died between 30-33 AD. (Do not attempt the math. It will never make sense to the rational mind.) The beginning of his ministry coincided with the end of John the Baptist's sojourn in the desert (approximately 30 AD). Jesus taught his disciples a new brand of religion, unlike that of the Pharisees and teachers of the law. This new covenant with mankind superceded the old Jewish covenant and therefore abolished the law and its symbol, circumcision. Because of this radical new philosophy and the fact that Jesus was hailed as the Son of God, the Pharisees and teachers of the law had Jesus arrested for blasphemy. The Romans, represented by Pilate, were forced to carry out the will of the Jewish people, the crucifixion of Jesus.

Three days after the crucifixion, Jesus appeared to Mary, Peter, James and the other apostles. For many weeks, Jesus explained the Scriptures behind his death and resurrection, and laid the foundation for His Holy Church. From that time forward, the Holy Spirit would cleanse the souls of all those who called upon His name. This grace was certainly a familiar concept for the apostles, for Jesus had taught them these very things for over three years while he worked his wonders in the land of Israel.

Oh, those silly apostles! Within days of Jesus' return to heaven, the apostles were preaching at the Temple and slowly returning to their pre-Jesus beliefs. Was the law necessary? Must everyone be circumcised? The Old Testament Scriptures said yes, but Jesus said no. If it were not for the conversion of Paul, the teachings of Jesus may have been lost forever. Paul met Jesus in a vision and came to understand the true teachings of Jesus. It was now up to Paul to teach the apostles the truth, his gospel received directly from the Risen Christ.

God even tried to help Paul in re-converting the apostles to Jesus. In Acts chapter 10, Peter was shown a vision which convinced him to include a Gentile, Cornelius, into the church without circumcision. Peter explained his actions to James, the brother of Jesus, but James was slow in understanding. Paul had to convince James at the Council of Jerusalem to fully accept Gentiles. James finally believed and the church became one in Christ, Jews and Gentiles together. Thanks to Paul, the Jews were put back on the path instituted by Jesus.

This traditional view claims that Jesus preached the NEW religion, the apostles lapsed into the OLD religion (Judaism), and Paul once again preached the NEW religion. This logic is questionable in that all contradictory evidence in the New Testament is ignored and all other historical documents, such as Josephus' writings, are totally discounted. When we take the whole of the New Testament and Josephus together, we arrive at a totally different place. In the hypothesis put forward in this book, Jesus taught the OLD law, the apostles followed Jesus' teachings, and it was Paul who introduced the NEW religion. That is why the Jews turned their backs upon Paul as related in the book of Galatians.

So how did the traditional viewpoint become so ingrained in our minds? Much of the problem has to do with our understanding of the New Testament. We assume that the Gospels should be read first as this is the history of Jesus. But these four documents were not written until the early second century, and they have an unmistakable anti-Jewish bias. The first documents to be read are the first four letters of Paul: Romans, 1 and 2 Corinthians and Galatians. In these documents, we are given the Pauline philosophy, but also some history of Paul's relations with Peter and James. Paul claimed that his gospel was something that man did not invent. In fact, Paul's gospel was obtained through the Risen Christ, not from Peter and James, the Pillars of the Jerusalem church. In the book of Galatians, Paul admitted that the Jews turned their backs upon him and his gospel. This is totally different than the sanitized version of history as depicted by Acts.

In conjunction with Paul's slanted history of events, one must read Josephus' works, *The Jewish War* and *Antiquities of the Jews*, written well before the Gospels. Josephus never wrote of a Jewish party which resembled the Gospel movement led by Jesus. In fact, Josephus did not mention Christianity at all, but he did write about Jewish revolutionaries who often were crucified. These figures were fully Jewish in nature, following the law and preaching circumcision. When this is taken into consideration, the traditional story of Christianity becomes very hard to believe.

◆ ◆ ◆

After the death of Jesus at the hands of Roman authority, the apostles gathered in Jerusalem and preached a new and radical message. Peter said, "Therefore let all Israel be assured of this: God has made this Jesus, whom you crucified, both Lord and Christ." (Acts 2:36) According to Acts, about three thousand were added to their small band in one day. But what of the thousands who did not believe the apostles? What were they thinking? Why did they refuse to believe?

Jerusalem was the spiritual center of Judaism in the first century AD. All Jewish sects were represented: the Essenes, Pharisees, Sadducees, and the Fourth Philosophy of Judas the Galilean. For the Jesus movement to gain ground among the people, it had to compete with these groups. If one was a member of another group, it would have been so easy to ask the question: where is Jesus now? After all, Jesus' crucifixion would have turned away a multitude of potential followers. It may have been much easier to follow living leaders as opposed to a resurrected one.

Even though resurrection was accepted by Essenes, Pharisees and the Fourth Philosophy, the claims of Peter and the apostles must have seemed incredible. A dead man had risen and was now both Lord and Christ. Those who overcame their grave doubts became disciples, but to the unbelievers, Jesus was dead, never to return.

At the very beginnings of the church, these passing days, weeks, months and years made it a certainty that Christianity would not survive within the Jewish boundaries. If Jesus was standing at the right hand of the Father as Stephen claimed (Acts 7:56), then the Jews could logically expect him to help in their fight against their Roman oppressors. Opponents of the Jewish Christians must have reveled whenever an event did not warrant an answer by Jesus. This must have embarrassed and maddened the disciples, yet Jesus still did not return.

Even at the writing of Revelation, many Christian Jews believed that Jesus would return and defeat the Romans.

> With justice he judges and makes war. His eyes are like blazing fire, and on his head are many crowns.... He is dressed in a robe dipped in blood, and his name is the Word of God. The armies of heaven were following him.... Out

of his mouth comes a sharp sword with which to strike down the nations.... Then I saw the beast [Rome on the seven hills] and the kings of the earth and their armies gathered together to make war against the rider and his army. (Revelation 19:11-20)

The beast referred to above is none other than Rome. In Revelation 17:5-9, the writer clarifies what is represented by the seven heads of the beast. "The seven heads are seven hills on which the woman sits." The seven hills are the seven hills of Rome. No other explanation makes sense.

Jesus was to return in glory and defeat Israel's opponents, namely Rome, the most powerful nation on earth. However, according to history, the Roman army surrounded Jerusalem and beat down its walls, destroying the Temple and those brave enough to fight to the last. In 73 AD, the last vestige of resistance against Rome was shattered at Masada. The small group of Jewish resistors committed suicide rather than becoming toys for Roman cruelty. And still, Jesus did not come!

The Jesus movement among the Jews was doomed to failure. Unless he returned in glory and power, the hope of his return would dim with each passing event. Could the Jews be blamed? The disciples of Jesus did promise a powerful return with Jesus at the right hand of God. Only God could have defeated Rome. When God did not intervene, the credibility of Jesus was obliterated.

This book will attempt to answer the questions we have today concerning the very early church. Did Jesus preach against the Everlasting Covenant with the Jews or did that come from Paul? How did an entirely Jewish movement become a Gentile enterprise? When and why did this happen? Could the Jews have been blamed for believing that Jesus was still dead?

THE FOURTH PHILOSOPHY

Josephus is the source for nearly all information concerning first-century Israel. His two major works are the *Jewish War* and *Antiquities of the Jews*. The *War* focuses mainly on the years leading up to the war with Rome and the eventual conflict with Rome (66-73 AD). *Antiquities* is divided into twenty books. The Old Testament stories are the focus of the first eleven books. Book twelve introduces Judas Maccabee and his brothers, and their fight for Jewish independence. Books seventeen through twenty relate the stories of Herod the Great, up to the beginnings of the war with Rome.

Near the end of Herod the Great's life, Josephus began his testimony concerning Judas the Galilean and his new philosophy, termed the Fourth Philosophy.

This Fourth Philosophy dominated the narrative of Josephus. From 4 BC to 73 AD, Josephus wrote of Judas, his sons and his grandson. No other rabbi was given such lavish treatment, yet very few now remember anything about Judas the Galilean.

A few examples of this memory loss will make my point. Alvar Ellegard, author of *Jesus—One Hundred Years Before Christ*, does mention that Josephus included a fourth philosophy, "that of the Zealots," but he says little else of the movement or its founder, Judas the Galilean.(1) Instead, he focuses on the Essenes and tries in vain to tie Jesus exclusively to this group and the Righteous Teacher of 100 BC. Many scholarly books do this one better: they totally ignore the Fourth Philosophy. A Harvard educated Ohio State University professor has the *Foundations of Christianity* in his library. This book, written in 1970 by J. Bruce Burke (Michigan State University) and James B. Wiggins (Syracuse University), actually details five forms of Judaism: the Pharisees, the Sadducees, the Essenes, Hellenistic Judaism and Pauline Christianity.(2) Missing from their list is the Fourth Philosophy of Judas the Galilean or Jewish Christianity. Indicted in this gross omission are the Ivy League, the Big Ten and the Big East. In fact, most scholars from all sections of this country and abroad have little to say about Judas the Galilean.

But not all scholars are ignorant of Judas the Galilean. S.G.F. Brandon wrote this in *The Trial of Jesus of Nazareth*, "Judas, himself a Galilean, would doubtless have been a hero of Jesus' boyhood, and it is likely that Jesus knew many of the followers…because they were zealous for the God of Israel—men who had taken to the desert and whose exploits were eagerly recounted as the latter-day Maccabees."(3) Brandon did not identify Jesus with Judas because he held the traditional dating for Pilate and Jesus' crucifixion. This traditional dating made it impossible for Brandon to associate a 6 AD Judas with a 30 AD Jesus. Therefore, further investigation into the similarities between the two men was never entertained.

It is interesting to note that the story of Jesus and the apostles is curiously missing from Josephus' first-century account. Did Jesus really exist? If he did exist, and if he was an influential teacher, a Messiah figure, could Josephus have flat out ignored him? This would be like recounting Yankee baseball history and omitting Babe Ruth. I believe Jesus did exist, but was given another name by Josephus. Could Jesus have been the title or nickname for Judas the Galilean?

Judas the Galilean and his followers did the same things that Jesus and his apostles did: temple cleansings, crucifixions, prisoner releases, and teachings. The names were the same. There were Simons, Judases and James in both movements. It will be my job to relate the many similarities between this Fourth Philosophy and Jewish Christianity. One thing is certain: Josephus called Judas the Galilean a wise man and a clever rabbi, but never once mentioned Jesus' life. I believe Josephus was obsessed with Jesus, but referred to him by the outsider's name of Judas the Galilean.

WHY JUDAS WAS FORGOTTEN

The New Testament recounts the story of Jesus just as Josephus tells the story of Judas the Galilean. When Judas or Jesus did not return to rescue the Jews from the Roman army, the influence of the Fourth Philosophy or Jewish Christianity waned in Jewish circles. How could a Jew put his faith in a resurrected Messiah who refused to be King? The Jewish war with Rome also thinned the ranks of the fanatical followers of Judas/Jesus.

As for the recording of the Fourth Philosophy, Josephus was the only contributor. His references to the movement were often derogatory in nature. Although he did call Judas the Galilean a clever rabbi and a wise man, the term most used to describe the movement was bandits. According to Brandon, this may be the reason why later (current) scholars have overlooked the connection between the Fourth Philosophy and Jesus.(4) Jesus could never have been associated with such evildoers! Even though Jesus was crucified between two bandits, we are led to believe there was nothing in common between Jesus and these poor souls.

The obvious bias of Josephus against the followers of Judas the Galilean has colored our view of these nationalists. However, Brandon stated that the view of these nationalists may have changed after World War II, where the French Resistance worked against Nazi occupation by using tactics involving "assassinations and murder."(5) It depends on who you consider good and who you consider bad. If the Nazis were evil then the resistance was good, even though murder was a useful tool in the nationalists' arsenal. Many Jews considered the Roman occupation of Israel as evil, so that the movement of Judas may have been viewed favorably by the masses. If we view it more favorably, then one large hurdle has been overcome in our attempt to tie Jesus to this popular movement.

By 75 AD, the Fourth Philosophy (Jewish Christianity) was smashed. What was left of Christianity after the Jewish war were the congregations founded by Paul. But this Christianity was much different than the original Jewish brand. The law was not central to this religion, and Jesus was a spiritual redeemer, not an earthly Messiah. That is why Paul's version of Jesus' teachings survived while the original was lost to history.

Pauline Christianity distanced itself from the Jewish model partly due to theological differences (grace vs. law), and due to practical concerns, Jews being persecuted throughout the Roman Empire. Before the Jewish war, Jews were expelled or persecuted in Rome in 19 AD, 50 AD and 64 AD. The Roman historian, Suetonius, said that because the "Jews at Rome caused continuous disturbances at the instigation of Chrestus, he [Claudius] expelled them from the city."(6) It was the <u>Jewish Christians</u> who were persecuted by Claudius. The most famous persecution occurred in 64 AD, after the Great Fire. Nero mercilessly tortured the Christians, again the Jewish Christians. After the Jewish war, Jews were persecuted throughout the Empire. These persecutions forced the Gentile Christians to disassociate themselves from Judaism: Jesus changed from a Jewish revolutionary and Messiah to an other-worldly redeemer.

We will examine Paul, his teachings and his relationship to Cephas, John and James, the Pillars of the early Jewish Christian church. It will become obvious that Paul taught an entirely new religion, our current Christianity. Lost were the original apostles. Lost was Jesus. And lost was Judas the Galilean. In their places moved mythical characters, created to advance the Gentile Christian message.

Throughout this book, the Gospels and Acts will be shown to be full of contradictions and falsehoods. By compiling a large collection of curious events (coincidences), I hope to unsettle the traditional views of Christianity. Any one coincidence can happen by mere chance, but the sheer volume of chance events will boggle the mind. When this is digested, the reader will have to reevaluate his/her views on Christianity. Each person will have to ask this fundamental question: Is Jesus Dead? If Jesus is physically dead and not resurrected, then what does that mean to you spiritually? Is it possible that a dead Messiah figure can inspire, just as the mythical Jesus has inspired people throughout the ages? These questions are important to the believer but cannot be answered by history. They can only be answered by the lessons you learn from history. For example, Jesus taught us to love our neighbors as ourselves. Does Jesus' death diminish his message?

2

JESUS IN HISTORY

Jesus was the most influential person who lived and taught in first-century Israel. It would seem logical that he would have been written about by contemporaries. But that part of the Jesus story is puzzling. How could this giant of his time be ignored by historians such as Josephus, Tacitus and Suetonius? This treatment of Jesus is akin to omitting Babe Ruth from baseball greats of the 1920's and 30's or Hitler from the causes of World War II. Surely no historian would make such glaring mistakes of omission. Unfortunately, Jesus has been ignored by history other than the New Testament.

The only mention of anything related to Jesus by Tacitus concerned the Fire of Rome in 64 AD. Nero blamed the Christians for the fire and mercilessly murdered them in retaliation. From this, we know that the followers of Jesus were scattered throughout the cities of the Roman Empire, but nothing further concerning Jesus was revealed. (*Annals* xv.44) Suetonius also mentioned the Jews who were followers of a "Crestus," causing disturbances in Rome around 50 AD. (*Twelve Caesars*, Claudius 25) But once again, Jesus was not detailed in any way. It is interesting to note that the Jews who followed "Crestus" or Christ were causing disturbances in Rome. In the traditional view of Christianity, the Christians were law abiding, meek individuals. However, this report by Suetonius puts the Jewish Christians in the same camp as those from the Fourth Philosophy. One reason for this disturbance in Rome could have been a reaction against the government for the crucifixion of two of Judas the Galilean's sons. (*Ant*. 20.102)

Josephus wrote about Jewish history, from the beginnings to the war with Rome, ending in 73 AD. Surely, Jesus would prominently appear in his history. After all, Jesus was a sensation according to the Gospels. Jesus walked on water, raised people from the dead, healed the blind and crippled, produced matter in the feeding of the five thousand, and his teachings confounded all the teachers of the day. Josephus would have had a field day with this subject matter. Amazingly, there is nothing written about Jesus except one questionable passage which seems more like a later creed than the skeptical writings of Josephus. This passage is reproduced below.

> Now, there was about this time Jesus, a wise man, if it be lawful to call him a man, for he was a doer of wonderful works—a teacher of such men as receive the truth with pleasure. He drew over to him both many of the Jews, and many of the Gentiles. He was [the] Christ; and when Pilate, at the suggestion of the principal men amongst us, had condemned him to the cross, those that loved him at the first did not forsake him, for he appeared to them alive again the third day, as the divine prophets had foretold these and ten thousand other wonderful things concerning him; and the tribe of Christians, so named for him, are not extinct at this day. (*Ant.* 18.63,64)

According to this lone passage about Jesus, Josephus appeared to be a believer, calling Jesus a wise man and the Christ. Josephus must also have believed in the resurrection if this passage is legitimate. If this were the case, then Josephus would have mentioned Jesus and his movement throughout his narrative of the Jews. After all, we know that the leader of the Christian movement after Jesus was his brother, James. James was a powerful force in Jerusalem as noted in Acts 21:17-21 and *Ant.* 20.200. If Christianity was so powerful in Jerusalem and abroad, then Josephus could not have been blind to it all.

In fact, the passage above was a forgery, replacing something else from the pen of Josephus.(1) In this section of Josephus, the years 19 through 37 are curiously missing. The beginnings of the church have been removed and this spurious passage was inserted. Why was this done? A careful reading of Josephus shows that the historian did speak to a powerful movement in Judea and beyond. This movement was led by Judas the Galilean, not Jesus of Nazareth. The forgery and the expunged material simply helps hide the true history of the time. Was Judas the Galilean the historical Jesus? Josephus wrote about Judas, from his first public mission to his followers' last stand at Masada (73 AD). It is remarkable that Josephus omitted one detail from the story of Judas, that being his death. Could the spurious Jesus passage have replaced the story of Judas' death?

The following pages list forty similarities between Jesus of Nazareth and Judas the Galilean. Some are general in nature and others quite specific. Although any such listing does not prove a 100% foolproof case, the odds overwhelmingly favor my hypothesis that Jesus was simply the title for Judas the Galilean. Of these forty similarities, let's assume that there is a one in two chance of each event happening to Jesus in the time of Pilate and Judas a generation earlier. The mathematical formula for this would be 2 to the 40th power, or put simply: there would be one chance in 1.1 trillion that Jesus and Judas were separate individuals. Although my case is not 100% certain, this would come very close—99.999….%. And consider this: would the release of prisoners in 4 BC (the Barabbas event) be only one chance in two or would it be one chance in a thousand, or a million? Likewise, the release of prisoners on the Passover would not be one in two but one in three, in that three pilgrim festivals were celebrated by the Jews each year. As you can see, the one chance in 1.1 trillion of Jesus and Judas being separate people is a gross understatement of the odds favoring my hypothesis. To put it another way: would you risk your life savings on a lottery where you had only one chance to lose out of 1.1 trillion?

To further illustrate the odds against Judas and Jesus being separate individuals, just two similarities will be considered. Josephus stated that Judas was the author of the Fourth Philosophy. (The other three philosophies—the Sadducees, Pharisees and Essences—were founded in the second century BC.) To begin a new philosophy was no ordinary undertaking. According to Josephus, this one new philosophy dominated the Jewish scene until the war with Rome had ended. In that particular time frame, 4 BC–73 AD, Josephus never wrote one word about Christianity. Could Christianity have been like the Stealth bomber, hovering about, but never seen? The odds of this would be one in a million, conservatively. A second event concerning Barabbas also has long odds. Josephus wrote in the *War* and *Antiquities* of a Barabbas-style prisoner release in 4 BC but never again mentioned such an event. Again, could this have occurred under the leadership of the ruthless Pilate in 30 AD? The odds of this would be a million to one, conservatively. Thus, these two similarities, when put together, would yield the formula 1,000,000 to the 2nd power, or one chance in a trillion. How do you ignore these odds?

SIMILARITIES—JUDAS THE GALILEAN AND JESUS

1. Jesus was born in 8-4 BC (Matthew) and in 6 AD at the Census of Cyrenius (Luke). Judas was mentioned by Josephus in 4 BC (Temple Cleansing—*Ant.* 17.149-167) and in 6 AD, regarding the census of Cyrenius (*Ant.* 18.1-10). In Chapter Four, the birth narratives in Matthew and Luke are both proved inconsistent with the reign of Pilate and the ministry of John the Baptist. Neither account appears historical. These two birth narratives were placed in an era when Judas was active as an adult. The reason for this deception is clear: to move the adult Jesus thirty years away from Judas the Galilean and thus hide the Messiah's true identity. This misdirection by the Gospel writers has worked brilliantly. Very few scholars have even considered Jesus outside of the 30 AD time frame.

This is even more disturbing considering Jesus' brother, James, was purported to be 96 years old in 62 AD. Even if this is a slight exaggeration by ten years, James' birth can be estimated to be around 35-25 BC. Jesus was the older brother and could not have been born any earlier than 25 BC.

2. Both Jesus and Judas cleansed the Temple in Jerusalem. (Matt. 21:12,13)(*Ant.* 17:149-167) Actually, Judas probably cleansed the Temple twice. The first cleansing was the Golden Eagle Temple Cleansing where Matthias and he were captured by Herod the Great. The second cleansing can be deduced from inference. Judas the Galilean's son, Menahem, followed his father's modus operandi and seized an armory before marching on Jerusalem. Menahem promptly cleansed the Temple after being hailed as Messiah by his followers. It is most probable that Judas the Galilean marched on Jerusalem after 6-7 AD (after the census) and cleansed the Temple as a Messianic act. It is interesting to note that the Gospel of John placed the Temple cleansing at the beginning of Jesus' career (John 2:12-25) while the Synoptic Gospels have it at the end of his ministry. What are the odds of two separate men cleansing the Temple once, not to say twice. Outside of the cleansing in 4 BC (Judas) and the cleansing by his son, Menahem, Josephus does not record one other Temple cleansing from 4 BC to 66 AD. It was certainly not an everyday occurrence.

The 4 BC Temple Cleansing concerned the Golden Eagle which was a graven image paying homage to Rome. The Slavonic Josephus verified that the Golden Eagle was in honor of Caesar and was even named "the Golden-winged Eagle."(2) Josephus stated that Pilate brought his standards into Jerusalem in 19 AD, right before the crucifixion of Jesus. These standards had the eagle upon them, the symbol of Rome. In both Temple cleansings, the power of Rome was attacked by Judas/Jesus. (See Chapter Six—One Temple Cleansing or Two?)

3. Jesus and Judas were both called the Galilean. Actually, Jesus was referred to as Jesus of Nazareth, a city located near Sepphoris in Galilee. It is possible that this is a corruption of Nazirite as there are no references to Nazareth in the Old Testament or in Josephus. In fact, John Crossan stated that in addition to Josephus' silence concerning Nazareth, "it is never mentioned by any of the Jewish rabbis whose pronouncements are in the Mishnah or whose discussions are in the Talmud."(3) Jesus' disciples were called Galileans (Mk. 14:70) and it may have been a sleight-of-hand which changed Jesus the Galilean to Jesus of Nazareth. In John 7:41, the crowd asked, "How can the Christ come from Galilee?" And the leaders

had the same reservations about Jesus. "Look into it, and you will find that a prophet does not come out of Galilee." (John 7:52)

Judas the Galilean was mentioned in several passages by Josephus (*War* 2.118; *War* 2.433 and *Ant.* 20.102). Josephus did state that this Judas was from Gamala, across the river Jordan (*Ant.* 18.4) but he was known as the Galilean, as attributed by the above references. Galilee was a hotbed for revolutionaries. Both Jesus and Judas would have had a similar background, influenced by those who had struggled for years against Herod the Great.

4. Judas opposed the Roman tax and Jesus was crucified for the charge of opposing the tax. (Luke 23:2)(*Ant.* 18.4) The era of Judas (4 BC–19 AD) related to the tax issue. At the Barabbas-style prisoner release, the Jewish crowd demanded the release of prisoners, the easing of annual payments and the removal of an onerous sales tax. (*Ant.* 17.204-205) Judas then led a tax revolt at the time of the census (6 AD) but this did not end the extortion by Rome. Tacitus stated that Judea was exhausted by its tax burden (16-18 AD). (*Annals*, ii.42) This struggle against Roman taxation was well documented by both Tacitus and Josephus.

Jesus did not oppose every tax, but his hatred of Roman taxation is beyond doubt. "Give to Caesar what is Caesar's and to God what is God's" was <u>not</u> a pro-tax message. Jesus was saying this: take your money with Caesar's portrait and leave our country. This statement went well beyond a yes or no answer to the tax question. To "Give God what is God's" harkened the Jews back to the days of Judas Maccabee and his struggle for Jewish independence. This is why Jesus was crucified by the Romans.

Paul, on the other hand, taught his disciples to pay their taxes to Rome without hesitation (Rom. 13:1-7). This accommodation to Roman taxation is totally opposite the view of Judas/Jesus. Many people read Paul's view into the interpretation of Jesus' statement, "Give to Caesar what is Caesar's and to God what is God's." But we must remember that Jesus was crucified and that death was not a result of upholding Roman taxation.

5. According to Josephus, Judas founded the Fourth Philosophy during his fight with Herod the Great and Rome (*Ant.* 18.1-10). Jesus was credited with the founding of Christianity, a new religion. This religion of Jesus was never mentioned by Josephus, an amazing omission.

The Fourth Philosophy joined the earlier philosophies of the Pharisees, Sadducees and Essenes. This Fourth Philosophy was similar to that of the Pharisees except that followers of Judas were extremely nationalistic. Also, Judas' disciples shared some practices with the Essenes. Thus, the nationalistic movement had drawing power away from the other philosophies. This may explain why John the Essene was a leader in the war against Rome. Essenes were known as pacifists, so the mention of a warlike Essene has confounded scholars. This John the Essene was no doubt influenced by the Fourth Philosophy.

In reading the New Testament, one must admit that Jesus was often quite friendly with the Pharisees. He did blast those who loved themselves more than their fellow Jews, but his overall feelings for the Pharisees was positive. "You are not far from the kingdom of heaven," Jesus said to one Pharisee (Mark 12:34). In addition, Jesus preached using parables, a mode of teaching practiced by the Pharisees. Thus, like Judas, Jesus was very close to the Pharisees in belief and action.

6. Josephus detailed the life but not the death of Judas while mentioning the death but not the life of Jesus. Josephus invested much effort in recounting Judas' life, even touching upon the lives of his sons, Judas, Simon and Menahem and his descendent, or grandson, Eleazar. (*Ant.* 20.102; *War* 2.433,434; *War* 7.253) It is probable that the death of Judas was removed by a Gentile Christian who believed the death of Judas by crucifixion might attract too much attention. In chapter nine of my earlier book, *Judas the Galilean*, the death of Jesus in Josephus was shown to be a late third or early fourth century addition. The question is: was the spurious Jesus passage a replacement for Judas' death by crucifixion? The death of Judas by crucifixion should not be doubted. Judas fought against Rome and such actions were punishable by crucifixion. In addition, Judas' two sons, James and Simon, were crucified a generation later (46-48 AD).

7. Both Judas and Jesus had a second-in-command, Sadduc and James the Just, respectively. This organizational model was fashioned after the Maccabees. Mattathias was the leader and his son, Judas, was his lieutenant. After Mattathias died, Simon took his place and Judas Maccabee was elevated to the leadership role. In the later Fourth Philosophy, Matthias and Judas worked together. After Matthias was martyred, Judas filled this position with Sadduc. In the Gospel accounts, Jesus picked Simon Peter as his second-in-command, although a closer investigation shows that James was actually the second. (See Chapter Fifteen, James, the Sadduc.) When Jesus died, his brother, James, assumed the leadership role and Cephas (Peter) then became the lieutenant. The dual leadership may have safeguarded the respective movements. If one of the leaders was captured or killed, then there would still be someone in charge.

It must also be noted that both the terms Sadduc and Just were related to the concept of Righteousness. Surely these terms were titles which described the leaders.

8. The followers of Jesus and Judas were zealous for the Law. (Acts 21:20)(*Ant.* 17.149-154) It is true that Paul taught his Gentile followers that the law was unnecessary. However, the Jewish Christians clearly denounced that teaching and removed Paul and his followers from fellowship. (See Galatians)
Some forty years after the death of Judas (19 AD), a splinter group of the Fourth Philosophy, known as the Zealots, appeared on the scene (late 50's AD). Like their name suggests, these individuals were obsessed with the Law. This is comparable to the description in Acts 21:20, where the followers of James were zealous for the Law.

9. Zealots and Sicarii arose from Judas' Fourth Philosophy. The names of two of Jesus' apostles were Simon the Zealot and Judas Iscariot (a garbling of Sicarios). Since the Zealots and Sicarii are not introduced until the late 50's and early 60's, titles of that sort would not have been used in Jesus' time (4 BC–19 AD). These names were placed on Apostles by Gentile Christians, nearly one hundred years after the facts. In addition, the nickname Sons of Thunder denotes a power associated with the Fourth Philosophy, not the mild Christianity of the Gospels.

10. The movement of Judas was centered in Jerusalem and Galilee. Judas began his career in Jerusalem, teaching young men at the Temple. He convinced his students to tear down the Golden Eagle from the Temple and was arrested by Herod. (*Ant.* 17.149-167) Judas was later released by Archelaus and then fled to Galilee. Until his return to Jerusalem, Judas was centered in Galilee where he was crowned Messiah by his followers and where he led a tax revolt against Rome. (*Ant.* 17.271-272 and 18.1-10)

Jesus was also in Jerusalem at the start of his career, according to John. He then returned to Galilee where he was proclaimed Messiah and spent the majority of his career. Jesus eventually returned to Jerusalem, where he was captured and crucified.

The later centers of Judas' movement were also Jerusalem and Galilee. In fact, Josephus noted that Eleazar was sent by his leaders in Galilee to teach King Izates true Judaism, which included circumcision. King Izates had previously been taught by Ananias that he could become a full Jew without circumcision. The Jewish Christian model practiced circumcision. Note that Paul and Cephas had a similar disagreement in Galatians, caused by men being sent by James. James may have been centered in either Galilee or Jerusalem.

11. Jesus spent three days at the Temple at the age of twelve. He was "sitting among the teachers, listening to them and asking them questions. Everyone who heard him was amazed at his understanding and his answers." (Luke 2:41-52) Judas taught young men at the same Temple. Judas was "the most celebrated interpreters of the Jewish laws and…well beloved by the people, because of [the] education of their youth." (*Ant.* 17.149) How many other men also taught at the Temple? It is possible that Judas' early career as teacher was made legend by placing his wisdom and knowledge within the body of a twelve year old.

12. Judas and Jesus were both called wise men by Josephus. (*Ant.* 17.152 and *Ant.* 18.63) As the Jesus passage was a late third or early fourth century addition, the use of wise man was taken from the description of Judas and Matthias. It must also be noted that Josephus did not freely use the term wise man. He called himself a wise man as well as the assassin of Caligula. If Josephus called himself a wise man then this indeed was a great compliment.

13. Disciples of both Jesus and Judas were willing to die for their respective cause. The Neronian persecution reported by Tacitus and the description of the Fourth Philosophy by Josephus show a willingness to die happily for God. Jesus said, "Blessed [are] the ones being persecuted because of righteousness, for theirs is the Kingdom of God." (Matt. 5:10) In the same way, Judas and Matthias stressed the rewards of righteousness if they were to be punished by Herod. (*Ant.* 17.149-167) The followers of Judas the Galilean gladly accepted death for the sake of righteousness. (*Ant.* 18.23-24)

Unlike the Fourth Philosophy (Jewish Christianity), Paul's Gentiles were taught to pay taxes to Rome and to follow their rulers (Nero and other madmen). Paul's philosophy of acting like a Gentile to the Gentiles and like a Jew to the Jews is totally contrary to Judas' and Jesus' teachings. Judas/Jesus was who he claimed to be. He never acted a part as did Paul.

14. Both teachers assigned a high value to the sharing of wealth or pure communism. (Matt. 6:19-27; Acts 2:42-45; Acts 4:32-37; James 5:1-6)(*Ant.* 18.7; *War* 2.427)(Essenes—*War* 2.122) In fact, this was the central message in "Love your Neighbor as Yourself." How could one love his neighbor if he let that neighbor go hungry or be unclothed?

Members of the Fourth Philosophy were known as bandits by Josephus, for they exploited the wealthy, a type of Robin Hood. During the war with Rome, the debt records were burned in order to free those enslaved to the wealthy by their debt.

At the beginning of the church, disciples were urged to share everything in common (Acts 2:42). This approach to living is in line with the Kingdom of God as preached by Jesus. Also, the feeding of the five thousand was simply the sharing of one's food with another. It had nothing to do with hocus pocus. In addition, the book of James favored the poor over the rich. (James 5:1-6)

15. The sons of Judas and the "brothers" of Jesus were named James and Simon. How easy it would have been for an early Gospel writer to change children into brothers and a wife into a mother. This would have been done for several reasons. First, by making sons and a wife into brothers and a mother, the Gospel writers made Jesus into a younger man, that of about thirty. Secondly, to follow in Paul's footsteps, one had to be celibate. Although marriage and sex had no negative connotations in Jewish society, it was difficult for the later church to accept the fact that God's Son had sex which resulted in children (mini-gods). Thirdly, it was easier to disassociate Jesus from brothers and a mother. A good father and husband would have been more understanding with his wife and his own children. (See Chapter Nine—You Will Indeed Drink From My Cup).

16. The sons of Judas were put to death by crucifixion. The only other individual mentioned by name to be crucified was Jesus. Also, two apostles were to drink the same cup as Jesus, namely crucifixion. (Matt. 20:20-23)(*Ant.* 20.102) This is fully explained in Chapter Nine.

This is very significant because crucifixion was a form of punishment doled out by the Roman authorities. One was crucified because of political activity, not for religious beliefs. In fact, the Romans allowed all types of religions as long as they did not oppose Rome and its tax machine. Jesus preached against Roman taxation and was proclaimed King or Messiah. The two sons of Judas the Galilean would have been crucified for the same reason: resistance against Rome.

17. The movements of Judas and Jesus expanded throughout the Roman Empire. The Fourth Philosophy of Judas was responsible for the war against Rome. Although centered in Jerusalem and Galilee, Judas' followers were numbered throughout the Empire and suffered greatly during the Jewish war. We know that Paul's Gentile churches were scattered amongst the great cities, but the Jewish

Christian movement must have been much greater. While Paul was the lone apostle to the Gentiles, the influence of Cephas and others must have reached a great multitude. In fact, the early church would have placed most of its resources in the "conversion" of the Jewish community to the Way of Righteousness.

Note also that Suetonius tied the rebellious, trouble-making Jews to Chrestus, or Christ. (Suetonius, *The Twelve Caesars*, Claudius 25) This passage definitively connected the Fourth Philosophy to Christ. While this particular disturbance was at Rome, it seems most probable that all large Jewish congregations of the Diaspora would have contained an element sympathetic to the nationalism of Judas the Galilean/Jesus.

18. The movements continued after the deaths of Judas and Jesus. It is interesting that Acts downplayed the movement of Judas the Galilean, saying that Judas was killed "and all his followers were scattered." (Acts 5:37) (See Chapter Ten—Theudas and Judas the Galilean). In reality, the Fourth Philosophy of Judas did not end with Judas' death but grew to a great degree according to Josephus. (*Ant.* 18.1-10) So the speech by Gamaliel in Acts was an attempt by Luke to alter history. The author of Acts did not want people to associate the Roman destruction of the Fourth Philosophy (70 AD) with the Gentile Christian movement of the second century. It is true, however, that when the story of Acts was written (early second century), the followers of Judas the Galilean had been smashed and scattered.

19. Both Judas and Jesus were considered fine teachers of the Law. (Matt.5:17-20, Mk. 12:28-34)(*Ant.* 17.149; *War* 1.648) Judas followed the basic teachings of the Pharisees as did Jesus. From the Gospels, we know that Jesus used parables in relating his message, in line with Pharisaic practices.

Jesus said that the two greatest commandments were to love God and to love thy neighbor. To love God involved obeying God and the law handed down by God to Moses. To love thy neighbor included sharing one's possessions, so that no one was left hungry. In addition, both Judas and Jesus followed Judas Maccabee in his interpretation of the Sabbath: the Sabbath was made for man, not man for the Sabbath. Judas Maccabee permitted his disciples to defend themselves if attacked on the Sabbath. Likewise, Jesus preached that it was proper to do good on the Sabbath. In fact, Jesus was reprimanded by some Pharisees for breaking the Sabbath laws as he fled from Herod. Jesus quoted the Old Testament story of David eating consecrated bread in order to maintain strength in his flight from the authorities. Jesus had good reason to follow David and Judas Maccabee; he was a marked man. Both Jesus and Judas Maccabee would not have flouted the Sabbath law for any old reason.

20. Herod the Great planned to execute Judas after the Temple Cleansing. Luckily for Judas, Herod ordered to have his prisoners put to death after his own death, in order to create great sorrow in Israel. After Herod's death, his advisors reneged on the insane plan. (*Ant.* 17.149-167) Herod the Great tried to kill the baby Jesus. (Matt. 2) Herod's goal of eliminating Jesus ended with his death. In both stories, an elderly paranoid Herod tried to destroy elements he perceived as being a threat to his rule. Of course, the infant narrative was not actual history but rather a replay of Moses' infancy.

21. In the trial of Matthias in the Temple Cleansing, the High Priest was also named Matthias. This Matthias had once relinquished his office for a day, a day celebrated by a fast, because of a dream where he had sexual relations with his wife. Pilate washed his hands of responsibility on a single day because of his wife's dream concerning Jesus' innocence. (Matt. 27:19-24)(*Ant.* 17.166) In both cases, a dream sequence was used to remove responsibility for a short period of time. In the case of Pilate, this conveniently shifted the blame from the Romans to the Jews. The Jews supposedly said, "Let his blood be on us and on our children." (Matt. 27:25) Unfortunately, this has been used as an excuse to persecute the Jews throughout history.

22. Herod the Great sent Matthias, Judas and the rebels to Jericho for questioning concerning the Golden Eagle Temple Cleansing. There he heard the reasons for the uprising. (*Ant.* 17.160) Pilate sent Jesus to Herod for questioning. (Luke 23:6,7) The Jesus story was told only by Luke. Luke had a tendency to take events from Josephus and incorporate them into the fictional story of Jesus and the early church. There were two Temple cleansings, the Golden Eagle and the one recorded in the Gospels. And two trials or interrogations also occurred, one before Herod the Great and the other before Pilate. Luke simply combined these two trials in his Gospel. (See an analysis of Acts for further tampering by Luke—Chapter Fourteen.)

23. Under Herod the Great's son, Archelaus (4 BC), prisoners were released to appease the Jewish mob. One of these prisoners may have been Judas the Galilean. (*War* 2.4 and *Ant.* 17.204-205) This same story was repeated at the trial of Jesus. In that story, Pilate released Barabbas to the mob instead of Jesus.

(Matt. 27:15-26) One point must be noted: the Romans did not release political prisoners; they crucified them. On the other hand, the release of prisoners by Archelaus rings true as he was dealing with the remnants of the Matthias and Judas following. It is here that the crowd would have wished for Barabbas, the son of the Father. (See Chapter Seven—Barabbas.)

24. In the Gospel story, Barabbas led an insurrection in the city, Jerusalem. (Mark 15:7 and Luke 23:19) Shortly before the prisoner release of 4 BC, Matthias and Judas led the Golden Eagle Temple Cleansing, an insurrection in the city, where many of the rebels had been burnt alive while others, Judas included, were held for later punishment. (*Ant.* 17:149-167; 17.204-206)

Insurrections in the city of Jerusalem were not commonplace in the time frame noted. From 4 BC to 50 AD, the only ones recorded were the Golden Eagle Temple Cleansing (4 BC) and the one supposedly led by Barabbas. This should reinforce the statement that Barabbas was really a nickname for Judas/Jesus. Both insurrections were aimed at the power of Rome. The Golden Eagle was a symbol of Rome and Barabbas of Gospel fame was undoubtedly a member of the Fourth Philosophy. Judas and Barabbas were very popular with the Jewish crowd, who were anti-Roman.

25. The trial of Jesus and the release of Barabbas occurred at the Passover feast. (Mark 14:12) The release of prisoners in 4 BC also coincided with Passover. (*Ant.* 17.213) As there were three Jewish pilgrim festivals (Passover, Pentecost and Tabernacles), the odds of this "coincidence" is one in three.(4)

26. King Herod died a week or so before the Passover feast. At his death, Herod was clothed in purple, with a crown of gold upon his head and a scepter in his right hand. (*Ant.* 17.197) Before his death, Jesus was mocked by the Roman soldiers who put a purple robe on him and wove a crown of thorns to be placed upon his head. A staff was used to beat him. (Mark 15:16-20)

27. Jesus was mocked by the Roman soldiers. (Mark 15:16-20) Herod the Great was afraid that the people would mourn his death in "sport and mockery" only. (*Ant.* 17.177) The Gospels and Acts often used information from Josephus or the letters of Paul to flesh out the story of Jesus and his church. Jesus not only wore the same garb as Herod, but was also treated as poorly by his adversaries.

28. In the Gospels, the crowd (Pharisees etc.) preferred Barabbas over king Jesus. (Mark 15:1-15) This was not only an endorsement for Barabbas but also demonstrated an intense hatred for Jesus. Anyone would have been chosen over Jesus.

Josephus described the crowd as followers of Matthias and Judas, who preferred these teachers over king Herod. (*Ant.* 17.204-206) The disciples really loved Judas and Matthias but their hatred of Herod and all he stood for was unmatched. Their hatred of Herod corresponds to the Gospel story where the Chief Priests and the Jews hated Jesus.

29. In the infancy story, Jesus was born at the time of a star rising in the east. (Matt. 2:2) Scholars are not sure when and what this star was. In the story of the Golden Eagle Temple Cleansing, there was an eclipse of the moon (4 BC). This was the only mention of an eclipse of the sun or moon by Josephus. (*Ant.* 17:167) It is possible that the celestial event of Jesus' birth was merely this eclipse mentioned by Josephus.

30. Joseph returned to Israel after the death of Herod the Great but was afraid to settle in Judea because of Archelaus. Having been warned in a dream, Joseph moved his family to Nazareth, in Galilee. (Matt. 2:19-23) The New Testament often moved characters by using dreams, miracles or visions. For example, Philip was whisked away after baptizing the eunuch in Acts 8:39-40. Peter's visit to Cornelius' house in Caesarea was preceded by a vision in Acts chapter 10. And the Magi did not return to King Herod because they were warned in a dream (Matt. 2:12).

After being released by Archelaus, Judas went to Sepphoris in Galilee, where he led an uprising against the son of Herod. (*War* 2.56) Sepphoris was in the tetrarchy of Herod Antipas, not under the control of Archelaus. Since Archelaus was waging war upon the followers of Judas and Matthias, the move to Galilee was prudent in that it allowed Judas to reorganize without fear of being attacked by Archelaus. The events in Josephus and the New Testament both occurred because Herod the Great had died and the country was in unrest.

31. Jesus was proclaimed Messiah or King, in Galilee, or close by. Before the Transfiguration, Jesus and the Twelve were in Caesarea Philippi (Matt. 16:13) and afterwards they traveled to Capernaum. (Matt. 17:24) After Jesus was proclaimed King, he marched to Jerusalem.

Judas was also proclaimed King in Galilee, around Sepphoris. This was done after he captured Herod's armory and equipped his followers. (*Ant.* 17.271-272;

War 2:56) He also may have marched upon Jerusalem, but this would be deduced by examining the behavior of his son, Menahem, who proclaimed himself King after capturing Herod's armory at Masada. He then marched straight to Jerusalem. (*War* 2.433) Judas the Galilean's entrance to Jerusalem may have been in 19 AD, so his kingship may have actually lasted twenty-two years, from 4 BC to 19 AD. This is different than Jesus who went directly to Jerusalem. However, the Gospels may have telescoped the career of Jesus into a few short years just as Josephus compressed the seventy-five year movement created by Judas into a few paragraphs. (*Ant.* 18.1-10)

32. The Gospels do not mention the early life of Jesus, except for the one story in which he taught at the Temple at the age of twelve. Otherwise, no information was given from 6 AD (Census) to 26 AD (Pilate). This lack of information reproduces Josephus' *War* where nothing is written from 6 AD (Census) to 26 AD (Pilate). (*War* 2.167-169) Josephus barely expanded on this paucity of information in *Antiquities*, where he listed the Roman procurators during this twenty year stretch, but little else. (*Ant.* 18.26-35) It is possible that these missing years from Josephus could have been the result of "pious" editing. The actual crucifixion of Judas the Galilean may have been deleted. Note that Josephus detailed the deaths of Judas' three sons, James, Simon, and Menahem and his descendent Eleazar. With each of these occasions, Josephus referred back to Judas the Galilean. It is hard to believe that Josephus omitted the circumstances behind the death of Judas.

33. When Jesus was arrested, he was brought first to Annas, the father in law of Caiaphas and former High Priest. (John 18:12-24) This Annas was appointed High Priest in 7 AD by Cyrenius and Coponius, in the days of the census. Opposing the census and Annas was none other than Judas the Galilean. It would seem that Annas would have been much more interested in the death of Judas the Galilean than the Gospel Jesus. But why would the ex-High Priest take a leading role in the arrest of Jesus? Under the governorship of Gratus (15-18 AD), four different High Priests were appointed. This musical chairs approach to the High Priesthood must have maddened the religious people of the day, including Jesus. This may have been one reason why Jesus picked this time to enter Jerusalem. Note that Annas was calling the shots the whole time. (See Chapter Three—Pilate's Reign.)

The Gospel of John may have inadvertently connected Jesus with this old adversary. The Synoptic Gospels are careful to avoid mentioning Annus, preferring to have the whole affair tried before Caiaphas and the elders. Annas certainly lends credence to my hypothesis, in that he was an earlier figure (7-15 AD), and his reign coincided with the rise of a nemesis, Judas the Galilean.

34. In the Golden Eagle Temple Cleansing, Matthias and Judas were captured by Herod the Great. Matthias was put to death by fire and Judas was eventually released to the Jewish crowd in a Barabbas-style prisoner release. Once released, Judas assumed the leadership role once held by Matthias. Judas' role was then given to Sadduc.

In the book of Acts, Matthias replaced Judas Iscariot as one of the Twelve. (See Chapter Eight—Judas Iscariot). While the Josephus story has Judas replacing Matthias, the Acts' version has Matthias replacing a Judas. This Matthias was never mentioned in the Gospels and was absent from any further activities in Acts. Matthias was just a name taken from Judas the Galilean's past and playfully included in the Jesus story.

35. Many members of the movement had nicknames. Sadduc was a priestly title denoting righteousness while James was given the nickname Just. (*Ant.* 18.4) Judas the Galilean was known as Jesus; Simon as Cephas (Peter), which means rock; and Saul as Paul. These internal nicknames would not have been known or used by outsiders. Thus, Josephus wrote of Judas, Simon and Saul, not Jesus, Cephas and Paul.

Nicknames were also used in the Maccabean movement. Judas was nicknamed Maccabee or the Hammer. Since the Fourth Philosophy (Jewish Christianity) was based upon the Maccabean movement, the use of nicknames should be expected.

Other nicknames in the Jesus movement included the Sons of Thunder, James the Just, Simon the Zealot and James the Younger. Thomas or twin may have referred to a Judas. A combination of Judas and Thomas may produce Thaddeus or Theudas.

36. Many religious scholars have questioned the silence of Jesus before Pilate. When charged with a crime, Jesus made no reply, to the amazement of Pilate (Mark 15:3-5). Unlike Paul, who made a speech everywhere in Acts, Jesus remained silent. The only mention of this type of behavior in Josephus concerned Simon, who had been summoned to answer charges by Agrippa. Simon, too, made no reply to the charges. (*Ant.* 19.334) (This Simon-Agrippa episode was the basis for the Simon Peter-Cornelius story of Acts chapter 10).

Silence was a way to protect the movement. Under interrogation, members of the movement would not betray their compatriots. The questioning of Jesus may have been much more severe than we are led to believe by the Gospel accounts. Pilate and his henchmen would have liked information and they no doubt tortured Jesus. He, however, did not betray his friends. The Fourth Philosophy, represented by Simon in the Simon-Agrippa episode, also was famous for its steadfast loyalty to God and fellow members. "They also do not value dying any kind of death, nor indeed do they heed the deaths of their relations and friends, nor can any such fear make them call any man Lord." (*Ant.* 18.23-25) In short, they would rather die than betray God and their fellow disciples.

37. Jesus was crucified between two bandits. The bandit was Josephus' term for members of the Fourth Philosophy. This term bandit did not refer to thieves or highwaymen but rather to terrorists (freedom fighters) or those seeking political turmoil.(5) That Jesus was crucified between these two should not surprise. Jesus was their leader.

John Crossan admits that Jesus was an apocalypticist, but that did not mean that Jesus advocated violence. He concludes that if Jesus were a military threat then Pilate would have captured a large number of Jesus' disciples with him and crucified them as well.(6) There are two fundamental errors in Crossan's reasoning. First, the Judas the Galilean/Jesus movement was not violent as compared to the later Fourth Philosophy as dominated by the Zealots and Sicarii. (See Chapter Sixteen—The Fourth Philosophy.) The early version of the Fourth Philosophy as preached by Judas/Jesus would rid Israel of Roman occupation by the power of God, not by armed rebellion or by assassinations. Secondly, Crossan does not recognize that Jesus was placed in the middle of two bandits. Obviously, Rome had captured some of Jesus' disciples as they hung to his left and to his right. By placing Jesus in the middle and by attaching the charge against him, King of the Jews, Pilate was attacking the Fourth Philosophy head on.

The treatment of the bandits in the Gospels is not consistent. John 19:18 simply said that Jesus was crucified with "two others—one on each side and Jesus in the middle." John had nothing more to say about these two. Mark and Matthew tell a different tale. They state that "those crucified with him [the bandits] also heaped insults on him." (Mark 15:32) In this, Mark and Matthew placed the bandits along with the High Priest, aligned against Jesus. But no one does the story better than Luke.

> One of the <u>criminals</u> who hung there hurled insults at him. "Aren't you the Christ? Save yourself and us!"
> But the other <u>criminal</u> rebuked him. "Don't you fear God," he said, "since you are under the same sentence? We are punished justly, for we are getting what are deeds deserve. But this man has done nothing wrong."
> Then he said, "Jesus, remember me when you come into your kingdom."
> Jesus answered him, "I tel! you the truth, today you will be with me in paradise." (emphasis mine)

Three major discrepancies can be noted from the above passage. First, Luke called the two criminals and not bandits. This made the two men common criminals and not part of a religious or political movement, that being the Fourth Philosophy. Secondly, one of the criminals hurled insults but the other now sided with Jesus, even saying that Jesus had done nothing wrong, thus exonerating Jesus. Thirdly, this second criminal was pardoned by Jesus, a Pauline move. Jesus always preached a lifelong commitment to God. All of a sudden, he now accepted deathbed conversions. Again, this was added to make Jesus accept the Pauline notion of faith; saved by faith, not by works.

38. In Acts 5:37, Judas the Galilean was killed "and all his followers were scattered." This passage was meant to minimize Judas' influence, giving the impression that Judas' movement ended with his death. However, Josephus clearly stated that Judas' movement grew and expanded over the next fifty to sixty years.

After Jesus was captured, his disciples fled and some denied their association with him (Peter). Even after the crucifixion, the disciples were forlorn and in hiding. It seems as if both movements acted the same way after their leaders were killed.

39. This next to last coincidence may be the smoking gun behind the New Testament version of Jesus. In the Gospels, John the Baptist introduced Jesus to the world in 29-30 AD, per the dating of Luke. In fact, this is the reason why scholars look nowhere else for Jesus. It is just a given that Jesus' ministry began around 30 AD.

According to the Slavonic Josephus, this same John came baptizing in the Jordan in 6 AD, right before the mention of Judas the Galilean.(7) In addition, the Pseudoclementine *Recognitions* acknowledge John right before describing the various Jewish sects. Josephus describes these same sects right after his introduction of Judas the Galilean. So the 6 AD time frame for John the Baptist is attested to by more than one source.

Could this John the Baptist have been baptizing and proclaiming different Messiahs in both 6 AD and 30 AD? The odds of that would be millions to one. The only logical conclusion is that Jesus and Judas the Galilean were the same person. (See Chapter Five—John the Baptist.)

40. This last coincidence is the smoking gun, part 2. In the Gospel of Matthew, the Magi were drawn to Jerusalem by a star. This was near the end of Herod the Great's reign, about 4 BC. These Magi found the baby Jesus but did not return to Herod to report their findings. Herod was incensed and ordered the slaughter of all the baby boys in the vicinity of Bethlehem, two years old and younger.

In the Slavonic Josephus, Persian astrologers went to Herod the Great to point out the star in the sky and its significance. Herod had them promise to return to him after finding the infant. The astrologers were warned by the stars to avoid Herod. In his rage, Herod wanted to kill all the male children throughout his kingdom. His advisors convinced him that the Messiah would come from Bethlehem, so that the slaughter was confined to only Bethlehem. This passage occurred in the early years of Herod, between 27-22 BC.(8)

If Jesus was born in 25 BC, then he would have been 30 years old at the time of the census (6 AD). This is the exact time when John baptized in the Jordan and proclaimed the coming of the Messiah. This date was also marked by the nationwide tax revolt led by Judas the Galilean or should I say, the Messiah, Jesus.

ASSUMED DISSIMILARITIES

1. Jesus was not married while Judas had at least three sons, James, Simon and Menahem. (These three were named by Josephus, but Judas probably fathered more sons and daughters.) However, it would have been consistent with Jewish practices if a wife and family were following Jesus, not a mother and brothers. Pharisees and even one sect of the Essenes practiced marriage as a way to uphold God's command to be fruitful and multiply. (Gen. 1:28) Jesus' own movement also married and had children according to Paul's testimony in 1 Corinthians 9:5. The wedding in Cana may have been the wedding feast of Jesus and Mary. Note that Jesus and Mary were concerned about the wine situation, a likely concern for those involved with the wedding. (John 2:1-10) In addition, Cana was halfway between Judas' power base (Sepphoris) and the birth place of his wife, Mary Magdalene (Magdala). This may explain why Jesus first appeared to Mary Magdalene after the resurrection (Mark 16:9). Their love for each other was far greater than any other tie.

2. Jesus was a healer, a miracle worker. However, some of the miracles, such as the feeding of the five thousand, may have been distorted accounts of actual history. Jesus taught his disciples to share with one another, and this turned into the hocus pocus of Gospel lore. People want to believe that Jesus created matter out of thin air. But the <u>sharing</u> explanation is consistent with Jesus' teachings.

Josephus does not mention this miracle worker trait concerning Judas. However, Judas must have been extremely charismatic to develop such a massive following. In addition, Josephus claimed that the most onerous innovators (rebels) were the miracle workers. These miracle workers were part of Judas' Fourth Philosophy. Thus, Jesus would have fit in nicely next to Theudas or The Egyptian or the other miracle workers. (*Ant.* 20.98; *Ant.* 20.160; *Ant.* 20.167,168; *Ant.* 20.169-172 and *Ant.* 20.188)

3. Jesus started his ministry at the age of thirty (Luke 3:23) and preached for three years before his crucifixion. However, this age is not reliable. Per Luke's history, Jesus was born in 6 AD and died in 39 AD, two years after Pilate left Judea. Luke probably meant to use 6 BC and the thirty-three years would have placed Jesus at the hands of Pilate in 27 AD. The thirty years was just a number to get Jesus to the Pilate era.

Judas would have been approximately thirty years old at the census of Cyrenius. He was probably the junior member with Matthias, possibly a young man of twenty in 4 BC. If Judas was crucified in 19 AD, then his age would have been a respectable forty-three. Even in his early career, Judas would have had great respect among the people because of his earlier affiliation with Matthias. In addition, Judas' little brother, James the Just, would have been between forty and fifty-three years old in 19 AD. (Legend has James being murdered in Jerusalem in 62 AD at the age of ninety-six. However, this may be an exaggeration as the same fourth-century church historian claimed that James was a lifelong virgin, even though he was a married man. The only conclusion that can be made is that James was an old man at his death, somewhere between 80-96.) Thus, there is no discrepancy concerning age. Judas the Galilean was probably a robust middle-aged man at his death. And the age of Jesus as reported by Luke probably described Judas/Jesus in the time of the census of Cyrenius.

SIMILARITIES—JUDAS THE GALILEAN AND JUDAS

Many scholars do not believe that Judas the Galilean was the same Judas as was described in the Golden Eagle Temple Cleansing. (Please note that this has nothing to do with the mythical Judas Iscariot.) In *War* 1.655, Josephus claimed that the rabbis were put to death, although not mentioning them by name. However, in *Ant.* 17.167, only Matthias died and it appears as if Judas was either imprisoned or on the run. If imprisoned, he was undoubtedly released by Archelaus as part of the Barabbas-style prisoner release in 4 BC (*War* 2.4). Either way, he was free until recaptured by Pilate in 19 AD.

There is one scholar who believes that the Golden Eagle Judas may well be Judas the Galilean. Robert Eisenman, author of *James, the Brother of Jesus*, writes:

> This rabbi [Golden Eagle Judas] is hardly to be distinguished from Judas the Galilean subsequently, even though for Josephus Judas Sepphoraeus, together with another 'rabbi' he calls Matthias (again note the Maccabean names), are burned alive ('being guilty of sacrilege under the pretence of zeal for the law'), while Judas the Galilean goes on functioning and Josephus never does delineate his fate. Josephus (or his sources—this is forty years before Josephus was born), may have been mistaken about this detail, as later in the *Antiquities* he says only Matthias was burned. Here, Josephus portrays the people as preferring the burning of the rabbis and their followers rather than having 'a great number prosecuted', a point of view echoed in John 11:50's picture of Caiaphas' famous explanation to his fellow Chief Priests about Jesus: 'it profits us more that one man die for the people, rather than the whole nation perish.'(9)

The following passages from Josephus and the Gospels will bring these two Judases together.

1. There are two Gospel references which may describe Jesus fleeing from Herod Antipas. "At that time some Pharisees came to Jesus and said to him, 'Leave this place and go somewhere else. Herod wants to kill you.'"(Luke 13:31) And in Matt. 12:1-8, Jesus and his disciples picked heads of grain and ate them on the Sabbath, thus working on the Sabbath. As a defense, Jesus referred his critics to David, who ate consecrated bread while being chased by Saul. Jesus' argument seems to place him in the same position as David, fleeing from the authorities. These two passages may hearken back to Judas escaping the death sentence imposed upon Matthias and forty others. (*Ant.* 17.149-167) In fact, Judas was probably imprisoned by Herod and then released by Archelaus in the Barabbas scenario noted earlier. (*War* 2.4)

Since Herod Antipas was Tetrarch of Galilee from 4 BC–39 AD, the references to this Herod do not necessarily put Judas/Jesus in a later time frame. The above passages may also describe the efforts put forth by Herod Antipas to capture Judas after his escape from Jerusalem. After all, Judas did break into the armory at Sepphoris, supplying his followers with weapons and whatever money that was there. (*Ant.* 17:271,272) Therefore, Herod Antipas would have been after Judas in 4 BC as well.

2. Josephus mentioned a bandit leader named Judas, who led a rebel group at <u>Sepphoris</u> in Galilee, around 4-3 BC. This Judas attacked the royal armory and equipped his followers. (*Ant.* 17.271; *War* 2.56) The Golden Eagle Judas was the son of <u>Sepphoris</u>, per the account in *War* 1.648. In one instance, Sepphoris is a city, in another, a name. Also note that Archelaus released political prisoners to the populous, hoping to atone for his father, Herod the Great. (*War* 2.4) If Judas had been captured with Matthias, he might have been in prison and released. Shortly after this prison release, Josephus writes about Judas the bandit.

3. The teachings of Matthias and Judas were similar to those of Judas the Galilean. Both were obsessed with following the Law and keeping the Temple pure. They also would gladly die rather than worship idols or Caesars. (*Ant.* 17.151; *Ant.* 18.23) Note also that Matthias and Judas cleansed the Temple from an idol, the Golden Eagle, thereby confronting Herod the Great with sedition. In 41 AD, the Jewish fanatics were willing to go to war with Rome if Caligula placed a statue of himself in the Temple. (Tacitus, *Histories*, V.9) The followers of Hezekias, Judas the bandit's father or grandfather, also had a presence at the Temple. (*Ant.* 14.168)

The tie between Judas and Judas the Galilean is assured when we consider the symbolism of the Golden Eagle. Not only did this represent the power of Herod the Great, but its placement in the Temple area was a not too subtle way of paying homage to Rome. (The Eagle was the symbol of Rome.) Judas and Matthias, by tearing down the Golden Eagle, were proclaiming war upon Rome. This same mentality was present at the Census of Cyrenius where Judas the Galilean and Sadduc opposed Roman taxation.

This secure connection is further cemented by the Slavonic Josephus. Additional data concerning the Golden Eagle Temple Cleansing was included in this account. The Golden Eagle was placed in the Temple as an honor to Caesar. In addition, Judas and Matthias patterned themselves after the Maccabees in resistance against a foreign power and in their willingness to die for their cause.(10) This is identical to the Fourth Philosophy of Judas the Galilean.

4. The High Priest in 4 BC at the Golden Eagle Temple Cleansing was Joazar (*Ant.* 17.164). Joazar persuaded the people to accept the Roman taxation of 6 AD which was opposed by Judas the Galilean. (*Ant.* 18.3) In both cases, the High Priest was supporting the Roman presence in Judea. Joazar could be considered the Evil Priest of the Dead Sea Scrolls. However, his replacement, Annas (7-15 AD), makes an even better Evil Priest.

5. Matthias and Judas worked as a team. Judas the Galilean also had a second-in-command, Sadduc. (*Ant.* 17.149; *Ant.* 18.4) This organizational structure was modeled after the Maccabees. Mattathias and Judas led rebels against the Greek occupiers beginning around 195 BC. When Mattathias died, his son Simon replaced him. Thus, Judas Maccabee and Simon were then the leaders of the movement. In the New Testament, Jesus appointed Peter as his second-in-command, although a closer reading of Paul's writings shows that James was the leader and subsequently the second to Jesus. After Jesus' death, James and Peter led the Jewish Christian movement. In all the above cases, the movements were led by two men. When one died, the other became leader and a replacement was added to the team.

6. Matthias and Judas were referred to as wise men by Josephus, a high honor indeed. (*Ant.* 17.155) Judas the Galilean was called a clever rabbi by Josephus in *War* 2.433. These words of honor are especially important because Josephus opposed Judas the Galilean. Josephus wrote his history for the Romans. However, even though he did not agree with the politics of Judas, he admired him greatly.

7. The son of Judas the Galilean broke into King Herod's armory in Masada (66 AD) just as Judas, the bandit, had done in Sepphoris (4-3 BC). (*War* 2.433; *War* 2.56) This definitely links the 4 BC Judas with the 6 AD Judas the Galilean. And this also shows that Judas the Galilean would have been active at the time of the Golden Eagle Temple Cleansing of 4 BC.

8. The father or grandfather of Judas, the bandit, was Hezekias (Ezekias). This Hezekias was put to death by Herod the Great. Hezekias' followers petitioned at the Temple for justice in regards to Herod's actions. These followers of Hezekias had a presence in Galilee and in Jerusalem, just as Matthias and Judas in 4 BC and Judas and Sadduc in 6 AD. In addition, King Hezekiah purified the Temple, so the name Hezekias may hearken back to this as well.

9. Matthias and Judas resemble Mattathias and Judas Maccabee in that both cleansed the Temple and the names are similar. Judas the bandit and Judas Maccabee were both terrible to all men. (*Ant.* 12.314; *Ant.* 17.272) And Judas the Galilean and Sadduc were also based upon the Maccabean precedent of a leader and a second-in-command.

10. After the death of Matthias and the imprisonment of Judas, their followers petitioned Archelaus for the release of Judas (Barabbas) and for tax relief. (*Ant.* 17.204-205) Judas the Galilean led his followers in opposing the Census tax of Cyrenius. (*Ant.* 18.1-10) This concern for tax relief is very important. It was one of the cornerstones of the movement. Note also that Jesus was crucified for his refusal to pay taxes to Rome.

CONCLUSION

From the above, it appears as if the Jewish historian, Josephus, was quite specific concerning Jesus and his followers. He did not use the nicknames with which we are so familiar. Jesus was Judas, Cephas was Simon, and Paul was Saul. However, the context in which he placed these individuals makes it a near certainty that his history focused on what became known as Christianity.

The Fourth Philosophy of Josephus was really Jewish Christianity. The reason why this has been overlooked by scholars is because Christianity has always been defined by the Pauline definition (Gentile Christianity). However, it is clear that Cephas and James worked in Galilee and Jerusalem. Their message was purely Jewish with one addition: Jesus was resurrected and would someday return. This was an appealing message in the beginning, but as time wore on, the Jews tired of waiting. The death knell for Jewish Christianity was the war with Rome. When Jesus failed to return in Judea's time of need, the remaining Jews lost faith in him.

The above forty similarities between Judas the Galilean and Jesus are supplemented by the many similarities between the Christians in Acts and the Fourth Philosophy in Josephus. In Chapter Fourteen, nineteen obvious alterations of history are noted. Some of the changes were to events reported by Josephus and some from Paul's accounts in Galatians. The combination of the forty coincidences between Judas the Galilean and Jesus of Nazareth and the rewriting of Acts should convince the reader that something strange has been going on for the past two thousand years.

3

PILATE'S REIGN

The traditional dating for Pilate's governorship is 26-37 AD. This is arrived at by adding up years contained in certain passages in Josephus. Per the existing documentation, Josephus stated that Gratus was appointed procurator shortly after the succession of Tiberius (14-37 AD). If Gratus arrived in 15 AD and served eleven years (*Ant.* 18.35), then his successor, Pilate, must have arrived in Judea in 26 AD. So the story goes.

This traditional dating of Pilate is crucial to support the Gospel story of Jesus. In Matthew, Jesus was born right before the death of Herod the Great, approximately 8-4 BC. Luke mistakenly placed the birth at the census of Cyrenius, or 6 AD. Also, Luke stated that the ministry of Jesus began in his thirtieth year. Assuming his ministry lasted three years, Jesus would have been thirty-three at his death. From the birth in 8-4 BC, the death would have occurred thirty-three years later, from 26-30 AD. This fits in quite nicely with the traditional dating for Pilate. (Note that Luke's dating would have placed the crucifixion at 39 AD, two years after Pilate.)

However, I believe there is overwhelming evidence within the writings of Josephus and Tacitus to question the later dating of Pilate. From an analysis of their histories, we will place the reign of Pilate in Judea from 18-37 AD. This early date will be shown to approximate the crucifixion of Judas/Jesus. If this is the case, then the Gospel Jesus would have been in his early twenties by Matthew's reckonings and twelve by Luke's. Surely, the early date for Pilate would spell trouble for the orthodox story of Jesus.

JOSEPHUS ON PILATE

In analyzing the dating for Pilate, the passage concerning Pilate's rise to power will be quoted in context in order to ascertain the proper year in which he arrived in Judea.

> He [Tiberius] was now the third emperor [14 AD]; and he sent Valerius Gratus to be procurator of Judea, and to succeed Annius Rufus. This man [Gratus] deprived Ananus of the high priesthood, and appointed Ismael, the son of Phabi, to be high priest. He also deprived him in a little time, and ordained Eleazar, the son of Ananus, who had been high priest before, to be high priest: which office, when he had held for a year, Gratus deprived him of it, and gave the high priesthood to Simon, the son of Camithus; and when he had possessed that dignity no longer than a year, Joseph Caiaphas was made his successor. When Gratus had done those things, he went back to Rome, after he had tarried in Judea <u>eleven</u> years, when Pontius Pilate came as his successor. (*Ant.* 18.33-35) (emphasis mine)

From the above passage, Gratus became procurator in 15 AD, right after the death of Augustus and the corresponding rise of Tiberius. Josephus stated that he appointed Ismael to be High Priest in 15 AD and quickly replaced him with Eleazar. This Eleazar held the office of High Priest for one year, from late 15 to late 16 AD. He was then replaced by Simon who also held office for no longer than a year (16-17 AD). In his final act, Gratus replaced Simon with Joseph Caiaphas (18-37 AD). After these appointments, Gratus returned to Rome. Per the years listed by Josephus, his governorship lasted only three years, from 15-18 AD. Note that this passage curiously listed his tenure at eleven years. After this, Pilate was introduced by Josephus to his readers.

Interestingly, the Gospel of John may provide valuable information concerning the above High Priests. At the arrest on the Mount of Olives, Jesus was bound and sent to Annas, where he was interrogated. After questioning, Jesus was then sent to the reigning High Priest, Caiaphas. (John 18:12-24) Per the account in Josephus, Annas was originally appointed High Priest by Cyrenius and Coponius in 7 AD, replacing Joazar. (*Ant.* 18.26) It is at this time that Judas the Galilean began his tax revolt. (*Ant.* 18.1-6) The arrest of Judas/Jesus would have concerned no one more than Annas.

Annas was deprived of the High Priesthood by Gratus in 15 AD. Of the other High Priests appointed by Gratus, Eleazar was the son (15-16 AD) and Caiaphas the son-in-law (18-37 AD) of Annas. The Gospel of John may have inadvertently given us a clue as to the year in which the crucifixion occurred. If Jesus were taken first to Annas, then it would appear that this Annas was still held in high esteem by other officials. In fact, Annas may have been the one calling the shots. This would have been true in 18 AD, but not so likely in 30-33 AD. In the later time frame, Annas may have been long since dead and/or Caiaphas would have been more firmly entrenched after being High Priest for twelve to fifteen years. In addition, the charge of tax revolt against Jesus rings true with the interrogations by Annas, the High Priest of Cyrenius and Coponius.

The author of the Gospel of John may have given us one last clue. Concerning the High Priest, Caiaphas, he wrote: "They bound him [Jesus] and brought him first to Annas, who was the father-in-law of Caiaphas, the high priest that year." (John 18:13) From Josephus' account of the High Priests, Annas was High Priest from 7-15 AD. However, during the governorship of Gratus, the High Priests served only one year. After Gratus, during the tenure of Pilate, Caiaphas may have served from 18-37 AD. So when John described Caiaphas as being High Priest that year, he may have unwittingly pointed to the year 18-19 AD.

If the tenure of Gratus actually spanned eleven years, and if Pilate became procurator beginning in 26 AD, then one would expect the following history related by Josephus to be post 26 AD. But that is not the case. Right after the introduction of Pilate, Josephus described how Herod the tetrarch had built the city of Tiberius. This city, under construction for nine years, was dedicated in 18 AD. (*Ant.* 18.36-38) After this, Josephus spent time discussing obscure Parthian history, leading into his mention of the death of Germanicus, the Roman general who was assassinated in 19 AD. (*Ant.* 18.39-54)

After this 19 AD reference, Josephus wrote about Pilate again. The first story concerned the introduction of standards into the city. The Jews vehemently opposed this action and forced Pilate to withdraw the standards. Next, Pilate used the Temple treasury for the purpose of constructing an aqueduct. The Jews were outraged, and many were slaughtered in their opposition.

After these two events, the spurious passage about Jesus follows. In traditional calculations, the passages about Pilate were early in his career, around 26-27 AD. The passage about Jesus would therefore be shortly thereafter, anywhere from 26-30 AD. This passage about Jesus is not authentic, but it may have replaced the original story of Judas the Galilean's death at the hands of Pilate.

This assertion is bolstered by the two episodes related by Josephus after the spurious Jesus passage. If Jesus was crucified in 26-30 AD, then the following sections of Josephus would logically be post 26-30 AD; but once again, that is not the case. The story of the Roman woman, Paulina, who was tricked into prostituting herself in the Temple of Isis coincides with a similar tale told by Tacitus. However, Tacitus firmly placed the dating to 19 AD.(1) Secondly, Josephus explained why the Jews were expelled from Rome. (*Ant.* 18.65-84) Compare these two mentions by Josephus to this 19 AD reference by Tacitus.

> There was a debate too about expelling the Egyptian and Jewish worship, and a resolution of the Senate was passed that four thousand of the freedman class who were infected with those superstitions and were of military age should be transported to the island of Sardinia, to quell the brigandage of the place, a cheap sacrifice should they die from the pestilential climate. The rest were to quit Italy, unless before a certain day they repudiated their impious rites. (Tacitus, *Annals*, II.85)

This same event was recorded by Suetonius, except that he stated that the "Jews of military age were removed to unhealthy regions, on the <u>pretext</u> of drafting them into the army."(2) The motives are slightly different but the events are the same. And this is the same event described by Josephus.

So once again, the narrative of Josephus returned to 19 AD. The explanation for this is simple. Pontius Pilate became procurator in 18 AD and the death of Judas/Jesus was shortly thereafter, in 19 AD. With this explanation, the text of Josephus makes perfect sense. The traditional Gospel story put Jesus at the hands of Pilate a decade later. So why did the Gospel writers need to tamper with history?

First of all, the story of Judas/Jesus being crucified under the governorship of Pilate was very early indeed. This element of the Jesus story could not be altered. The Gospel of Mark, therefore, used this original outline where Pilate was procurator. Mark did introduce other elements into his story, such as the 4 BC Barabbas incident, but his Roman procurator could not be changed. However, since Mark did not have a birth narrative, the actual dating of Pilate was not necessary. This purposeful imprecision of dating Pilate became outdated with the birth narratives of Matthew and Luke. According to these Gospels, Jesus could not have died before 26-30 AD. When these were set in stone, all other documents had to be adjusted.

The pious editors simply went to work on Josephus, the only source of evidence concerning the early movement. The term of Gratus was extended from three years to eleven even though the text can be calculated to three years. By doing this, Christians throughout the ages have discounted the problems noted above, that the Pilate and Jesus texts fall within the discussion of Judea in 19 AD. The death of Judas the Galilean was expunged and replaced with the obvious counterfeit passage of Jesus. This explains why the life of Judas the Galilean was detailed by Josephus but his death was not covered. And this also explains why only the death of Jesus was included in the writings of Josephus.

The greatest editing actually occurred after the 19 AD narratives. From 19-37 AD, all information was erased from Josephus. This corresponds to the early church as found in Acts chapters 1-9. What Josephus had to say about the early church activity is anybody's guess. But we can be sure it would have differed wildly from the book of Acts. In Chapter Fourteen, I have noted the inaccuracies and plain misrepresentations given by the author of Acts. This revisionist history was achieved by utilizing a different time frame, that of Judas the Galilean. Without this shift in perspective, it would have been impossible to ascertain the truth. And that is why the section covering the years 19-37 AD was deleted from Josephus. Without his valuable information, the detective work would be insurmountable for those trying to find the flesh and blood Jesus. Luckily, tracking Judas the Galilean exposed these clever tricks.

WHO WAS PILATE?

Not much is known about Pontius Pilate outside of the few mentions in the New Testament and a sketchy outline in Josephus. As discussed above, Pilate became governor of Judea in 19 AD. His first acts were provocative in nature. He brought the Roman standards into Jerusalem, forcing the conservative Jews into a corner. Were they willing to stand up to the blatant attempt to sully their religion? The standards had the image of an eagle on them, a symbol of the power of Rome and a graven image. The Jews called Pilate's bluff, and he was forced to remove the offensive standards, back to Caesarea. Next, Pilate used the Temple's monies to fund an aqueduct project. This may have been good government; but once again, the conservative Jews were outraged. It is at this point that Josephus details the death of Jesus. Pilate may have been instructed to do anything in his power to catch Judas/Jesus. The standards and the Temple funds, along with the High Priest musical chairs, could have lured Jesus to Jerusalem. Pilate knew that Jesus would only be caught when cornered, and this action could only take place in Jerusalem.

The New Testament adds little to our understanding of Pilate. In one interesting episode, Pilate's wife warns Pilate to steer clear of Jesus' trial.

> While Pilate was sitting on the judge's seat, his wife sent him this message: "Don't have anything to do with that innocent man, for I have suffered a great deal today in a dream because of him." (Matt. 27:19)

This dream sequence was necessary to pull Pilate away from the conspiracy against Jesus. First, dreams were seen as a way for God to communicate with people. Joseph interpreted Pharaoh's dreams, and everything in those dreams came to pass. Paul's gospel was based upon dreams and visions, and he took it as a sign from God. In the same way, we are to believe that God was communicating with Pilate through Pilate's wife. Second, in the dream, Jesus was pronounced innocent of all crimes. Certainly, this would have shaken Pilate.

The dream episode may have been lifted from the pages of Josephus. After the Golden Eagle Temple Cleansing, the High Priest, Matthias, was removed from his duties for a short while because of a dream he had concerning his wife. This dream made him unclean and unfit for duty. Both dreams had the effect of removing responsibility: Pilate washed his hands in the trial of Jesus while Matthias was replaced after the trial of Judas and Matthias.

A second important scene in the Jesus story concerns Pilate and Barabbas. From the New Testament account, Pilate was forced by the crowd to release Barabbas against his good judgment. Pilate tried to convince the Jews that Jesus had done nothing wrong (innocent man per his wife's dream), but they screamed for his crucifixion.

> Now it was the governor's custom at the Feast to release a prisoner chosen by the crowd. At that time they had a notorious prisoner, called Barabbas. So when the crowd had gathered, Pilate asked them, "Which one do you want me to release to you: Barabbas, or Jesus who is called Christ?" For he knew it was out of envy that they had handed Jesus over to him.... When Pilate saw he was getting nowhere, but that instead an uproar was starting, he took water and washed his hands in front of the crowd. "I an innocent of this man's blood," he said. "It is your responsibility!"
> All the people answered, "Let his blood be on us and on our children!"
> Then he released Barabbas to them. But he had Jesus flogged, and handed him over to be crucified. (Matt. 27:16-18; 24-26)

We have just examined Pilate's earliest actions concerning the Jews: the standards and the Temple funds. Both actions showed no sensibilities to the Jewish religion. Now we are expected to believe that Pilate cared about Jesus and tried to release him. This flies in the face of common sense. First, nowhere in Roman practice, anywhere in the Empire, did the efficient and often ruthless Roman government release prisoners to the wishes of the oppressed. Barabbas was a political prisoner, having stirred an insurrection in the city. This man would have certainly been crucified. Pilate would not have released him to the crowd. In fact, the only prisoner release written about by Josephus occurred in 4 BC, during the shaky reign of Archelaus. This may have been the real Barabbas incident. (See Chapter Six—Barabbas).

The whole point of Pilate's actions, which included Barabbas, the dream and the washing of his hands, was to shift blame from the Romans to the Jews. The Jews had welcomed Jesus into Jerusalem as Messiah. Now we are to believe that they turned their backs upon him, demanding that he be crucified! Nothing could be more illogical. Pilate and the High Priests were working together. The arrest and crucifixion of Jesus was Roman justice. Pilate was a severe and sadistic man; he deserved the blame along with his hirelings. According to Josephus, Pilate was recalled to Rome in 37 AD because of his slaughter of the Samaritans. (*Ant.* 18.85-89) The soft, sentimental Pilate was interesting literature, but not good history.

TIMELINE OF JOSEPHUS
(*Ant.* 18.26-84)

6 AD	Joazar—High Priest.
6–9 AD	Coponius—Roman Governor
6 AD	Judas the Galilean—Tax Revolt
7–15 AD	Annas—Appointed High Priest by Coponius
9–12 AD	Ambivulus—Roman Governor
12–15 AD	Rufus—Roman Governor
15–26(18) AD	Gratus—Roman Governor (**11 or 3 years**)
15 AD	Ishmael—Appointed High Priest by Gratus
15–16 AD	Eleazar—Appointed High Priest by Gratus
16–17 AD	Simon—Appointed High Priest by Gratus
18–37 AD	Caiaphas—Appointed High Priest by Gratus
26(18)–37 AD	Pilate—Roman Governor
18 AD	City of Tiberius built
19 AD	Germanicus poisoned
26(19) AD	Pilate—Roman effigies; sacred money for aqueduct
26(19) AD	Jesus Passage (replaced Judas the Galilean's death)
19 AD	Paulina Affair—corroborated by Tacitus

4

THE BIRTH NARRATIVES

Scholars, church historians and the clergy have invested much energy in avoiding the obvious discrepancies between the two birth narratives of Jesus included in the New Testament. Instead of concentrating on the areas of disagreement, these "scholars" tend to harmonize the two accounts, so that the Christian story appears to be historical to the uninformed. For example, most believe in the dating scenario presented by Matthew, where Jesus was born shortly before the death of Herod the Great. But they somehow also give credence to the census registration as related by Luke. This melding of accounts may make for an interesting Christmas play, but it does little to advance the quest for truth.

To fully understand the birth narratives, the dating of the Synoptic Gospels must be ascertained. All scholars agree that the first written Gospel in the present canon is Mark, dated between 70-105 AD, a generation before Matthew and Luke. Mark has no information concerning the birth of Jesus. This suggests that many components of the birth narratives were either not widely disseminated or not yet invented. Instead of an infancy story, Mark began his narrative with the story of John the Baptist. In Mark's Gospel, John preceded Jesus, preparing the Jews for the coming Messiah. Mark does not date John, just as he does not date Pilate or Caiaphas, the only other historically verifiable figures in his Gospel. All we can do is guess at the time frames, based upon the history of Josephus concerning John the Baptist, Pilate and Caiaphas.

The subsequent birth narratives of Matthew and Luke create dating problems which were nonexistent in the book of Mark. When was Jesus born? How old was he when he began his mission? And what year did he die? These questions can be answered by Matthew and Luke, but the answers actually create more questions.

The first question concerning the date of Jesus' birth is answered differently by Matthew and Luke. Matthew placed the birth before the death of Herod the Great. From Josephus, the date of Herod's death can be positively identified as 4

BC. Thus, Jesus' birth was some time before this as Matthew claimed the Magi consulted Herod <u>after</u> they had seen the king's star in the east.

> <u>After</u> Jesus was born in Bethlehem in Judea, during the time of King Herod, Magi from the east came to Jerusalem and asked, "Where is the one who has been born king of the Jews? We saw his star in the east and have come to worship him."
> ...When Herod realized that he had been outwitted by the Magi, he was furious, and he gave orders to kill all the boys in Bethlehem and its vicinity who were two years old and under.
> ...After Herod died, an angel of the Lord appeared in a dream to Joseph in Egypt and said, "Get up, take the child and his mother and go to the land of Israel, for those who were trying to take the child's life are dead." (Matt. 2:1-20) (emphasis mine)

From this account, Jesus was a young child at the time of Herod's death. Depending on his age, anywhere ranging from 2 to 5 years old, the birth can be estimated at 9-6 BC. The latest date could be 6 BC as Herod had all the children two years old or younger slaughtered. Again, 4 BC plus two years equals 6 BC.

Many historians doubt the Herod the Great story, as the massacre of the innocents appears to be a copy of the Moses story. Also, Josephus recorded that Herod's jealousy for his crown was much closer to home. Herod actually had his own children put to death. This does not prove that Herod did not visit with the Magi, but such data escaped the pen of Josephus. This in itself is unlikely as Josephus' history was full of odd and interesting stories. If there had been a star in the east (comet?) or a massacre of the innocents, then Josephus would have included every last detail. But even if some of the particulars of Matthew's version are fiction, at least the date is set between 9-6 BC. (The Slavonic Josephus does recount such a story, so there may have been a source common to both Matthew and the Slavonic Josephus. Therefore, this traditional Christmas story may be older than many suspect.)

Luke's Gospel had a much different date for Jesus' birth, in the time of the census. This census has been pinpointed at 6-7 AD, a good 11-15 years later than Matthew's Herod the Great narrative.

> In those days Caesar Augustus issued a decree that a census should be taken of the entire roman world. (This was the first census that took place while Quirinius was governor of Syria. And everyone went to his own town to register. So Joseph also went up from the town of Nazareth in Galilee to Judea, to Bethlehem the town of David. He went there to register with Mary, who was

pledged to be married to him and was expecting a child. While they were there, the time came for the baby to be born, and she gave birth to her <u>firstborn</u>, a son. She wrapped him in clothes and placed him in a manger, because there was no room for them in the inn. (Luke 2:1-7) (emphasis mine)

This passage has long been used to explain why Mary and Joseph ended up in Bethlehem if they originally lived in Nazareth. It was convenient to use the census to move the couple, but this device has too many associated problems. For instance, making people walk to their respective home town to register would have been a logistical nightmare, even in this day of computers. The Romans would have registered people where they worked, thus saving a mass migration and unbelievable paperwork.

The census of Cyrenius has been dated to 6-7 AD. (*Ant.* 18.1,2) In light of the Matthew dating of 9-6 BC, this discrepancy surely destroys the inherent perfection of the New Testament. Scholars have tried to explain this obvious error, but the best attempt came from William Barclay, the famous Bible commentator. He admitted that Luke slightly erred in his mention of this particular census. He believed that Luke meant to be referring to another census, one fourteen years earlier.(1) So by this correction, Barclay moved Luke's birth date to 8 BC. This date would be consistent with that of Matthew, and therefore, must be correct.

Before we agree on the Barclay interpretation, let's logically see where Luke's dating takes us. If Jesus was born in 6-7 AD and his career lasted thirty-three years, then Jesus would have been crucified in 39-40 AD. This is two to three years after Pilate was sent back to Rome. In addition, this later date would have made the spread of Christianity across the world impossible in such a short time. Therefore, it is safe to throw out the written word of Luke in favor of Barclay's explanation of Luke.

According to Matthew and Barclay, the birth of Jesus must have been at 8 BC. Luke recorded that Jesus was thirty years old when he started his ministry. (Luke 3:23) If this is true, then the ministry of Jesus began in 23 AD. And most Bible scholars argue that Jesus spent three years in disseminating his gospel to the people. If that is true, then Jesus was crucified in 26 AD. Pilate came to Judea in 26 AD according to traditional dating, so the death of Jesus in 26 AD is consistent with Pilate's reign. It seems as if we have the answer to the dating problem.

However, one more item must be reconciled to the above dating of Jesus' ministry. According to Luke 3:1, John began his ministry of repentance in the fifteenth year of the reign of Tiberius Caesar. Tiberius became Caesar in 14 AD. So John's ministry began in 28-29 AD, two to three years <u>after</u> the death of Jesus.

But that is impossible, the preachers would surely say. John introduced Jesus to the world according to all four Gospels. (Luke 3:1-23)

If the Luke version of the birth is taken as fact, then Jesus began his ministry in 36-37 AD, after John the Baptist, but also after the reign of Pilate. If Matthew's version is followed, then Jesus died before John the Baptist began his ministry, but this death at least fell within the time frame of Pilate. Either way, the birth of Jesus at such a time of 8 BC or 6 AD does not follow our other information provided by the New Testament.

Then which is correct? My answer is neither. If one logically dates either scenario, then insurmountable problems emerge. The largest of these problems concerns John the Baptist. It is interesting to note that most scholars forget to analyze John's message in terms of the church's message <u>after</u> the death of Jesus. In Acts 2:38, Peter said this to the crowd, "Repent and be baptized, every one of you, in the name of Jesus Christ so that your sins may be forgiven." How is this different from John's ministry? "He went into all the country around the Jordan, preaching a baptism of repentance for the forgiveness of sins." (Luke 3:3)

Both John the Baptist and Peter were baptizing for the forgiveness of sins. Josephus clarified that the baptism did not forgive sins but was an outward sign of an inner repentance. (*Ant.* 18.117) Peter's message came shortly after the death of Jesus. Is it possible that John also preached after the death of Jesus and not before? Could John have been ushering in the return of Jesus as were the apostles? This is part of the answer to the dating problem. John the Baptist came after Jesus. This explains the following passage, where John compared himself to Jesus, the Jesus of heaven and not of the earth. This is similar to the Jesus in the book of Revelation. (Rev. 14:14-20)

> "I baptize you with water for repentance. But after me will come one who is more powerful than I, whose sandals I am not fit to carry. He will baptize you with the Holy Spirit and with fire. His winnowing fork is in his hand, and he will clear the threshing floor, gathering the wheat into his barn and burning up the chaff with unquenchable fire." (Matt. 3:11,12)

This definitely sounds like a judgment scene where Jesus will separate the good from the bad. This judgment was used as an incentive for repentance and a change in lifestyle. I have no doubt that John would have said this. But it was spoken well after Jesus' death. Looking at it another way: if John believed in the superiority of Jesus before they even met at the water baptism, then why did John still have disciples in the time of Paul? It seems to me that John's whole movement would have stopped the moment he baptized Jesus in the Jordan. If John did baptize Jesus, he nevertheless continued his own ministry. And according to Josephus, John was definitely on the scene many years <u>after</u> the death of Jesus!

The Jewish historian placed John's death at approximately 35-36 AD, far beyond the lifetime of Jesus. And the writings of Paul further cement this. In Corinthians, Paul complained that there were divisions in the church. One of the teachers, Apollos, may have been a disciple of John. Paul said, "I planted the seed, Apollos watered it, but God made it grow." (1 Cor. 3:6) Acts 18:24-26, identified Apollos as a Jew who taught of Jesus accurately but knew only of John's baptism. This later ministry of John was no doubt contemporaneous with Paul but not with that of Jesus.

So when John the Baptist preached in the desert in the 30's, preparing a way for the Lord, he was preparing the people for Jesus' return in glory. This repentance and the associated baptism was necessary in the leaders' eyes. This leads us to another troubling question. Why did the Gospel writers mislead us concerning John the Baptist's role in the Jesus movement? The answer can once again be uncovered from the writings of Paul.

In 1 Corinthians, a fight for supremacy among the teachers was ongoing. Although Paul said he welcomed the competition, a full reading of his positions clearly state that he believed the teachings of Cephas, James and John the Baptist to be inferior to his own. John the Baptist preached a baptism of repentance while he (Paul) preached a baptism of the Holy Spirit. The Gospel writers simply made John the Baptist subservient to the earthly Jesus as Paul believed John's teachings to be inferior to his own. This rewriting of history is not at all unusual for the Gospels or for Acts. Most of the story has been lifted from the pages of Josephus or from Paul's letters.

From the above, it is a certainty that Luke's version of the birth at 6 AD is incorrect. Also Matthew and Barclay's version of 8 BC cannot be correct since it puts Jesus well before John the Baptist. But this error may really be accurate. In Chapter Three—Pilate's Reign, a compelling case has been made to place the governorship from 18-37 AD. This earlier introduction of Pilate may also relate to an earlier crucifixion of Jesus. Without the birth narratives to set the historical dating of Jesus, the death can be placed anywhere within the era of Pilate. As has been shown in Chapter Three, the early date of 19 AD appears to be the most likely case. And if Jesus died in 19 AD, his birth would have been well before the Matthew date of 8 BC.

It should also be noted that commentators never doubt the age of Jesus, that being thirty. Is it possible that his ministry began at thirty but lasted five, ten or even twenty years? The Gospels themselves telescope Jesus' career into a one to three year ministry. But this may be good literature rather than good history. One church legend has James, the brother of Jesus, being 96 years old at his stoning in 62 AD. Even if this is an exaggeration of ten or so years, that means James must have been born somewhere between 35-24 BC. Since Jesus was the firstborn, it follows that he must have been born before James, possibly between 36-25 BC. Therefore, the age of Jesus in 5 BC would have been twenty to thirty. It is here that we should look for the historical life of Jesus and the beginning of his ministry.

The birth narratives brought Jesus into the world in the days of Herod the Great and at the time of the census. Josephus also introduced a character in these exact time periods. Judas the Galilean cleansed the Temple right before Herod's death (*Ant.* 17.149-167). He was arrested by Herod and later released to the Jewish crowd in a Barabbas-style prisoner release. Judas was then hailed as Messiah in Galilee before starting a nationwide campaign against Roman taxation, at the census (6 AD). (*Ant.* 18.1-10) This lengthy passage by Josephus claimed that this Judas founded his own philosophy, named the Fourth Philosophy. (The other three philosophies were the Sadducees, the Pharisees and the Essenes.) Thus, Josephus has two major sections covering Judas the Galilean, one at 4 BC and the other at 6 AD, the exact times of the birth narratives.

Could Jesus have been the nickname or title for Judas the Galilean? Josephus never mentioned Jesus or Christianity but was obsessed with Judas the Galilean and the Fourth Philosophy. It is my belief that Judas and Jesus were two names for the same man. But why would the Gospel writers go to such lengths in hiding this connection? It was their purpose to distance Jesus from anything Jewish and from his actual past. Even though Jesus was a Jewish Messiah, the Gospels portray him as fighting against the ancient religion in favor of his own vision. As you read the rest of this book, you will become aware that this new Christian vision came from the revelations of Paul and not from the life of Jesus.

TIMELINES

MATTHEW AND BARCLAY

```
Jesus    Herod      Tax                Jesus  Jesus  John         John
Born     Dies       Revolt             Begins Cruc.  Begins       Killed
{--------------- 30 Years ---------------------}
                                       {-------------- Pilate ---------------}
|----------------------------------------------------------------------------|
8         4          6                 18     23     26       29       37
BC                   AD
```

There are several problems associated with Matthew's version of Jesus' birth. First, Jesus' ministry would have occurred between 23-26 AD, many years before John the Baptist (29-36 AD). This flies in the face of the New Testament Gospel accounts. Second, if Jesus was the firstborn (Luke 2:7), then James, the brother of Jesus, must have been born around 7 BC or later. According to tradition, James was a very old man of 96 at his death in 62 AD. If James had been born in 7 AD, then he would have been just 68 in 62 AD, not so very old to promulgate a tradition of extreme old age.

LUKE

```
Jesus               Jesus at            John           Jesus John   Jesus
Born                the Temple          Begins         Begins Killed Cruc.
{----------12 Years ----------}{--------------- Pilate -----------------}
|----------------------------------------------------------------------------|
6                    18                  29             36    37     39
AD
```

The Gospel of Luke's birth narrative is obviously wrong. Not only does it contradict Matthew (an internal Bible problem), but the dating defies logic. If Jesus was born in 6-7 AD, then he died in 39-40 AD, several years after Pontius Pilate returned to Rome. In addition, this later ministry cannot jibe with Luke's own timetable in Acts. For example, If Paul converted a few years after this later crucifixion, then Paul's ministry started around 42 AD. By Paul's own reckonings in Galatians, approximately 17 years passed from his conversion to the Council of Jerusalem, placing this at 59 AD. Additional time passed as there was a disagreement with Cephas in Antioch (Galatians) and his own personal letters to the Galatians and Corinthians were written subsequently. Thus, Paul's arrival in Jerusalem could not have been before 60 AD. But again, that is later than the book of Acts would allow. According to Acts, Paul was in Jerusalem shortly after the Egyptian (58 AD), during the governorship of Felix (58-60 AD).

One other point must be made: the later the date for Jesus' ministry, the more unlikely that the gospel would have spread to other parts of the world, from 40-60 AD. For example, Suetonius claimed that the Jews who followed a Chrestus (Christ) were causing disturbances in Rome around 50 AD. It seems as if the Jewish Christian movement had reached the major cities in the Roman Empire and were quite organized. This would take time even in an era of instant communication. It is not feasible that the spread of Jewish Christianity could have occurred in only a few short years.

UNTERBRINK'S HYPOTHESIS

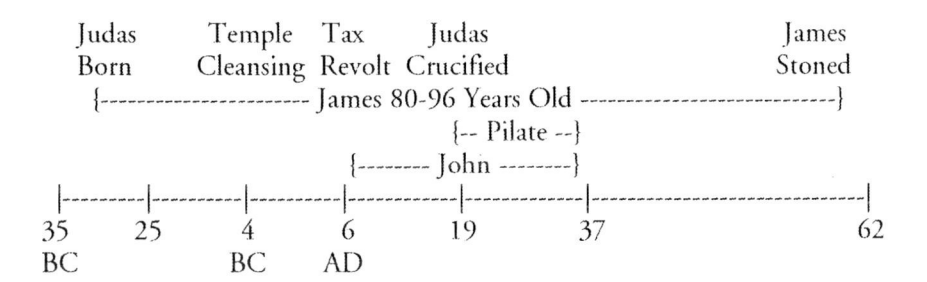

```
Judas       Temple    Tax      Judas                              James
Born        Cleansing Revolt   Crucified                          Stoned
{---------------------- James 80-96 Years Old ----------------------}
                               {-- Pilate --}
                           {-------- John --------}
|---------|----------|----------|-------------|--------------|----------------------------|
35        25         4          6             19             37                           62
BC                   BC         AD
```

My timeline begins a generation earlier than either Matthew or Luke. However, this takes into account the advanced age of James in 62 AD. (James' age of ninety-six at his death may be a slight exaggeration as the same historian stated that James was a lifelong virgin, even though Paul reported that James was married in 1 Cor. 9:5. Although the exact age may be questioned, surely James was an old man, ranging in age from 85-96 at his death.) Thus, James' birth could have been anywhere between 35-24 BC. Since Judas/Jesus was the older brother, his birth date would be between 36-25 BC.

The Slavonic Josephus has the same birth narrative as Matthew, that of the star of Bethlehem and the massacre of the innocents by Herod.(2) However, according to the Slavonic version, the Persian astrologers came to search for the infant somewhere between the tenth to fifteenth year of Herod's reign. This translates to 27-22 BC. As the infant was approximately two years old at the meeting with Herod, the birth was somewhere between 29-24 BC. This dating is also consistent with the age of James, noted above.

Was there really a star of Bethlehem? The traditional dating for Jesus has no one explanation for the star. Guesses range from Halley's comet (12 BC) to the conjunction of planets to the eclipse of the moon. In short, there is no definitive answer in the 6 BC time frame. In the 29-24 BC time frame, the same may be true. There is a coin dated 19 BC, honoring the "Divine Julius," which shows a comet with 8 rays. This comet may be a previous comet during the reign of Julius Caesar or may be representing a contemporary event.(3) In any event, the exact dating of Judas/Jesus in this earlier period may not be any easier than the failed attempts to pinpoint Jesus in 6 BC.

It is possible that the star legend has more to due with prophecy than any real celestial event. Eisenman states:

> "…the Star Prophecy is highly prized at Qumran. In the War Scroll it is directly applied to a Messianic 'no mere Adam'. In the Damascus Document, 'the Star' is tied to 'the Sceptre' and 'the Staff'…"(4)

Josephus blamed this Star prophecy for the Jewish war, as the Jews believed that the prophecy was about a Jew who would overturn the existing world order. Josephus, on the other hand, attributed this prophecy to Vespasian, the future Emperor of Rome.

> But what more than all else incited them to war was an ambiguous oracle, likewise found in their sacred scriptures, to the effect that at that time one from their country would become ruler of the world. This they understood to mean someone of their own race, and many of their wise men went astray in their interpretation of it. The oracle, however, in reality signified the sovereignty of Vespasian, who was proclaimed emperor on Jewish soil. (*War* 6.312,313)

The Slavonic Josephus gives the same message with the following: "For some thought it [meant] Herod, others the crucified miracle-worker [Jesus], others Vespasian."(5) Obviously, the early followers of Judas/Jesus attributed the Star prophecy to Jesus. Could the birth narrative somehow derive from this oracle? Could this legend have been invented, and then placed in the Slavonic Josephus in context to the time of Jesus' real birth? This seems to be the most likely explanation for the Star of Bethlehem.

One other interesting point must be made about the time period in question, 29-24 BC. In 27 BC, Augustus was proclaimed Caesar. The virgin birth by Mary paralleled the story of Augustus' mother as told by Suetonius.

> Suddenly a serpent glided up, entered her, and then glided away again. On awakening, she purified herself, as if after intimacy with her husband..., and the birth of Augustus nine months later suggested a divine paternity....Publius Nigidius Figulus, the astrologer, hearing at what hour the child had been delivered, cried out: "The ruler of the world is now born." Everyone believes this story.(6)

The Star of Bethlehem story may have been rooted in a combination of the Star prophecy and the competition between the ruler of Rome (the deified Augustus) and the Messiah of the Jews (Jesus). This Star of Bethlehem may have been an early story, maybe circulated during the lifetime of Jesus. After all, Judas/Jesus was a clever rabbi, and he used the scriptures to his own advantage. In the Gospels, Jesus rode into Jerusalem on a donkey, knowing full well that this was a Messianic action. In Chapter Five, John the Baptist will be shown as a member of Judas the Galilean's Fourth Philosophy. John introduced Judas/Jesus before his nationwide campaign against Rome, also a Messianic act. In short, the Star of Bethlehem could have been a cleverly invented story to give Judas/Jesus a miraculous beginning.

If Jesus was born in 25 BC, then he would have been thirty years old in 6 AD, the time of the census of Cyrenius. At this same time (6 AD), the Slavonic Josephus introduced a wild character (John the Baptist) who baptized in the Jordan and who foretold of a future Messiah.(7) This was the exact time when Judas the Galilean began his nationwide tax revolt against Rome. If the Slavonic Josephus' dating is correct, then Jesus and Judas were the exact same age and both were preceded by John the Baptist. This only confirms my hypothesis that Jesus and Judas were the same person.

The death of Judas/Jesus in 19 AD falls within the revised rule of Pilate (See Chapter Three—Pilate's Reign), but precedes the Gospel John the Baptist by a decade. As noted above, John introduced Jesus to the world in 6 AD, and then proceeded to outlive Jesus by seventeen years, from 19 AD to his death in 36 AD. The later John preached a post—Jesus message of repentance. Therefore, this is consistent with the Slavonic Josephus and Josephus' dating of John. Jesus would have been approximately 21 years old at the Golden Eagle Temple Cleansing, 22-30 when proclaimed Messiah in Galilee, 30 at the Census of Cyrenius and 43 at his death in 19 AD. Thus, the Jewish Christian church would have had its roots in 19 AD versus the traditional dating of 33 AD. This earlier date would also account for the spread of Jewish Christianity around the world. In addition, only this timeline can reconcile Paul's ministry to Josephus and the Pseudoclementine *Recognitions*. (See Chapter Sixteen—The Fourth Philosophy for timelines for the early church and Paul, beginning in 19 AD.)

5

JOHN THE BAPTIST

John the Baptist is perhaps the most important figure in the quest to unravel the riddle of the historical Jesus. According to the Gospels, John's life and death had a close proximity to Jesus' life and death. And the dating of John's ministry is crucial in determining the years in which Jesus preached the Kingdom of Heaven. Therefore, it is necessary to investigate everything written about John in the earliest known documents. We will first lay out the traditional viewpoint concerning John, coming straight from the various Gospels. Then, an alternative history will be proposed based upon the Gospels and other early writings, such as *Antiquities*, the Slavonic Josephus and the Pseudoclementine literature.

THE TRADITIONAL VIEW

> The angel answered, "The Holy Spirit will come upon you, and the power of the Most High will overshadow you. So the holy one to be born will be called the Son of God. Even Elizabeth your relative is going to have a child in her old age, and she who was said to be barren is in her sixth month. For nothing is impossible with God...
> At that time Mary got ready and hurried to a town in the hill country of Judah, where she entered Zechariah's home and greeted Elizabeth. When Elizabeth heard Mary's greeting, the baby [John] leaped in her womb, and Elizabeth was filled with the Holy Spirit. In a loud voice she exclaimed: "Blessed are you among women, and blessed is the child you will bear! But why am I so favored, that the mother of my Lord should come to me? As soon as the sound of your greeting reached my ears, the baby in my womb leaped for joy. Blessed is she who has believed that what the Lord has said to her will be accomplished."...Mary stayed with Elizabeth for about three months and then returned home. (Luke 1:35-56)

The Gospel of Luke has incredible detail concerning the parents of John as well as the reason for naming the child John. The above passage details the relationship between Mary and Elizabeth and their soon to be born sons, Jesus and

John. There are three major points to be gleaned from the above passage and Luke's earlier recorded history of the family. First, John and Jesus were related to one another. From this, a close relationship between the two families is assured. Second, John was to be born six months before Jesus. This means that the two would have started their ministries at the age of thirty (Luke 3:23). Third, both Elizabeth and her fetus were aware that Mary carried the Son of God in her womb. If John believed in Jesus as a fetus, then he would surely believe in him as an adult!

> In the fifteenth year of the reign of Tiberius Caesar—when Pontius Pilate was governor of Judea, Herod tetrarch of Galilee, his brother Philip tetrarch of Iturea and Traconitis, and Lysanias tetrarch of Abilene—during the high priesthood of Annas and Caiaphas, the word of God came to John son of Zechariah in the desert. He went into all the country around the Jordan, preaching a baptism of repentance for the forgiveness of sins....
>
> John said to the crowds coming out to be baptized by him, "You brood of vipers! Who warned you to flee from the coming wrath? Produce fruit in keeping with repentance."
>
> ...The people were waiting expectantly and were all wondering in their hearts if John might be the Christ. John answered them all, "I baptize you with water. But one more powerful than I will come, the thongs of whose sandals I am not worthy to untie. He will baptize you with the Holy Spirit and with fire. His winnowing fork is in his hands to clear his threshing floor and to gather the wheat into his barn, but he will burn up the chaff with unquenchable fire." (Luke 3:1-17)

The above passage describes John preparing the way for the Messiah, or for Jesus. This was in fulfillment of the prophet Isaiah (Isaiah 40:3-5). According to Luke, John's ministry began in the fifteenth year of the reign of Tiberius. Tiberius came to power in 14 AD, so John's emergence came in the year 28-29 AD. The beginning of Jesus' ministry can be dated to his baptism by John, around 29-30 AD. (Luke 3:21-23) Since both Jesus and John were thirty years old, their birth dates <u>must</u> be approximately 2-1 BC. Unfortunately, per Chapter Four, Matthew's birth date for Jesus was 9-6 BC while Luke's was 6 AD. No matter how you figure, these dates do not make sense. Something must be wrong!

John's message of repentance was ideal for its purpose, to usher in the day of the Messiah. John was simply preparing the people for Jesus' arrival. Not all people were thrilled by John's message. Those in power would have been threatened by a new Messiah, and were therefore resistant to John's message. However, John was not sensitive to their reservations. He called them a brood of vipers. This straightforward approach would eventually earn John a place in prison. But one thing is certain: John believed Jesus to be the Messiah. This steadfast belief is consistent with the earlier story of Elizabeth and Mary, where the fetus, John, leaped in Elizabeth's womb.

Luke's and Matthew's versions of John's description of the coming Messiah are unusual, as the one to come appears to be a resurrected Messiah, with judgment at hand. "His winnowing fork is in his hands to clear his threshing floor and to gather the wheat [the righteous] into his barn, but he will burn up the chaff [the wicked] with unquenchable fire." Thus, it is left open to our guess whether John was ushering in the earthly Messiah or the heavenly Messiah. In context, we will accept the earthly Messiah, but keep the resurrected Messiah in our thoughts for further analysis.

The Gospel of Mark did not refer to a judgment scene and added the following colorful description of John:

> John wore clothing made of camel's hair, with a leather belt around his waist, and he ate locusts and wild honey. (Mark 1:6)

According to Barclay, the mode of dress was to remind the people of the days of the great prophets, who lived the simple life apart from the luxuries of this life. Elijah wore "a garment of hair and a leather belt around his waist." (2 Kings 1:8) The food was either actual locusts and honey or carobs and sap from certain trees.(1) Regardless, the diet was simple, as John relied on God to provide from nature.

John the Baptist was indeed an interesting character. He introduced the Messiah to the world and was not afraid to criticize those in positions of power. This unwillingness to live comfortably with the world eventually led John to prison and to his death.

> But when Herod heard this [talk of John raising from the dead] he said, "John, the man I beheaded, has been raised from the dead!"
> For Herod himself had given orders to have John arrested, and he had him bound and put in prison. He did this because of Herodias, his brother Philip's wife, whom he had married. For John had been saying to Herod, "It is not lawful for you to have your brother's wife." So Herodias nursed a grudge against John and wanted to kill him. But she was not able to, because Herod feared John and protected him, knowing him to be a righteous and holy man. When Herod heard John, he was greatly puzzled, yet he liked to listen to him. (Mark 6:16-20)

After this part of the narrative, where Herod was infatuated with John, we are told of John's death. Herodias tricked her husband, Herod, into granting Herodias' daughter a wish after she pleased him with a dance. The girl asked for John the Baptist's head on a platter. In this way, the Gospel writers deflected blame away from Herod and toward his wife, Herodias.

From the above passage, John was doing what he knew best. He was being a social critic. Unlike Paul, who entertained Bernice and Agrippa, those Herodians accused of an incestuous relationship, John never hesitated to criticize actions he deemed inconsistent with the Law of Moses. This criticism enraged Herodias, and she eventually got her way: the death of John the Baptist.

One more passage needs to be examined. This concerns John's attitude towards Jesus while John languished in prison.

> When John heard in prison what Christ was doing, he sent his disciples to ask him, "Are you the one who was to come, or should we expect someone else?" (Matt. 11:2, 3)

This passage should confuse the reader. Throughout the story of John, he was sure of his own role in history and certain of Jesus, the Messiah. The fetus, John, leaped in his mother's womb upon hearing Mary's words. The man, John, baptized with water but promised that Jesus would baptize with the Holy Spirit. How could it be that John now doubted his role as well as the mission of Jesus? To go one step further: why did John even have disciples at this point? If he truly believed in Jesus, then he would have become part of the Jesus movement. But he did not. John had his own separate movement, one of repentance and baptism. The question is: why?

TRADITIONAL TIMELINE

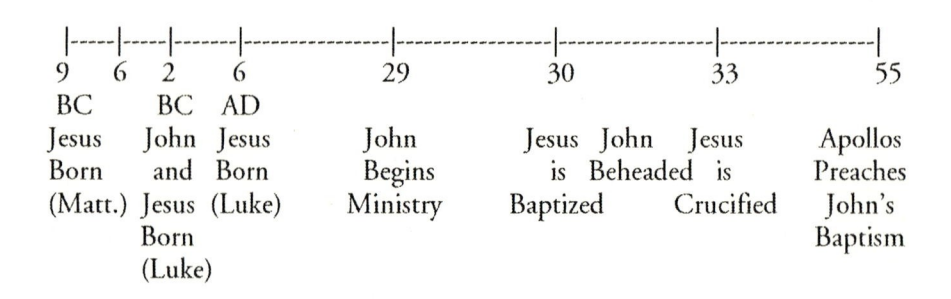

9 BC	6 BC	2 BC	6 AD	29	30	33	55
Jesus Born (Matt.)	John and Jesus Born (Luke)	Jesus Born (Luke)		John Begins Ministry	Jesus is Baptized	John is Beheaded	Jesus is Crucified	Apollos Preaches John's Baptism

The following problems emerge when considering the Gospel story of Jesus and John the Baptist.

1. Since Jesus and John were the same age at the beginning of their respective ministries (thirty years old), their birth dates can be calculated to 2-1 BC. This is inconsistent with the birth narratives related by Matthew and Luke. Matthew's birth of Jesus was between 9-6 BC while Luke had the birth at 6-7 AD. Either way, these cannot be reconciled to the John the Baptist story.

2. If we accept Matthew's dating for Jesus' birth, then Jesus' ministry would have started in 22-25 AD with his crucifixion occurring between 25-28 AD. Both dates are before the beginning of John's ministry as recorded by Luke. Obviously, one or both accounts are false.

3. If John was convinced that Jesus was the Messiah, then why did his own movement continue? After baptizing Jesus, and recognizing the Holy Spirit, we would expect both John and his disciples to jump onto the Jesus bandwagon. But they did not. In addition, the Gospels even share that John had his doubts about Jesus. If this is true, then the earlier stories about John's certainty might have been embellished.

4. According to the book of Acts, John had disciples into the 50's. (Acts 18:24) This episode related that Apollos taught about Jesus accurately but knew only the baptism of John. This explanation for Apollos answers the statement made by Paul in 1 Cor 3·6, "I planted the seed, Apollos watered it, but God made it grow." If Apollos was preaching the baptism of John, then we must ask ourselves these questions: did not John die before Jesus, and did not Jesus' apostles baptize in the Holy Spirit after Jesus' death? Put another way, the baptism by John should have been long forgotten. He was before the resurrection of Jesus and before the baptism of the Holy Spirit. Why would anyone use the baptism of John at this late date? This cannot be explained by the traditional timeline.

WHAT REALLY HAPPENED

From the traditional story, there are several discrepancies which cannot be explained, particularly the dating of events. However, the main thrust of the John the Baptist passages is clear: John came to announce the coming of the Messiah. But was this proclamation by John before the earthly Jesus came onto the scene, or was John proclaiming a return of the resurrected Jesus? From the Gospel accounts, both can be argued. In Mark, John appears to be ushering in the coming of the earthly Messiah, but Matthew and Luke invoke imagery of the Messiah at judgment, similar to the scenes in the book of Revelation. Is it possible that John the Baptist preached his message of repentance before the earthly Jesus and again after the crucifixion, to prepare his hearers for the return of a conquering Jesus? I believe that is exactly what happened. But if John died before Jesus, as tradition claims, then such a proposal is impossible. But what if John died after Jesus?

Before we answer the question concerning the death of John, we must make an attempt to pinpoint the beginning date of John's ministry. In the Gospel of Luke, John's ministry began in the fifteenth year of Tiberius' reign, or approximately 29 AD. That is why most scholars have placed Jesus' ministry at 30 AD, even though the birth narratives do not yield such a beginning date. The other three Gospels are silent on the year that John's ministry began. Josephus also has no information concerning the early years of John. Maybe Josephus did not think John important, or maybe such information was expunged from his record. After all, a charismatic character like John would have been very interesting material for Josephus. So we are left with only one source which flat out contradicts Luke's dating, and that source is the Slavonic Josephus.

The Slavonic Josephus was composed in Russia a thousand years after the events, but most scholars believe that it was not an original Russian document, but rather a translation from Greek or Aramaic. Was this from Josephus himself or by an early Jewish writer? No one will ever know for sure. Essentially, this version of Josephus contains the seven books of the *War*, but other information is included as well. This information was either part of the original Josephus or from the pen of a first-century Jew. Either way, the following passage about John the Baptist's beginnings is fascinating.

> Now at that time a man went about among the Jews in strange garments; for he had put pelts on his body everywhere it was not covered with his own hair; indeed to look at, he was like a wild man. He came to the Jews and summoned them to freedom, saying: "God hath sent me, that I may show you the way of the Law, wherein ye may free yourselves from many holders of power. And there will be no mortal ruling over you, only the Highest who hath sent me." And when the people heard this, they were joyful. And there went after him all Judea, that lies in the region round Jerusalem. And he did nothing else to them save that he plunged them into the stream of the Jordan and dismissed them, instructing them that they should cease from evil works, and [promising] that there would [then] be given them a ruler who would set them free....

> And when he had been brought to Archelaus and the doctors of the Law had assembled, they asked him who he [was] and where he [had] been until then. And to this he made answer and spake: "I am pure; [for] the Spirit of God hath led me on, and [I live on] cane and roots and tree-food." But when they threatened to put him to torture if he would not cease from those words and deeds, he nevertheless said: "It is meet for you [rather] to cease from your heinous works and cleave unto the Lord your God." (2)

The similarities between this John and the Gospel John include the following items. First, this John covered his whole body in pelts and appeared as a wild man. This description is not quite as dignified as the Gospels, where John dressed like one of the prophets of old. In addition, John's diet of cane, roots and nuts approximates the locusts and honey of the Gospels. According to Barclay, the locusts and honey could have been carobs and sap from certain trees. Regardless, this picture emerges: an unusual preacher not at all at home with the comforts of this life. In fact, this John's appearance was so unlike others that he must have stood out, like a true prophet.

Also, like the Gospels, John preached repentance to the crowds gathering around the river Jordan, and "plunged them into the stream." The passage goes on to talk about those who disapproved of John. His response to them was similar to the Gospel rebuke of the vipers. In both versions, John promised a ruler who would set them free, an attractive message to the crowds but a dangerous threat to the ruling authorities. In short, this Slavonic Josephus depiction of John has the same charm and power of the Gospels.

However, there are three major differences between this John and the Baptist of the Gospels. First, this John had a political agenda while the Gospel Baptist was centered strictly on repentance and baptism. This John said, "God hath sent me, that I may show you the way of the Law, wherein ye may free yourselves from many holders of power. And there will be no mortal ruling over you, only the Highest who hath sent me." This philosophy to remove the Herodians and Romans in favor of God was the same as the Fourth Philosophy of Judas the Galilean. In the *War* and *Antiquities*, Josephus wrote the following about Judas the Galilean.

> ...it was that a certain Galilean, whose name was Judas, prevailed with his countrymen to revolt; and said they were cowards if they would endure to pay a tax to the Romans, and would, after God, submit to mortal men as their lords. This man was a teacher of a peculiar sect of his own, and was not at all like the rest of those their leaders. (*War* 2.118) (emphasis mine)

> ...yet there was one Judas, a Gaulonite, of a city whose name was Gamala, who, taking with him Sadduc, a Pharisee, became zealous to draw them to a revolt, who both said that this taxation was no better than an introduction to slavery, and exhorted the nation to assert their liberty.... But of the fourth sect of Jewish philosophy, Judas the Galilean was the author. These men agree in all things with the Pharisaic notions; but they have an inviolable attachment to liberty; and say that <u>God is to be their only Ruler and Lord</u>. (*Ant.* 18.4,23) (emphasis mine)

There can be no doubt about it: the Slavonic John the Baptist held the same philosophy as Judas the Galilean. Since Judas was the leader of the movement, it follows that John was a disciple of Judas, albeit a wild one at that. By identifying John as a member of the Fourth Philosophy (later known as the Zealots) a later saying about John by Jesus may finally come into focus. "From the days of John the Baptist until now, the kingdom of heaven has been forcefully advancing, and forceful [violent] men lay hold of it." (Matt. 11:12) It is quite likely that Jesus was referring to the Fourth Philosophy which he championed.

The location of the Slavonic passage is after *War* 2.110. The above introduction to Judas the Galilean was eight verses later. The passage also dates itself by saying that John was brought before Archelaus. This meeting was shortly before Archelaus was summoned to trial for his atrocities against the Jews and Samaritans. In his ninth year (6 AD), he was banished to Vienna, a city in Gaul. (*War* 2.111) This Archelaus was the son of Herod the Great and ruled from 4 BC to 7 AD. Thus, John's ministry began in 6 AD, right before Judas the Galilean led his tax revolt against Rome. This can only mean that John's Messiah was none other than Judas the Galilean.

In support of the Slavonic Josephus passage, the *Recognitions of Clement* states, "For the people [Israel] was now divided into many parties, ever since the days of John the Baptist." (3) These groups were then denoted as the Sadducees, the Samaritans, the scribes and Pharisees, and even some of John's disciples. It should be noted that in *Antiquities* and in the *War*, Josephus wrote of the Jewish sects right after introducing Judas the Galilean and his Fourth Philosophy. Josephus mentioned four philosophies: the Sadducees, the Pharisees, the Essenes and the Fourth Philosophy of Judas. Is it just coincidence that the *Recognitions* recounted the different Jewish sects right after mentioning John the Baptist? Or is it possible that the *Recognition's* placement of John the Baptist came from a source similar to the Slavonic Josephus? This is clear: both the Slavonic Josephus and the *Recognitions* place John the Baptist before Judas the Galilean and before the enumeration of the Jewish philosophies.

In addition, we are given one last piece of information concerning John. When threatened by torture, John did not flinch but kept on preaching. This, too, was a hallmark of the Fourth Philosophy of Judas the Galilean. "They also do not value dying any kind of death, nor indeed do they heed the deaths of their relations and friends, nor can any such fear make them call any man Lord." (*Ant.* 18.23) These followers of Judas did not fear torture and death, just as this John refused to be bullied by the authorities. Such a stance was indeed dangerous, but it played well with the masses.

Considering all the other similarities between Judas and Jesus as enumerated in Chapter Two, this John the Baptist revelation may be the smoking gun. This moves the Jesus movement back to 6 AD, to the exact time of Judas the Galilean. Only the most stubborn believer will not recognize that Judas was the Messiah whom John was recommending to the people. My contention throughout this book is that Judas the Galilean and Jesus were two names for the same person. The John passage simply certifies this.

The next mention of John the Baptist outside of the Gospel record comes once again from the Slavonic Josephus. Here John appears without being summoned and interprets a dream by Philip, tetrarch of Trachonitis.

> While Philip was [still] in possession of his dominion, he saw a dream,—how an eagle tore out both his eyes. And he summoned all his wise men. But when each interpreted the dream differently, there came to him suddenly, without being summoned, that man of whom we have previously written, that he went about in skins of animals and cleansed the people in the waters of the Jordan. And he spake: "Give ear to the word of the Lord,—the dream which thou hast seen. The eagle—that is thy venality; because that bird is violent and rapacious. And that sin will take away thy eyes which are thy dominion and thy wife." And when he had thus spoken, Philip died before evening and his dominion was given to Agrippa. (4)

This passage tells us two things about John. First, his outspoken qualities were still very much at work. He blasted Philip for his unholy and evil life and then predicted a cruel ending for the man. And on cue, Philip immediately died. Whether or not this story is believable is left to one's own judgment. However, the most important point concerns the dating. Philip died in 34 AD. That means that John the Baptist was still roaming the land after at least twenty-eight years (6-34 AD).

The Slavonic Josephus and *Antiquities* relate the next mention of John, this time in relation to Herod and Herodias. In the Slavonic Josephus and in the Gospels, John accused Herod Antipas of unlawfully marrying his brother's wife. He was then imprisoned and put to death. The Slavonic Josephus framed the argument as being between Herod Antipas and John while the Gospels placed more blame upon Herodias, that vengeful woman. The whole affair may be best explained by Josephus in his *Antiquities*. After explaining the Antipas and Herodias affair, Josephus then wrote about John. Josephus never mentioned why John was imprisoned by Antipas, but from the other sources and from his placement of the John story, we can assume it had something to do with Antipas' relationship with Herodias.

> Now, some of the Jews thought that the destruction of Herod's army came from God, and that very justly, as a punishment of what he did against John, that was called the Baptist; for Herod [Antipas] slew him, who was a good man, and commanded the Jews to exercise virtue, both as to righteousness towards one another, and piety towards God, and so to come to baptism; for that the washing [with water] would be acceptable to him, if they made use of it, not in order to the putting away [or the remission] of some sins [only], but for the purification of the body; supposing still that the soul was thoroughly purified beforehand by righteousness. Now, when [many] others <u>came in crowds about him, for they were greatly moved [or pleased] by hearing his words. Herod, who feared lest the great influence John had over the people might put it into his power and inclination to raise a rebellion (for they seemed ready to do anything he should advise), thought it best, by putting him to death</u>, to prevent any mischief he might cause, and not bring himself into difficulties, by sparing a man who might make him repent of it should it be too late. Accordingly he was sent a prisoner, out of suspicious temper, to Macherus, the castle I before mentioned, and was there put to death. Now the Jews had an opinion that the destruction of this army was sent as a punishment upon Herod, and a mark of God's displeasure against him. (*Ant.* 18.116-119) (emphasis mine)

This description of John the Baptist by Josephus sets the story straight. Although Josephus did not relate exactly why John was imprisoned, we must assume it was due to John's criticism of Antipas' relationship to Herodias. The Slavonic Josephus stated: "But he accused Herod incessantly wherever he found him, and right up to the time when [Herod] put him under arrest and gave orders to slay him."(5) These accusations against Herod Antipas were serious in nature. John was not a lone voice in the wilderness at this point in time. Josephus plainly stated that John had many followers who were willing to do anything John wished. Herod had John put to death in order to stop a rebellion.

This motive of Herod is much different than the Gospel account. In the Gospels, Herodias wanted to kill John, and Herod tried to protect him. Herodias succeeded in having John beheaded much to the distress of Herod. (Mark 6:19-29) Why did the Gospels shift blame from Herod Antipas to his wife Herodias? Surely, the Gospels wanted to take away any political ramifications from the story. According to Josephus, Herod was afraid of the crowds that followed John. These crowds were dangerous and could be turned against Herod with only a word from John. Herod did what any insecure ruler would do: he killed the leader of the opposition! So the Gospels did to John what they successfully did to Jesus. They depoliticized him.

The Gospel account of John the Baptist also turned the Jews against John, similar to the treatment of Jesus. In Matthew 21:23, Jesus supposedly said, "Truly I tell you, the tax collectors and the prostitutes are going into the kingdom of God ahead of you. For John came in the <u>Way of Righteousness</u> and you did not believe him, but the tax collectors and the prostitutes believed him." What an incredible rewrite of history! The Josephus passage said that the people were ready to do anything John wanted, and that it was Herod (the tax collector) and Herodias (the prostitute) who put John to death. In reality, the people did believe in John and his message of repentance and righteousness. John came in the Way of Righteousness, often referred to as the Way. This was the same Way of Righteousness that Jesus also followed.

The Gospels successfully denigrated the Jews in their relations to Jesus and John. In regards to Jesus, it was the Jews who pressured Pilate to crucify, thereby shifting blame from the Romans to the Jews. In the case of John, the Gospels stated that the tax collectors and prostitutes admired him and would surely attain the Kingdom of God before any of the Jews. Most scholars have not argued against this Gospel presentation, because it is in line with Paul's relationship with the Jews. The Jews did hate and hound Paul (see Galatians), and his refuge was with Gentiles who believed in his vision of Christ. Paul was an Herodian (tax collector)! That is the reason why the Gospel story of Jesus and John has been slanted against the Jews in favor of the tax collectors and prostitutes.

There are other revealing clues within the above Josephus passage. First, the dating of John's death can be placed at 35-36 AD. This is five or so years later than the Gospel story and many years <u>after</u> the death of the Gospel Jesus. Earlier, we found that the beginning of John's career was in 6 AD, not 29 AD as claimed in the Gospels. Now we find that the end of his career was in 36 AD, not 31 AD per the Gospels. This is an interesting trend. So instead of a short two year ministry, John's influence in Judea lasted for thirty years (6-36 AD). Could Jesus' ministry have lasted beyond the three years assigned to him by the Gospels? Why not? My Judas the Galilean hypothesis states that Judas' career lasted from 4 BC–19 AD, an amazing twenty-two years. If John was careful enough to avoid arrest for thirty years, then it is entirely possible for Judas the Galilean as well.

Second, in 35-36 AD, John had a considerable following. His disciples were willing to follow him anywhere. This again poses problems for the Gospel story. According to the Gospels, John introduced Jesus to the world, was imprisoned shortly thereafter and was then put to death by the whims of a wicked woman. In reality, John's fame began in 6 AD and grew over the next thirty years. In 6 AD, he introduced Judas the Galilean to the world, because he was a member of the Fourth Philosophy of Judas. If John was really related to Jesus as claimed by Luke, then this familial connection was consistent with the Maccabean movement where family members were all working together. It is entirely possible that Judas sent his cousin, John, out to proclaim himself (Judas/Jesus) Messiah. This pre-planning would be no different than Jesus' arrival into Jerusalem on a donkey. Both events could be found in the Old Testament Scriptures, in Isaiah 40:3 and Zechariah 9:9, respectively. To make sure the people understood John's importance, Jesus said, "And if you are willing to accept it, he [John] is the Elijah who was to come." (Matt. 11:14) Jesus also said this, quoting Malachi 3:1, "I will send a messenger ahead of you, who will prepare your way before you." (Luke 7:27) All this talk of John the Baptist was merely a way for Jesus to solidify his Messianic claim. Josephus called Judas the Galilean a clever rabbi, and certainly this use of John the Baptist, imbedded in Scripture, to support his goals, was clever.

However, John outlived Judas the Galilean. If Judas was crucified in 19 AD, then John's ministry would have lasted another seventeen years. During these years, John's influence may have grown even though he was inside the Fourth Philosophy movement. This may explain the Gospel descriptions of John's message to the crowds. In the later years of John, John would have been proclaiming the return of the resurrected Jesus, the Jesus who would judge with a winnowing fork. (Matt. 3:11,12) Thus, John's baptism may have been before Judas/Jesus in 6 AD and after Judas/Jesus' death, from 19-36 AD.

There is one other possibility. According to the *Recognitions*, some of John's disciples separated themselves from the movement and proclaimed John as the Messiah.(6) Since Jesus died in 19 AD and John's ministry lasted until 36 AD, it is very possible that some questioned the validity of Jesus' Kingship, as Jesus was dead. This may also explain why John had such a large following. A live Messiah would have been preferable to a dead Messiah in many Jews' minds. Certainly, some of John's disciples believed that he, John, was the Messiah. Josephus claimed that John was put to death because Herod Antipas was afraid of John's influence over his myriad of disciples. Undoubtedly, this was why the New Testament writers expended so much energy in placing John behind Jesus (and Paul) in importance.

This following of John in 36 AD may also explain why Apollos knew of John's baptism. Everyone in this era knew of John's baptism. It also helps date the letters of Paul. If Apollos was teaching people about Jesus and using John's baptism, then John's influence was still strong. This suggests that the Apollos incident was fairly close to the date of John's death (post 36 AD). Traditionally, the letters to the Romans, Corinthians and Galatians are assigned a date of approximately 55 AD. I believe these letters were written in the early 40's, much closer to the time of John the Baptist's death.

Finally, Josephus described John's baptism. John's baptism did not remove sins but was simply a purification of the body, "supposing still that the soul was thoroughly purified beforehand by righteousness." (*Ant.* 18.117) The baptism was a confession before men of an inward change towards God. This is consistent with Deuteronomy Chapter 30, where the circumcision of the heart was a willingness to follow God. This is righteousness before God. This is the same message as preached by Judas the Galilean and Jesus throughout the Gospels. Josephus stated: "[John] was a good man, and commanded the Jews to exercise virtue, both as to righteousness towards one another, and piety towards God." These are the two greatest commandments: love thy neighbor as thyself and love God with all your heart, soul and strength. In philosophy, John and Judas/Jesus were inseparable.

REVISED TIMELINE FOR JOHN THE BAPTIST

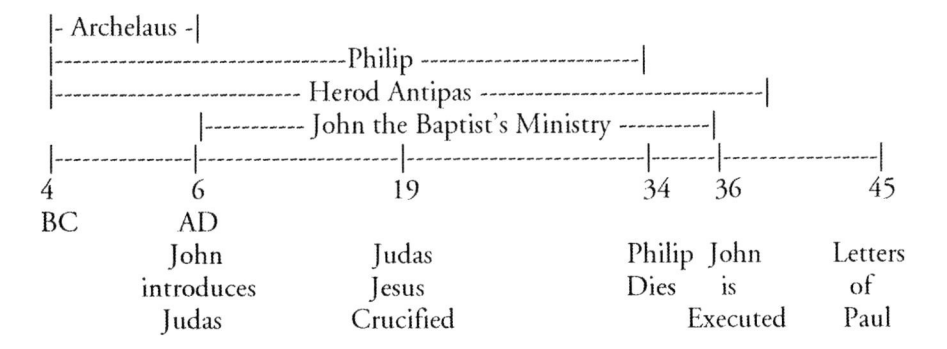

```
|- Archelaus -|
|-------------------------------Philip ----------------------|
|--------------------------- Herod Antipas ----------------------------|
            |----------- John the Baptist's Ministry ----------|
|------------|---------------|---------------------------|---------|----------------|
4            6               19                          34        36               45
BC           AD
             John            Judas                       Philip    John             Letters
             introduces      Jesus                       Dies      is               of
             Judas           Crucified                             Executed         Paul
```

The above timeline represents all information concerning John the Baptist. The problems associated with the traditional timeline are all solved.

1. There is no longer a problem with the dating. The traditional dating could not be reconciled to all the other dates given in the New Testament. From the revised timeline, there is no need to know the ages or birth dates of John or Judas the Galilean. Both came onto the national scene at the time of the census or 6 AD. John had the same philosophy as Judas the Galilean and was strategically used to announce the coming of the Messiah, Judas.

The dating in the New Testament is dependent on the dating of John. However, the three possible birth dates for Jesus are different: Matthew 9-6 BC; Luke 6-7 AD and Luke's Baptist dating, 2 BC. The only purpose of these inconsistent dates is to place Jesus in a later time frame, closer to 30 AD. By doing this, Jesus is separated from his true history, that of Judas the Galilean. And embarrassing revelations about Paul are swept beneath the carpet. (This dirt is exposed in Chapters Twelve and Thirteen.)

2. Even after Judas/Jesus died, John continued preaching his message of repentance. However, now, it was for the return of the resurrected Jesus. This is unknowingly confirmed by Matthew and Luke, who make the coming Messiah judge the good and evil on the threshing floor of Judgment Day.

3. John was alive when Philip died (34 AD) and was put to death by Herod Antipas in 35-36 AD. This is at least 5 years after John's Gospel death, several years after the Gospel crucifixion of Jesus, and 17 years after the actual crucifixion of Jesus.

The historical death of John the Baptist plays havoc with the Gospel story. In reality, John was alive and well, and on the loose long after Jesus was crucified. Thus, many of the Gospel passages about John are placed into an earlier time frame (30 AD). This was done to overcome the problems of John's great popularity around 35 AD. Therefore, the Gospels presented John and his followers as being disciples of Jesus, right up to the time of John's death.

4. This later death of John makes the references to Apollos and water in 1 Corinthians more relevant. John had a great following until his death. Therefore, his baptism would probably be well known and still be used into the 40's.

5. This new timeline confirms that Jesus was a title for Judas the Galilean. John's introduction in 6 AD confirms this. It is doubtful that John prepared the way for Judas the Galilean and later for a figure named Jesus of Nazareth. No! Judas and Jesus were one in the same.

6

ONE TEMPLE CLEANSING OR TWO?

What exactly did a Temple cleansing mean, and how did this affect the government, the religious leaders and the masses? There were three Temple cleansings reported by Josephus and the Gospels. The first occurred in 4 BC, during the latter reign of Herod the Great. Herod had erected a Golden Eagle to adorn the Temple as an honor to Caesar.(1) To the religious fanatics of the time, this Golden Eagle was a graven image and had to be torn down. In addition, the nationalists understood that the Eagle represented the power of Rome, a not so subtle attack on their liberty. Matthias and Judas the Galilean convinced their students to undertake this dangerous mission, the desecration of Herod's Eagle. The attempt occurred near the end of Herod's life. In fact, Herod's ill health may have emboldened the rebels. In any case, this was an affront to Herod's power and his appointed religious establishment. The tearing down of the Golden Eagle was both a political and religious statement, and played favorably among a section of the populace.

Where was the Golden Eagle located? According to John Crossan, Herod's Temple might have appeared to be an impregnable fortress, which may have alarmed the Roman. To assure the Romans of his fidelity, Herod may have placed the Golden Eagle somewhere between the sanctuary and the city, as a symbol of submission to Rome.(2) Thus, the tearing down of the Golden Eagle also had political implications concerning Rome. This undoubtedly ties this 4 BC Golden Eagle Judas to the Judas the Galilean as described by Josephus at the time of the census (6 AD). Judas had a long history in his fight against Rome.

The second Temple cleansing is recorded in the Gospels, where Jesus drove the money changers from the Temple. By doing this, Jesus was overturning more than just tables: the selling of sacrificial animals was sanctioned by the existing High Priesthood, represented at that time by Caiaphas and Annas. This High

Priesthood certainly received a handsome profit from the selling of doves, etc., at an exorbitant rate. Jesus declared that they were thieves, preying upon the innocent masses. This would have been a popular action to the masses, but taking control of the Temple placed him at odds with Caiaphas and Annas, and those who controlled the High Priesthood, Rome. Predictably, Jesus paid with his life. Coincidentally, Josephus (or a later interpolator) placed the crucifixion of Jesus right after Pilate had entered the city with the Roman standards. Upon these standards were effigies, the bronze eagle which represented Rome.

The third Temple cleansing occurred in 66 AD, at the beginning of the Jewish war with Rome. Menahem, the son of Judas the Galilean, marched upon Jerusalem as Messiah and cleansed the Temple. (*War* 2.433,434) This action was reminiscent of Jesus' entry into Jerusalem, per the Gospels. Once again, the Temple cleansing represented a political and religious coup. The Romans would once and for all be expelled from the country. Menahem was killed and his followers escaped to Masada, where they would play one last act in the drama against Rome: mass suicide under the leadership of Eleazar, the grandson of Judas the Galilean.

As can be seen from the above examples, a Temple cleansing was a very serious undertaking. It was meant to show that a new order was being instituted. Of course, the old order did not want to be replaced. In stable governments, coups are not the norm. But Judea was a hotbed of religious fanatics. The risking of a few lives was viewed as a gift to God, to purify the Temple and to lead God's people. Unfortunately, these acts normally led to crucifixions and disillusionment.

◆   ◆   ◆

Did Jesus cleanse the Temple once or twice in his career? This seems a moot point in that a Temple cleansing represented an affront to the ruling elites. And these ruling elites usually had their way. Caiaphas and Annas were High Priests during Jesus' lifetime, and they had the complete support of Rome as long as they maintained order. Their attitude towards Jesus would have been one of contempt and fear. A popular uprising could cost them their lucrative posts. The question is this: Could Jesus have challenged these High Priests twice?

To answer this question, it is important to understand Jesus' mode of operation. Was his career primarily based in Galilee and was he only in Jerusalem in the last week of his life? Or did Jesus spend more time in Jerusalem early in his career before settling in Galilee to raise his army of supporters?

The conventional wisdom is that Jesus cleansed the Temple once, <u>after</u> he entered Jerusalem as the Messiah in the last week of his life. That is the consensus of the Synoptic Gospels.

> Jesus entered the temple area and drove out all who were buying and selling there. He overturned the tables of the money changers and the benches of those selling doves. "It is written," he said to them, "'My house will be called a house of prayer,' but you are making it a 'den of robbers.'" (Matt. 21:12-13)

This cleansing had more importance than just a few moneychangers. By entering Jerusalem as Messiah, Jesus' first act was to cleanse the Temple of all impurities, and this included all activities sanctioned by the High Priest, Caiaphas. In effect, Jesus was saying, "Your time is over. Step aside for the new Messiah." Needless to say, this act of Temple cleansing was an act of insurrection, and the ruling elites would deal with it with ruthlessness; they would call in Rome's help.

Rome was not an innocent bystander in the Jesus story. Their efficient governing was due to strict discipline. As for religion, Rome generally accepted all kinds, as long as they supported the government. You could teach just about anything as long as you freely paid your taxes to Rome. However, the religion of Jesus was not at all sympathetic to the Roman cause. Remember, Jesus was crucified for claiming to be King (Messiah) and for his refusal to pay taxes. Jesus' "Give to Caesar what is Caesar's, and to God what is God's" was a call for the Romans to leave. Take your money and leave our land. So you see, the Temple cleansing pitted Jesus against Rome (Pilate) and his henchmen, led by the High Priest (appointed by Rome).

One thing is certain: Jesus cleansed the Temple after his arrival in Jerusalem, the week of his crucifixion. Now the next question is not so easy. Did Jesus cleanse the Temple at the beginning of his career? If he did, then he risked the same ire of Caiaphas and Pilate. Yet it seems as if Jesus walked away from this encounter.

> When it was almost time for the Jewish Passover, Jesus went up to Jerusalem. In the temple courts he found men selling cattle, sheep and doves, and others sitting at tables exchanging money. So he made a whip made out of cords, and drove all from the temple area, both sheep and cattle; he scattered the coins of the money changers and overturned their tables. To those who sold doves he said, "Get these out of here! How dare you turn my Father's house into a market!" (John 2:12-16)

This passage has much in common with the Synoptic Gospels' portrayal of Jesus at the Temple. Note that his actions were the same and the main purpose of the cleansing was to rid the temple area of the unsavory market. This does not mean that Jesus opposed the selling of sacrifices. However, those that sold were doing so for a tidy profit, and it was this greed factor which enraged Jesus. Again, this would have struck home against the High Priest, Caiaphas.

The Gospel of John's timing of the Temple cleansing is at the beginning of Jesus' ministry, <u>before</u> John the Baptist. If this is true, then there must have been two Temple cleansings. But once again, why did Jesus escape this time?

The answer to this question of two Temple cleansings may be answered by Josephus. Even though Josephus never wrote about the life of Jesus, he did mention another individual throughout his history of the Jews. Judas the Galilean cleansed the Temple at the beginning of his career.

> There was one Judas, the son of Saripheus, and Matthias, the son of Margalothus, two of the most eloquent men among the Jews, and the most celebrated interpreters of the Jewish laws, and men well-beloved by the people, because of their education of their youth; for all those that were studious of virtue frequented their lectures every day. [Judas and Matthias]…excited the young men that they would pull down all those works which the king [Herod the Great] had erected contrary to the law of their fathers…. So these men persuaded [their scholars] to pull down the golden eagle. (*Ant.* 17.149-152)

At the beginning of Judas the Galilean's career, he and his co-teacher, Matthias, convinced their students to tear down the Golden Eagle which Herod had adorned the Temple. This man made image was contrary to the law and had to be removed according to the teachers. Herod's men arrested the students and the two rabbis. Matthias was put to death and Judas was imprisoned. After the death of Herod, Judas was released by Herod's son, Archelaus, in a Barabbas-style prisoner release. Judas escaped with his life and headed towards Galilee, where he was proclaimed Messiah by his disciples.

Judas the Galilean built his organization over time. He escaped in the Barabbas-style prisoner release in 4 BC and was shortly thereafter proclaimed Messiah. Judas' following grew, but it did not become a nationwide movement until 6 AD. So unlike Jesus, his ministry was already at 10 years before he was a household name. In 6 AD, Judas began a tax revolt against Rome, an audacious act of rebellion. The High Priest at this time was Joazar who was replaced by Annas in 7 AD.

Most people assume that Judas the Galilean was killed in 6 AD, but there is absolutely no evidence which supports this. Acts chapter 5 does suggest that Judas was killed at the time of the census, but that whole account is proved to be a fabrication in Chapter Ten. Josephus does not mention the death of Judas; but if he were killed at the time of the census, then this would have been noted. The pious editing of Josephus covered the dates 19-37 AD. During those years Josephus' history has been erased. However, the census affair is largely intact.

Josephus does state that Judas' movement was large and very powerful. Unlike the account in Acts chapter 5, Judas' philosophy grew to such an extent that the youth of the nation were consumed until the war with Rome, 66-73 AD. (*Ant.* 18.9,10) If that were the case, then it is very likely that the tax revolt was somewhat effective and Judas may have roamed the countryside for years.

Just look how fast we captured Osama Bin Laden. He masterminded the 9/11 attack and was public enemy number one. As of the writing of this book (2006), he still is a free man, even though the United States has the most sophisticated surveillance equipment in the world. It is hard to believe that a man could escape the power of the U.S. for 5 plus years. In contrast, even though the Roman army was the great power of the day, they would not have been able to track a preacher in the wilderness. Judas may have brought his message to Israel one town at a time, always on the alert for traps. A reading of the Gospels gives the same impression of Jesus. He was on the run even as he taught. Matthew 12:1-8 describes Jesus and his disciples breaking a Sabbath law. To defend himself against criticism, Jesus used the example of David, who was justified in eating consecrated bread because he and his companions were hungry and needed their strength to evade their pursuers. Thus, Jesus argued, the Sabbath was made for man, not man for the Sabbath. This was not a new teaching. Judas Maccabee also taught this principle as a way of protecting his forces on the Sabbath. If one could not fight when attacked, then one was a dead man. Judas the Galilean followed in the footsteps of Judas Maccabee, and Jesus appears to be from the same mold!

If Judas the Galilean evaded capture for years, then what could have been the occasion of his death. Judas had earlier cleansed the Temple because Herod the Great had erected a Golden Eagle in the Temple (4 BC). As mentioned earlier, Herod did not place the Golden Eagle in the Temple area to needlessly provoke the Jews. This Golden Eagle was homage to Rome and nothing more. This graven image and its meaning in the minds and souls of every Jew, drove Judas the Galilean to action. "You cannot serve both God and Rome" was Judas' mantra. In 19 AD, Pilate moved his army from Caesarea to Jerusalem in order to abolish the Jewish laws. "He introduced effigies, which were upon the ensigns, and brought them into the city; whereas our law forbids us the very making of images," (*Ant.* 18.55) This was the exact same thing which drove Judas to action in 4 BC. He could not stand around and let Pilate (Rome) do these things. This may have been the provocative action which brought Judas back to Jerusalem. After Pilate removed the effigies back to Caesarea, Judas may have entered the city as an emancipator. His first action would have been a Temple cleansing, just as he and Matthias had performed in 4 BC. Note that this is the exact point in Josephus' history where the spurious Jesus passage is located. This Jesus passage is an obvious third or fourth century insertion into the historian's story. I strongly believe that the death of Judas the Galilean would have been conveyed to the reader at this point.

Josephus recorded the crucifixion of Judas the Galilean's sons, the triumphant entry into Jerusalem and eventual death of another son and the Masada ordeal of a grandson. Why would Josephus not mention the death of the main character in his *War* and of the later books of *Antiquities*? If Judas reentered Jerusalem in 19 AD, he no doubt also cleansed the Temple a second time. And his reward for this would have been crucifixion. Judas' two sons, Simon and James, were also crucified by Rome. To assume that Judas died another form of death rather than crucifixion is a stretch indeed. Judas the Galilean was the ultimate revolutionary, the most hated of insurrectionists. Crucifixion was his only destiny!

The tie between Jesus and Judas the Galilean is very evident when we analyze the temple cleansings. It should also be noted that Judas the Galilean's life was chronicled by Josephus but his death was not mentioned (probably erased by pious editing). And just as unlikely, Jesus' death was recorded (pious editing) while nothing of his life was reported. Was Judas the Galilean the historical Jesus? Judas the Galilean was a Messiah figure who championed the cause of the little person, the poor. He led a tax revolt against Rome and was eventually killed for this (not recorded). Jesus also championed the poor and was crucified for being King (Messiah) and for his refusal to pay Roman taxes. These charges would have been the same for Judas and Jesus. Real history knows only of Judas the Galilean. The Gospels have changed this Judas into a much softer, even mythical, Jesus.

I contend that Jesus was just a title or nickname for Judas, meaning Savior. Just as Joshua (Jesus) led the Jews into the promised land, so too would Jesus lead the Jews against Rome and secure victory. Nicknames were used throughout the movement. Simon was nicknamed Cephas or Peter, which means rock. And James was nicknamed the Just, meaning the Righteous One. While the Gospels speak of Jesus and Peter, Josephus calls these same men Judas and Simon. Different names do not necessarily denote different people!

7

BARABBAS

No story is as questionable as that of Jesus and Barabbas. The New Testament pits Jesus against Barabbas (the son of the Father), in a popularity contest among the Jews. In fact, in many early manuscripts, Barabbas' first name was Jesus. So we have the good Jesus (son of the Father) versus the bad Jesus (son of the Father). And of course, the Jews opted for the bad Jesus. This unfortunate choice shifted the blame of Jesus' crucifixion from Rome to the Jews. When Pilate washed his hands of all responsibility, the Jews said, "Let his blood be on us and on our children." (Matt. 27:25) This blood has been the excuse for endless persecutions against the Jews over the subsequent centuries.

The connection between Jesus and Barabbas may have been conveyed in an early Christian story, as it is reported in all four Gospels. Or, it is possible that the early story was about an actual prisoner release, and Barabbas was simply a literary device, invented by the Gospels, to shift blame from Rome to the Jews. A representative passage from Matthew is as follows:

> Now it was the <u>governor's custom at the Feast</u> to release a prisoner chosen by the crowd. At that time they had a <u>notorious</u> [distinguished] prisoner, called Barabbas. So when the crowd had gathered, Pilate asked them, "Which one do you want me to release to you: Barabbas, or Jesus who is called Christ?" For he knew it was out of envy that they had handed Jesus over to him.
>
> While Pilate was sitting on the judge's seat, his wife sent him this message: "Don't have anything to do with that innocent man, for I have suffered a great deal today in a dream because of him."
>
> But the chief priests and the elders persuaded the crowd to ask for Barabbas and to have Jesus executed.
>
> "Which of the two do you want me to release to you?" asked the governor.
>
> "Barabbas," they answered.
>
> "What shall I do then, with Jesus who is called Christ?" Pilate asked.
>
> They all answered, "Crucify him!" (Matt. 27:15-22) (emphasis mine)

In Mark and Luke, it was also revealed that Barabbas had been imprisoned for insurrection and for murder. So Barabbas was a bad character, at least to the ruling authorities. In Matthew, Barabbas was given the description of a "distinguished prisoner," translated as notorious in the quoted version.(1) From the Roman standpoint and from Josephus' writings, this Barabbas was a revolutionary, designated as a bandit. (Jesus was crucified between two bandits!) Maccoby wrote this concerning Barabbas, "As a leader and distinguished man, Barabbas was probably a Rabbi like the Zealot leaders, Judas the Galilean and Zadok."(2) And according to Josephus, Judas and his former partner, Matthias, were known as the "most eloquent men among the Jews….and men well-beloved by the people." (*Ant.* 17.149) This tie between Barabbas and Judas the Galilean makes perfect sense as the Fourth Philosophy was intent on fomenting revolution. It also answers why the crowd asked for Barabbas: his movement was a popular one among the masses. Such a figure as Barabbas may have been a hero to some, but not to the Romans. That is why placing a member of the Fourth Philosophy in a bad light was standard fare for the Gospel writers and Josephus. They were writing to their Roman audience and hoped to gain their favor

This Barabbas, whether real or invented, had a huge problem: an uprising or revolt against Rome was punishable by death, death by crucifixion. The Romans had used crucifixion as a deterrent for years. Spartacus, the ex-gladiator, led a slave revolt in 73 BC. He threatened the status quo in Rome and was crucified along with 6,000 of his men. This method of punishment was inhumane as the victim often lived on for days. But the greatest deterrent was for the living. Rome's message was this: misbehave and you, too, may someday hang from a cross. It was a ruthless but extremely efficient tool for keeping order. Any bandit like Barabbas knew that such an ending was likely, for the Romans did not coddle revolutionaries.

If Rome's attitude towards insurrectionists was set in stone, then why did Pilate release Barabbas to the crowd? Was Pilate a soft-hearted man? From what is known through the writings of Josephus, Pilate was anything but kind. In fact, he was recalled to Rome because of his brutality. Perhaps the tradition of releasing prisoners trumped Pilate's hatred of the Jews. Once again there is a problem: nowhere in the Roman Empire did the Romans practice this supposed ritual of releasing a prisoner to the crowd. It is interesting to note that Matthew wrote that the prisoner release was the governor's custom to grant to the crowd at Passover while Mark 15:6 stated it was the custom at <u>every</u> Feast. (Josephus never mentions any prisoner release custom. For example, Herod the Great would have been as ruthless as the Roman procurators, and he did not release prisoners.)

Regardless of whose custom it was, or how often it was supposedly practiced, following such a ritual would defy logic for Pilate. Why would the Romans expend resources in capturing revolutionaries only to release them once again into the population?

Think of it this way: if the United States captured Bin Laden, would there be any chance of releasing him to the Arab crowds? Of course not; just imagine the outrage in the streets of America! Congress and the President would be summarily thrown out of office and replaced with hardcore opponents to terrorism. The same holds true for the efficient Roman government. They would not have released Barabbas, if he had truly been an insurrectionist. Thus, the traditional view of the Barabbas event has this one insurmountable problem: Rome, inefficiency and mercy did not mix.

Hyam Maccoby argued that the story of Barabbas was simply a purposeful garbling of a Jesus legend. Perhaps Jesus was imprisoned by the Romans for insurrection. (He was crucified for refusal to pay taxes and for claiming to be King or Messiah.) While in prison, his followers clamored for the release of Jesus, son of the father. Or simply put: release Jesus Barabbas! Jesus was known to have called God Abba, or Father. It is possible that the only prisoner with Pilate was Jesus, and Jesus was the one accused of insurrection against Rome.(3) This explanation makes more sense than the Gospel version because Pilate would have never released a dangerous criminal to the crowd. But if this scenario was true, then no prisoner release occurred. In this, Maccoby was on the right track: <u>there was no Barabbas prisoner release in the time of Pilate</u>. The supposed release of a dangerous revolutionary was simply a way to shift blame from the Romans to the Jews. Note that the Jews preferred a revolutionary to a peaceful king, and even clamored for crucifixion. This appears so unlikely considering the Jews had hailed Jesus as Messiah just a few days earlier. So does this mean that there was never a prisoner release? After all, this Barabbas prisoner release may have been an early legend about Jesus. There may have been some truth to the story.

There is one more explanation to the Barabbas question. It involves another character from the pages of Josephus, namely Judas the Galilean. In 4 BC, Judas and his co-teacher Matthias led an insurrection in Jerusalem. They instructed their followers to tear down Herod the Great's Golden Eagle which adorned the Temple. This Golden Eagle was Herod's homage to Rome, but it was seen as a graven image and a symbol of an occupying power, Rome. To Judas and Matthias, this removal of the Golden Eagle was a cleansing of the Temple, in the same way that Judas Maccabee (167 BC) cleansed the Temple when Antiochus Epiphanes polluted it with idols and unholy sacrifices. The result of Judas and Matthias' cleansing was arrest and imprisonment for the two teachers as well as their students.

Herod had Matthias put to death by the flame. Judas the Galilean was kept in prison for a special event. Herod was nearing the end of his life, and he had serious mental problems. He knew that the people of Judea hated him with a passion, and no one would mourn his death. Therefore, his demented mind arrived at a solution: arrest and imprison notable people throughout the kingdom and kill them on the day of his own death. In that way, all of Israel would mourn on the day of Herod's death. (*Ant.* 17.175-181)

After Herod's death, his advisors cancelled this mass killing. To this act of sanity, Judas owed his life. However, Judas still languished in prison. This continued to be the case as Herod's son Archelaus tried to win support from the people. Archelaus' power base was weak, so he tried to sway peoples' opinions by granting their requests. Concerning the aftermath of Herod's death in 4 BC, Josephus reported the following:

> Whereupon the multitude, as it is usual with them, supposed that the first days of those that enter upon such governments, declare the intentions of those that accept them; and so by how much Archelaus spake the more gently and civilly to them, by so much did they more highly commend him, and made application to him for the grant of what they desired. Some made a clamor that he would ease them of some of their annual payments; <u>but others desired him to release those who were put in prison by Herod, who were many and had been put there at several times</u>; others of them required that he would take away those taxes which had been severely laid upon what was publicly sold and bought. So Archelaus contradicted them in nothing, since he pretended to do all things so as to get the good will of the multitude to him, as looking upon that good will to be a great step towards his preservation of the government. (*Ant.* 17.204-205) (emphasis mine)

Unlike Pilate, Archelaus had reason to listen to the crowd. He needed the goodwill of the masses. Pilate had the power of Rome and cared little for the wishes of those he governed. The Jewish crowd asked three favors of Archelaus: the easing of their annual payments, the release of prisoners and the removal of a sales tax. In addition to the obvious prisoner release request, the crowd asked for the reduction or elimination of two taxes. This hatred of taxation ran throughout the ministry of Judas the Galilean and was also present in the charge against Jesus, as related in the Gospels.

After the prisoners were released, Judas escaped to Galilee and began building his forces. His dual messages of equality and of tax relief were popular and drew the poor to him. The poor were a majority in Judea so there was always a sympathetic ear to his preaching. This can also be argued for Jesus. Traveling among the small villages in Galilee, Judas the Galilean became Messiah, and later he would take his mission to Jerusalem, to confront Rome and their hirelings.

Was this prisoner release the actual Barabbas prisoner release? Judas was a revered rabbi just as Jesus was reported to be. He had just lost his co-teacher, or perhaps his father, to the flames of Herod the Great. Could Barabbas mean son of the father or Judas, the son of Matthias? Note that Judas Maccabee was the son of a Mattathias.

In addition, the prisoner release makes sense in the time frame of Archelaus but makes no sense with the Roman governor, Pilate. Pilate would never have released a dangerous criminal, but Archelaus did this very act as a way of gaining popular support from the masses.

The Slavonic Josephus offers a few insights into the Barabbas affair which support my hypothesis. According to this tradition, Jesus was captured by Pilate's guard at the insistence of the Jewish leaders. When Pilate questioned Jesus, he found him innocent of all crimes and summarily released him. This enraged the Jewish leaders, who then bribed Pilate with 30 talents. With money in hand, Pilate gave the Jewish leaders authority to crucify Jesus.(4)

It must be understood that this particular passage has been altered or greatly influenced by an early <u>Gentile</u> Christian, not unlike the Gospel presentation. The Romans were not totally innocent in the whole affair; in the process of capturing Jesus, Pilate killed many of the disciples, and Pilate did accept a bribe, allowing Jesus to be crucified. But the treatment of the Romans was quite friendly in relation to the author's portrayal of the Jews. The Jewish leaders were selfish, unscrupulous and blood thirsty in this account. Surely, this particular part of the Slavonic Josephus was slanted against the Jews, a Gentile position. (No early Jewish Christian would have painted such a picture of events. To the early Jewish Christians, Rome was the enemy. Rome crucified Jesus!)

If this was from an early Gentile Christian, then one would expect an orthodox interpretation of these last days of Jesus. But that is not the case! The Slavonic Josephus states that Pilate released Jesus. This release of Jesus is consistent with my contention that Judas was released by Archelaus. The difference being that the Slavonic Josephus placed Jesus' release at the hands of Pilate, an unlikely event. This telescoping of Judas/Jesus' life into the last days before Pilate was also done by the Gospel writers. The important point is this: the one being released was Judas/Jesus.

In the early Gentile church, the release of Jesus was still being preached. Note that there was not one mention of a character named Barabbas. Barabbas had not yet been invented by the Gospel writers. Although this Slavonic Josephus passage was from a sympathetic Gentile Christian, the details do not support the traditional Barabbas story. No, the tradition of Jesus' release was strong, and the author of this passage was relating the truth as he understood it.

The traditional story of Barabbas is not true, as determined by common sense and supported by the Slavonic Josephus. The Roman procurator, Pilate, would not have acted in such an irresponsible manner. Thus, this story is merely a twisted version of an earlier event in the life of Judas the Galilean. Maccoby wrote that Barabbas was probably a rabbi like Judas the Galilean. But Maccoby did not realize that Judas was part of a prisoner release. This Judas was nicknamed Jesus, and the chants of the Jewish crowd for Jesus Barabbas was real, a part of history. What was lost was the actual man of history, Judas the Galilean.

8

JUDAS ISCARIOT

No name in western civilization is as reviled as that of Judas Iscariot, the betrayer of Jesus Christ. But what do we know of this shadowy figure? Was he the one who fingered Jesus to the authorities as claimed by the Gospels or was he an invention of these later writers? But not only should the "who" be answered but the "why" as well. Why would one of the Twelve apostles, the handpicked disciples of Jesus, betray him to the opposition High Priests and the hated Roman oppressors? Our investigation must begin with the earliest documents and then go forward to the later writings.

The first mention of a betrayal of Jesus comes from the pen of Paul. The dating of Paul's letters range from 40-55 AD, at least a generation earlier than the Gospels. Per my dating, at least three generations passed. Paul's main letters (Romans, Corinthians and Galatians) can be dated to the early to mid 40's, while the Gospels were penned <u>after</u> the writing of *Antiquities* in 93 AD.

> For I received from the Lord what I also passed on to you: The Lord Jesus, on the night he was betrayed, took bread, and when he had given thanks, he broke it and said, "This is my body, which is for you; do this in remembrance of me." (1 Cor. 11:23,24)

Note that this information of the betrayal and the Last Supper came to Paul from the Risen Christ through revelations. This may comfort some, but it should raise an alarm to others. Most scholars date Corinthians in the 50's while I believe it to be from the early 40's.(1) Either way, this is an early date for the recording of a betrayal and for the Last Supper. An early date is usually helpful in determining whether information is reliable. However, there is no evidence that this was handed down to Paul from the Jewish apostles. In fact, in Galatians, Paul was quite vehement in claiming the superiority of his unique gospel. He categorically denied human intervention; he did not receive his gospel from any man! If that is the case, then the whole betrayal may be an invention of a very fertile yet unstable mind.

Just because Paul stated that the betrayal and Last Supper came from the Risen Christ, it does not mean that the whole story should be thrown out. It is possible that Paul's inspiration was used in interpreting events that had happened. The body and blood imagery may have been invention, but the Last Supper, a sharing of bread and wine, may have actually occurred. In the same way, the betrayal in Paul's imagination may have had an historical equivalent.

One other objection to the betrayal concerns the translation of betrayed from the Greek. According to the Greek lexicon, this could have been translated "handed over" or "delivered up," slightly different meanings than betrayed. It is very likely that Paul was not even referring to a betrayal, not to mention one by Judas Iscariot, one of the Twelve apostles. Paul could have simply meant that Jesus was captured. If this is the case, then all talk of Judas Iscariot is moot.

There are four distinct possibilities concerning this "handing over" process. The first involves the Romans and Pontius Pilate in particular. In Matthew 27:26, Pilate finally accepted the wishes of the crowd. "Then he released Barabbas to them. But he had Jesus flogged, and <u>handed him over</u> to be crucified." The same Greek word was used in Pilate <u>handing over</u> Jesus to be crucified. But does this tie into Paul's statement about that fateful night? The trial before Pilate occurred the next day, not the night of the Last Supper. Although it is tempting to attach Pilate and Jesus' crucifixion to Paul's description of the "handing over," the timing of events do not perfectly jibe.

The second possibility involves the Chief Priests, Annas and Caiaphas, those Jews aligned with Rome. In John 18:30, the Chief Priests said to Pilate, "If he were not a criminal, we would not have <u>handed him over</u> to you." Again, the same Greek word was used in "handing over" Jesus to Pilate. This occurred early in the morning. (John 18:10) This may very well be the answer to the how and why questions. The Chief Priests hated Jesus because he challenged their rule at the Temple. The trial before the Chief Priests occurred during the night and the "handing over" to Pilate happened at the end of the night. All these components are consistent with Paul's description of the Last Supper. Paul may have been referring to the Jews "handing over" Jesus to Pilate in general or to the High Priests in particular. Either way, this may have been the "betrayal" in Paul's mind.

This scenario is supported by the Slavonic Josephus.

> "The teachers of the Law were envenomed with envy and gave thirty talents to Pilate, in order that he should put him to death. And he, after he had taken [the money], gave them consent that they should themselves carry out their purpose."(2)

This may not be totally historical as it placed the blame for Jesus' crucifixion on the Jews. The only crimes committed by Pilate were greed and corruption. But the following should be noted. It was the Chief Priests and Jewish leaders who paid thirty talents to Pilate as a bribe, enabling them to crucify Jesus. The thirty talents correspond to the thirty pieces of silver supposedly paid to Judas. That Judas is not even considered in the above passage is revealing. Obviously, the traditional story of Judas was not known by the writer of this section of the Slavonic Josephus.

The third and fourth "betrayal" scenarios are similar in nature. The third involves one of the Twelve, Judas Iscariot. According to the Gospels, Judas "betrayed" Jesus on the night of his arrest. This has always been read into Paul's account, but Paul never mentioned Judas or one of the Twelve. The assumed interpretation of the Greek word for "handed over" is translated as "betrayed" because of the Gospel bias. This act would only be a betrayal if done by a disciple or friend. Pilate and the Chief Priests could not have betrayed Jesus although it can be argued that the Jews could have. Thus, the later interpretation of Judas Iscariot as the "betrayer" rules out the first two alternative explanations for Jesus being "handed over." We will further explore the Judas Iscariot possibility below.

The fourth possibility concerns an unknown disciple "betraying" Jesus. This may explain why Paul did not mention Judas Iscariot. The betrayal may have been well known by Paul's time but the myth associated with Judas Iscariot may not have been invented yet. This, too, will be further explored near the end of this chapter. In my opinion, the second and fourth scenarios make the most sense, as they fit into Paul's brief description of the "handing over" process.

But let us assume that a betrayal did occur. This assumption may be quite logical considering Jesus' mode of operation, always careful and on the run. For the Roman authorities to catch Jesus, they may have needed inside information. In the recent attempt to catch Osama Bin Laden, the United States spent tens of millions of dollars in an attempt to gather information from Afghan tribal lords. One can argue whether this was money well spent, but one point is perfectly clear: to catch an elusive figure is not easy and may require help from unexpected places. It is very likely that someone in the Jesus camp or on the periphery did provide some useful information to the High Priests and to the Romans. This information was no doubt rewarded with money. Thus, the motive for betrayal may have been purely financial.

Paul did not mention Judas by name but only said that Jesus was betrayed. The modern reader fills in this omission with Judas Iscariot, because that is the Gospel story. Yet it seems odd that Paul would not include the name of the betrayer if that person had some intimate connection with Jesus. Another passage by Paul may answer the question of whether an apostle betrayed Jesus.

> For what I received I passed on to you as of first importance: that Christ died for your sins according to the Scriptures, that he was buried, that he was raised on the third day according to the Scriptures, and that he appeared to Peter, and then to the <u>Twelve</u>. After that, he appeared to more than five hundred of the brothers at the same time, most of whom are still living, though some have fallen asleep. Then he appeared to James, then to all the apostles, and last of all he appeared to me also, as to one abnormally born. (1 Cor. 15:3-8) (emphasis mine)

Once again, Paul claimed his close ties to the Risen Christ. The beginning of the passage sounds like the apostles' creed and refers back to the Scriptures twice. These are the Old Testament Scriptures. Where in the Old Testament was it foretold of the Messiah dying for others' sins and where was the resurrection of Jesus mentioned? His audience was comprised primarily of Gentiles who would not have questioned Paul's supposed knowledge of the Scriptures. It may be argued that Paul referred to the Suffering Servant of Isaiah chapter 53; but to claim this as proof of a new religion took guts, or simply a personal revelation.

Regardless of how one views Paul, he does mention one very revealing fact concerning the betrayer. He wrote that Jesus appeared to Peter and then to the <u>Twelve</u>. If this was actually from the pen of Paul, then it blows away the story of Judas Iscariot. According to Mark 16:9-14, Jesus appeared first to Mary Magdalene, then to two disciples as they walked in the countryside and then to the <u>Eleven</u>. Note that there are several discrepancies between the Gospel account and that of Paul. If the New Testament documents have been doctored, then some of the problems can be explained. But as they stand, Paul definitely stated that Jesus appeared to <u>twelve not eleven</u> apostles. If this is true then there was no Judas Iscariot.

By examining the two accounts, one must question part of Paul's order. He never mentioned Mary Magdalene, which may have been a chauvinistic approach to the problem. And he uncharacteristically put a definite number on the apostles. Everywhere else in his writings he speaks of apostles, but always an indefinite number. Thus, it is possible that the Twelve number was added by a later, not too bright, commentator. The 500 disciples also is absent from the Gospel account, but may have been added to lessen the influence of James. Note that in the Gospels, Jesus appeared to two disciples on the road to Emmaus. These two were probably Peter and James, the brother of Jesus, the subsequent leaders of the church.

If these possible interpolations are removed from Paul's account, then it is much closer to the Gospel account. And if the Twelve in 1 Corinthians is bogus, then it is possible that Judas Iscariot actually betrayed Jesus. (However, it may be wishful thinking to assume the Gospel account is accurate.) Is there any other mention of the Twelve in church history? Can any source support the 1 Corinthians' account?

There is one non-canonical Gospel which does support the Twelve apostle scenario as reported by our version of 1 Corinthians. The Gospel of Peter said this about the apostles after the death of Jesus, "But we, the twelve disciples of the Lord, wept and grieved; and each one returned to his home, grieving for what had happened." (vs. 59) This Gospel was written in the early second century, in the same general time period as Matthew and Luke. Obviously, even by the early second century, some parts of the Christian world had not yet learned of Judas Iscariot and his supposed betrayal. If there was a Judas Iscariot, then his infamous story would have been known to all Christians. Judas could not have been forgotten by Paul or the churches who utilized the Gospel of Peter. The Gospel of Peter was eventually branded heretical, and as a result, removed from circulation. However, this one mention of the Twelve bolsters Paul's claim for the Twelve. The claim for the Twelve appears solid, but let us examine other aspects of Judas Iscariot.

The name Judas is revealing in that this name approximates Judah or the Jews. No other name could have been better suited for representing the Jews. In Paul's letters, he constantly denigrated the Jewish Christian movement as weak, and at one point wished that they would emasculate themselves (Gal. 5:12). The Synoptic Gospels pitted Jesus against the Jews even though he was a Jewish Messiah figure. And the book of John stated that the Jews were children of the devil (John 8:42-47). This betrayer was conveniently named Judas to condemn a whole nation, not just one man.

Iscariot is also a very interesting name. If the I and s are reversed, then we are left with sicariot, which approximates sicarios, or the assassins of the late Fourth Philosophy. Josephus said this group arose in the later 50's or early 60's and was bent on wreaking havoc with Roman authority. These assassins fought Rome with short knives, hidden within their tunics. They were the most fanatical of the Fourth Philosophy, but this splinter group was simply an offshoot of a larger resistance movement against Rome.

To place the blame of the betrayal on Judas Iscariot, squarely incriminated the Jews and particularly those Jews who rebelled against Rome. The Gospel writers knew of a betrayal and simply filled in the details, which distanced their cause (Gentile Christianity) from that of the Fourth Philosophy (Jewish Christianity). Thus the name Judas Iscariot was an invention of the Gospel writers, built upon the scant information provided by Paul.

In John 12:4-6, we learn of Judas' love of money.

> But one of his disciples, Judas Iscariot, who was later to betray him, objected, "Why wasn't this perfume sold and the money given to the poor? It was worth a year's wages." He did not say this because he cared about the poor but because he was a thief; as keeper of the money bag, he used to help himself to what was put into it.

According to John, Judas Iscariot was a thief. This is consistent with Josephus' description of members of the Fourth Philosophy, calling them bandits. This whole line of attack upon Judas was a backhanded slap at Judas the Galilean, the historical Jesus. The Gospel of John was stating that the bandits were opposed to Jesus, opposed to God. In addition, John asserted that Judas Iscariot was a hypocrite in that he really did not care for the poor. Once again, this ties exactly to Josephus' feelings towards the Fourth Philosophy.

One other sad note should be added concerning the mythical Judas Iscariot. According to the Gospel account, Judas committed suicide after betraying Jesus. In the most famous mass suicide in history, Eleazar, the grandson of Judas the Galilean, led the Sicarii to Masada, where they were surrounded by the Roman army. After putting up a valiant fight against this mighty army, Eleazar convinced his followers to take their own lives as opposed to letting the Romans slaughter them and their families. Approximately nine hundred men, women and children took part in this mass suicide. The Gospel story of the mythical Judas Iscariot committing suicide should not surprise us.

After Judas Iscariot committed suicide, the book of Acts said that a replacement was voted upon. Matthias was to become the twelfth apostle. In reality, the only person to be replaced was that of Jesus. He was succeeded by James, his brother. If Jesus was a title for Judas the Galilean, then James replaced his brother, Judas. Thus, a Judas was replaced. As for Matthias, this name comes from the Golden Eagle Temple Cleansing where Judas replaced Matthias as the leader of the movement. The New Testament writers must have laughed heartily at this twisted history. They had forever destroyed the name Judas, had incriminated the Jews and had minimized James' position in the early church. For good measure, they brought back the slain Matthias to take the place of a mythical Judas Iscariot.

If one reads the New Testament as it is written, the betrayer could not have been Judas Iscariot because Paul and the non-canonical Gospel of Peter said Jesus appeared to the Twelve. If the Twelve was a later interpolation in both writings, the story of Judas Iscariot also rings false. One thing is certain: the Gospel writers had no reservations in twisting dates, names and events to their own purposes. This was done in the case of Judas Iscariot as a way of creating a compelling story. And what a story it has been!

◆ ◆ ◆

Although Judas Iscariot can be disproved from the above, could there have been some sort of betrayal? The later Gospel writers may have inserted the mythical Judas Iscariot in the role of betrayer, replacing someone else. To answer this question, we must go back and try to understand Jesus' mindset as he entered Jerusalem.

> Rejoice greatly, O Daughter of Zion! Shout Daughter of Jerusalem!
> See, your king comes to you, righteous and having salvation, gentle and riding on a donkey, on a colt, the foal of a donkey. (Zechariah 9:9)

When Jesus entered Jerusalem, he proudly rode into the city on a donkey, fulfilling the prophecy of Zechariah. We should not be so naïve to think that Jesus was unaware of the Scriptures. Jesus knew exactly what he was doing. And the Chief Priest knew as well. This act was a claiming of the throne of Israel; the Messiah had come!

If Jesus believed himself to be king (he did), then there is reason to believe that Jesus foresaw victory on the Mount of Olives, not arrest and imprisonment. Scholars on the whole have ignored Zechariah chapter 14, where God promised to destroy the nations who fought against Israel.

> Then the Lord will go out and fight against those nations as he fights in the day of battle. On that day his feet will stand on the Mount of Olives.... This is the plague with which the Lord will strike all the nations that fought against

Jerusalem. Their flesh will rot in their sockets, and their tongues will rot in their mouths. On that day men will be stricken by the Lord with great panic. Each man will seize the hand of another and they will attack each other. Judas too will fight at Jerusalem. (Zechariah 14:3,4;12-14) (3)

Jesus believed in the prophecy of Zechariah when he rode the donkey into Jerusalem. I am convinced he also believed in Zechariah concerning this battle on the Mount of Olives. Note that God promised to intervene and the enemy would be stricken with great panic. In fact, the enemy was to turn upon itself. All the Jews had to do was start the fight and God would finish it.

According to Luke, at the Last Supper, before heading out to the Mount of Olives, the disciples said, "See Lord, here are two swords." "That is enough," he replied. For Jesus, two swords were plenty. Any fight that started would end with God on their side, a sure victory. So here we have it: Jesus and the disciples were ready to rumble, but it takes two to tango. It is at this point in time that the betrayer story had its genesis.

Although John played the party line in regards to Judas Iscariot, his betrayal scene is curiously different from the other Gospels.

> Leaning back against Jesus, he asked him, "Lord, who is it?"
> Jesus answered, "It is the one to whom I will give this piece of bread when I have dipped it into the dish." Then, dipping the piece of bread, he gave it to Judas Iscariot, son of Simon. As soon as Judas took the bread, Satan entered into him.
> "What you are about to do, do quickly," Jesus told him, but no one at the meal understood why Jesus said this to him. Since Judas had charge of the money, some thought Jesus was telling him to buy what was needed for the Feast, or to give something to the poor. As soon as Judas had taken the bread, he went out. And it was night. (John 13:25-30)

In John's story, Jesus dipped bread and gave it to Judas, who immediately went out to alert the High Priest. If Jesus believed in the prophecy of Zechariah, then the above scene with some follower (not Judas Iscariot, for Paul knew nothing of such a person) was necessary to arrange the fight on the Mount of Olives. Jesus fully expected God to come to his rescue as was promised. Thus, Jesus and his disciples prayed, hoping to prod God into action. When the armed guards of the Chief Priest arrived, Jesus expected to be exalted. Instead, he was arrested and imprisoned. God did not honor his promise to Jesus! That is the reason why Jesus groaned these unforgettable words as he hung upon the cross, "My God, My God, why have you forsaken me?"

Later Christians could not bear to accept the fact that Jesus had failed on the Mount of Olives. The original story had to be altered. First, Jesus had to believe that the fight on the Mount of Olives could not be won. Thus, Jesus was made to talk about his impending doom. Second, the one sent out to fetch the guard was made to be a betrayer. (This must have been done after Paul because Paul simply stated that Jesus was "handed over" or "delivered up," not betrayed.) This betrayer later took on the name Judas Iscariot as a way to incriminate the Jews in general and the Fourth Philosophy in particular. (Again, Paul stated that the Risen Jesus was seen by the Twelve, proving that there was no Judas Iscariot.)

As with most of the Gospel stories and Acts, there is some truth hidden beneath the surface. Although there was no Judas Iscariot, there may have been a person sent to alert the High Priest. Unfortunately, historians have accepted the Gospel version, never acknowledging that Jesus may have wanted to win the fight. The traditional story has to ignore the triumphal entry into Jerusalem and the cleansing of the Temple, for both acts were statements of Jewish kingship. Jesus wanted to be king. He had no desire to offer himself up as a sacrifice.

The above scenario of Jesus' true ambition is probably true, in that no real betrayal occurred. But somewhere along the line, a betrayal event did circulate among the early church. As will be explained in Chapter Fourteen, Acts and the Gospels often took events in history and twisted them into the stories we know today. For example, the story in Acts chapter ten of Peter and Cornelius was an attempt to place Paul's beliefs back into time. Thus, the conversion of Cornelius was an act of <u>inclusion</u> into the Church. The parallel version in Josephus concerned Simon and Agrippa, and the thrust of this historical event centered on <u>exclusion</u> from the Temple. The book of Acts turned an exclusionary event into an act of inclusion. This same type of trick may have also occurred with the betrayal.

There was only one Apostle who actually betrayed the Jewish Christian movement. That Apostle was none other than Paul. Paul was a member of the movement for approximately twenty years, and then was removed because of his teachings. According to Paul, all the Jews turned their backs upon him and his gospel. (Galatians) It was at this point that the war between Paul and James (and Cephas) began. The Pseudoclementine literature painted Paul as the "Enemy" of the Church. This was after Paul attacked James and almost killed him in Jerusalem, around the time of the Famine (mid to late 40's). This was the time when the sons of Judas the Galilean (James and Simon) were captured and crucified. It is quite probable that Paul had something to do with their capture. (See Chapters Eleven through Thirteen for support of this hypothesis.)

The betrayal of Jesus by Judas Iscariot never occurred. However, a betrayal of the sons of Judas the Galilean probably did happen. And there was only one man who could have perpetrated such an act. That man was Paul. Paul knew the leaders of the church, and he had a vendetta to settle. The Pseudoclementine literature did not simply make Paul the "Enemy" for no good purpose. Paul threatened the church with every word he spoke and every letter he wrote. No doubt, the tradition of Paul's betrayal was very deep. After the demise of Jewish Christianity (the Jewish war in 66-73 AD), the Gentile church had a monumental restoration project on its hands: how to make Paul the hero and not the villain of Christian history. Obviously, the betrayal of Paul had to be erased or somehow changed. This betrayal label was successfully transferred from Paul to the mythical Judas Iscariot. (Even Paul had never heard of Judas Iscariot!) This bait and switch methodology worked well throughout the Gospels and Acts. The betrayal switch was just one trick in a whole bag of tricks.

9

YOU WILL INDEED DRINK FROM MY CUP

What did Jesus mean when he said to James and John, "You will indeed drink from my cup."? Surely this was not meant to be taken literally but rather figuratively. To drink of my cup was to undergo my struggles, my pain. This cup was martyrdom, by crucifixion. Did Jesus predict the unfortunate deaths of James and John or was the whole scene invented long after his death as a way to explain the failures within the movement?

Before answering this question, we must first analyze the passage in question. The story is found in Mark 10:35-40 and Matthew 20:20-23. The only difference in the two versions concerns the mother of James and John, not mentioned in Mark, but a central figure in Matthew. Although Mark is the earlier version and often closer to the truth, we will examine the Matthew version as the mother of James and John may be the key to unraveling the passage and answering the above question.

> Then the mother of Zebedee's sons came to Jesus with her sons and, kneeling down, asked a favor of him.
> "What is it you want?" he asked.
> She said, "Grant that one of these two sons of mine may sit at your right and the other at your left in your kingdom."
> "You don't know what you are asking," Jesus said to them. "Can you drink the cup I am going to drink?"
> "We can," they answered.
> Jesus said to them, "You will indeed drink from my cup, but to sit at my right or left is not for me to grant. These places belong to those for whom they have been prepared by my Father." (Matt. 20:20-23)

It seems to be such a straightforward little story of a mother's love for her children, wanting them to succeed in life and in death. The traditional explanation is that John and James conspired with their mother to ask Jesus this great favor of being on his right and left in his kingdom. Whether they knew that the kingdom was not in this world is questionable. Jesus diplomatically refused their request because he said these places were already prepared, possibly for Moses and Elijah. The request caused a bit of dissention among the apostles, because all men have pride. Why should these two be treated any differently than the other ten? Jesus' answer supposedly diffused the hard feelings and one more lesson in humility was taught.

According to the traditional interpretation of this story, all was eventually resolved and a lesson was learned: humility trumps pride. To go beyond the traditional explanation, however, we must ask some simple questions. Who were John and James, the sons of Zebedee? Why was their mother interceding for them? And where in the world was the mysterious Zebedee?

In the Gospels, John and James, the sons of Zebedee, were members of the central three closest to Jesus. Along with Peter (Cephas), they always had the ear of Jesus. They went with Jesus to a high mountain and witnessed the transfiguration. (Matt. 17:1-9) They also were honored by Jesus by going to Gethsemane on the night of his arrest. (Matt.26:36-37) From the Gospel presentation, James, John and Peter were special and deserved recognition.

However, in Galatians and 1 Corinthians, Paul presented another central three with the same names, Cephas (Peter), James and John. Paul called these three the Pillars of the church. (Gal. 2:9) In Paul's earlier list (40 AD vs. 100 AD), James was the brother of Jesus and it can be argued that John was also a brother of Jesus. (1 Cor. 9:5 brothers) If Paul's list of the central three was correct, then the Gospel stories must be fabricated.

Determining the real James and John is central to unraveling the web of lies presented by the New Testament. By replacing Jesus' brothers with James and John, the sons of Zebedee, the Gospel writers could distance Jesus from his own family. This becomes even clearer in the Gospel of John where Jesus' brothers act no better than the brothers of Joseph, who sold him into slavery. Jesus' brothers wanted him to go to Jerusalem, to his death. (John 7:1-5) Also, by hiding Jesus' brothers in the Gospels, the writers tried to distance the early Christian movement from the revolutionary movement of Judas Maccabee and his brothers. This familial arrangement had a dangerous connotation to the ruling authorities. Since the later Gentile church wanted to distance itself from these revolutionary beginnings, a rewriting of history was necessary. James and John were just two names among many which received this unwholesome attention.

The Gospel brother pairing of James and John were called the sons of Zebedee and nicknamed the sons of Thunder. If this nickname had any true significance, then their father, Zebedee, must have been a magnificent man. The following is all we know about Zebedee.

> Going on from there, he [Jesus] saw two other brothers, James son of Zebedee and his brother John. They were in a boat with their father Zebedee, preparing their nets. Jesus called them, and immediately they left the boat and their father and followed him. (Matt. 4:21-22)

According to Matthew, Zebedee was a fisherman, not a great leader. His sons left him and were followed by his wife as well. This would have been extremely unusual for a wife to leave her husband to follow a traveling rabbi. It also shows that neither the sons nor the wife had great respect for the man titled Thunder. Titles or nicknames were attached to individuals based upon their personal attributes. Simon was nicknamed Cephas (Peter) because of his solid character, like a rock. Obviously, this Zebedee had not earned the title Thunder.

So far we have placed doubt upon James and John, the sons of Zebedee and upon Zebedee as well. What about the mother? To travel with the group without her husband would have been somewhat scandalous. In addition, the Gospels gave her much influence over her two sons and some over Jesus himself. (She felt comfortable enough to ask Jesus to elevate her sons above all other disciples.) But would an <u>unrelated</u> woman who had left her husband have much influence within a religious movement? That would be very doubtful in today's society not to mention the male dominated society of first-century Israel.

One other point must be made. Jesus asked the two brothers if they could drink the same cup as he. Jesus then said that they would drink the same cup. This cup was crucifixion. From Acts 12:2, James was put to death with the sword. John, however, survived an early death and supposedly wrote the book of Revelation on the island of Patmos, at the age of ninety. If this is so, then both James and John did not drink from the same cup. Was Jesus mistaken or have the Gospel writers purposely switched the sons of Zebedee with someone else's sons?

WHAT REALLY HAPPENED

The main parts of the cup story are accurate. There were two brothers (sons), a famous father (Thunder) and a mother who had incredibly close ties to Jesus. These brothers were crucified some years after Jesus was crucified. Thus, the prophecy of Jesus was 100 percent on the mark. The problem is: can these brothers be identified?

From the pages of Josephus, such a set of brothers did exist.

> ...the sons of Judas of Galilee were now slain; I mean of that Judas who caused the people to revolt, when Cyrenius came to take an account of the estates of the Jews.... The names of these sons were James and Simon, whom Alexander commanded to be <u>crucified</u>. (*Ant.* 20.102) (emphasis mine)

It is interesting to note that James and Simon were captured and crucified at the same time that Acts chapter 12 had James and Simon Peter being captured. In fact, the book of Acts is a series of events recorded in Josephus which are twisted to tell a quite different story.

These sons of Judas the Galilean would have been properly called the sons of Thunder, unlike the Zebedee story. Judas the Galilean dominated first-century Jewish history, forming a new philosophy and eventually challenging the great power of the day, Rome. Now that is Thunder!

The mother of James and Simon would have been the wife of Judas the Galilean. In Chapter Two, a clear tie between Jesus and Judas the Galilean has been established. So, in reality, the mother was the wife of Jesus. This makes much more sense. Imagine the scene: Jesus' wife asks her husband to elevate their sons to his right and left in his glory. Surely, this puts a little more pressure on Jesus' response: he has to live with this woman. Jesus never assigned them places, but left that chore up to God. After all, God could choose from Moses, David, Solomon and a great many other heroes of the past.

This one passage illustrates so many things about the Jesus story. Jesus was a family man just like all of his apostles. (1 Cor. 9:5) His wife, probably Mary Magdalene, tried to persuade Jesus to help out their sons. (It should be noted that Jesus first appeared to Mary after the resurrection.) This may explain the wedding of Cana in John chapter 2:1-11. Cana was situated halfway between Judas/Jesus' power base at Sepphoris and Mary's home town of Magdala. (In John, Mary is referred to as Mary of Magdala, while the Synoptic Gospels call her Mary Magdalene, meaning Mary of Magdala.) In addition, both Mary and Jesus were giving orders at the wedding feast, as if it were their own. Also, other post-Gospel traditions have paired up Mary and Jesus.

Jesus had sons who were very active in the early church. The Gospels claim that Jesus' brothers were James, Simon, Judas and Joseph. These were really his sons and his brothers were James and John, part of the Pillars of the church as described by Paul. (Galatians)

If my hypothesis is true, then Judas/Jesus married Mary early in his career. Certainly by the 6 AD census revolt, they may have had the four sons (brothers) as named in the Gospels. Simon and James were crucified between 46-48 AD, making them approximately 50-55 years old, mature major players in the movement. But what of the other two sons, Judas and Joseph? These two were partially hidden within the pages of Acts. Both appeared in context with James, the brother of Jesus, and were called Barsabbas. This means son of the bather. But the text might have read Barabbas or Barrabbas, son of the Father or son of the rabbi, respectively. Regardless, this nickname most likely referred to Judas/Jesus. And there was a good chance that Judas and Joseph were twins. Those names would have represented the Northern and Southern kingdoms, the Twelve tribes of Israel. In addition, in the Gospel list of apostles, there was a Judas, a Thaddeus and a Thomas, most likely the same person. Thomas is translated as twin. This may have been attached to Judas, so that Judas Thomas (Judas the twin) became Thaddeus or Theudas. So it is very possible that Judas/Jesus' son Judas (Theudas) was beheaded between 44-46 AD as recounted by Josephus. (*Ant.* 20.97-99)

The only other son of Judas the Galilean was Menahem. He rode into Jerusalem and cleansed the Temple like his father in 66 AD. If he, too, was born early in Mary and Judas/Jesus' marriage, then he would have been in his middle to late seventies by 66 AD. In my earlier book, *Judas the Galilean*, I assumed this was too old and concluded that Menahem was a grandson. However, upon further reflection, I now believe that Josephus was accurate in calling him a son. There is a good chance that Menahem was born much later than the other brothers, even later than the tax revolt of 6 AD. That is why he was not counted among them in the Gospel story. The Gospel story of the sons (brothers) was about Jesus' early career. If Menahem was fifty years old in 66 AD, then he must have been born around 16 AD. This much later birth of Menahem may also explain his name. Menahem means comforter, and this may refer to a child born to older parents. This supports my hypothesis that Judas the Galilean did not die in 6 AD but survived until 19 AD, when he was captured and crucified by Pilate. Menahem may be one more link between the historical Judas and the mythical Jesus.

If Jesus was the father of the two brothers who were crucified, then he was Judas the Galilean. This Judas cleansed the Temple, was proclaimed Messiah in Galilee, and he founded a new Philosophy which consumed the nation. It sounds like Jesus. It sounds like Thunder.

◆　　◆　　◆

So why was the story included in the Gospels? Did Jesus really foretell the future as reported by the Gospel writers? We now know that the two brothers were actually the sons of Judas/Jesus. They were crucified between 46-48 AD by Alexander. This would have been a major blow to the movement. Only a few years earlier, Theudas had been captured and beheaded. To counterbalance these unfortunate failures, the Fourth Philosophy did a little propaganda of its own. The oral traditions or earliest Jewish writings about Jesus were a work in progress. To explain the failures of the Sons of Thunder, the Jewish Christians simply argued that Jesus had predicted their deaths by crucifixion while still on earth. This explained the failures (not failures at all) and made Jesus even more awe inspiring. Our present day Gospels took these well known stories and changed a few names (James and Simon became James and John, the sons of Zebedee), preserving a legend but obscuring the true participants. In the end, we must admit that Jesus did not really foresee his sons' deaths. At that point in history, Jesus did not foresee his own death.

10

THEUDAS AND JUDAS THE GALILEAN

The handling of Theudas and Judas the Galilean by the author of Acts is perhaps the most confusing, most illogical and most dishonest literature one will ever come across. Its purpose was to mislead, so one must admire the desired effects over the past two thousand years. It has worked brilliantly: the histories of both Theudas and Judas the Galilean have been suppressed to the point that these two Jewish revolutionaries are insignificant footnotes, never even considered in the Jesus story.

But were they really only bit players in a much larger drama, or did Luke distort their true contributions to Jewish history by his own unflattering account? After all, their very mention means that some people still remembered them. Is it possible that both Theudas and Judas the Galilean were much more important than we can even imagine? Luke's take on these two is reproduced below.

> Having brought the apostles, they made them appear before the Sanhedrin to be questioned by the high priest. "We gave you strict orders not to teach in this name, he said. "yet you have filled Jerusalem with your teachings and are determined to make us guilty of this man's blood."
>
> Peter and the other apostles replied, "We must obey God rather than men!" The God of our fathers raised Jesus from the dead—whom you had killed by hanging him on a tree."....
>
> When they heard this, they were furious and wanted to put them to death. But a Pharisee named Gamaliel, a teacher of the law, who was honored by all the people, stood up in the Sanhedrin and ordered that the men be put outside for a little while. Then he addressed them: "Some time ago Theudas appeared, claiming to be somebody, and about four hundred men rallied to him. He was killed, all his followers were dispersed, and it <u>all came to nothing</u>. After him, Judas the Galilean appeared in the days of the census and led a band of people in revolt. He too was killed, and <u>all his followers were scattered</u>. Therefore, in the present case I advise you: Leave these men alone [Peter

and the apostles]! Let them go! For if their purpose or activity is of <u>human origin, it will fail</u>. But if it is from God, you will not be able to stop these men; you will only find yourselves fighting against God." His speech persuaded them. (Acts 5:27-40) (emphasis mine)

The supposed author of this passage on Theudas and Judas the Galilean was Gamaliel, a renowned teacher of the law. He came to the rescue of Peter and the other apostles after they had been detained by the religious authorities for preaching the message of Jesus of Nazareth. The apostles were brought to the Sanhedrin by the Sadducees and were being questioned by the High Priest. This part of the Sanhedrin wanted to put the apostles to death. Their opinion of the Jewish Christians had not changed since the crucifixion of Jesus. It was the Sadducees and the High Priest who arrested and condemned Jesus. (This trial of Jesus was at night and was not in front of the whole Sanhedrin.) Luckily for the apostles, this arrest was brought to the Sanhedrin, which consisted of Sadducees and Pharisees. Gamaliel, a leader of the Pharisees, convinced the whole Sanhedrin that the apostles should be freed. Unlike the trial of Jesus, the Sanhedrin was ruled by majority vote. Gamaliel had the full support of the Pharisees and thus saved the apostles.

This act by a Pharisee contradicts the traditional teachings concerning the Pharisees. In the Gospels, we are led to believe that the Pharisees hounded Jesus and were responsible for his capture and crucifixion. However, on the night of Jesus' arrest, Jesus was taken to Annas and Caiaphas and was then <u>handed over</u> (the same Greek word as applied to Judas Iscariot's supposed <u>betrayal</u>) to Pilate for crucifixion. The Pharisees had nothing to do with Jesus' arrest! That the Pharisees were not opposed to Jesus' movement can also be supported by Josephus. In *Ant.* 20.197-203, James, the brother of Jesus, was stoned to death by the illegal actions of the high priest, Annas. (This was the son of the Annas responsible for Jesus' arrest and crucifixion.) In response to the police action against James, the Pharisees petitioned to have Annas removed as High Priest. Thus, the friendly relations between Jesus and the Pharisees existed over several generations. But this raises a new question: if the Pharisees were not against the Jewish Christians, then why did Paul claim that he was a Pharisee before his conversion (Phil 3:5; Acts 23:6)? Was Paul the only Pharisee that persecuted the Church? This will be answered in Chapters Twelve and Thirteen.

Gamaliel's reasoning for rescue was simple: these men would fail miserably if they were not from God, and the converse, nothing could be done to stop them if God were on their side. Obviously, there was nothing in the apostles' message which was deemed blasphemous. The claims for the Messiah and for resurrection were both acceptable to the Pharisees. This was not true for the Sadducees. Jesus' claim for kingship (Messiah) and his cleansing of the Temple, were political attacks on the power structure, and they (Sadducees and High Priest) were the ones with the most to lose. The authorities agreed with Gamaliel only because the majority of the Sanhedrin sided with him. The apostles were set free after an obligatory flogging and a warning to stop preaching about Jesus. The use of Theudas and Judas the Galilean by Gamaliel was meant to show how unholy men failed who were not from God. The Pharisees were willing to take a wait and see attitude towards the Jesus movement.

According to the traditional timeline of the Gospels, this event took place shortly after the crucifixion, between 30-35 AD. If that was true, then how would it have been possible to know about Theudas? In *Ant.* 20:97-99, Josephus wrote that Theudas persuaded many people to follow him to the river Jordan, where he promised to divide the river as Moses had parted the Red Sea. This failed spectacle occurred during the reign of Cuspius Fadus, procurator from 44-46 AD. Theudas' attempt to alter the elements fizzled, and he was captured and beheaded with the sword, an unfortunate ending for an apocalyptic leader. Theudas' attempt at the miraculous was the first of many who tried to coax God into action. He was no doubt a member of Judas the Galilean's Fourth Philosophy, but his methods were different than the wait and see disciples. Like Jesus on the mount of Olives, Theudas wanted God to intervene into history. If only God would part the Jordan as he had done in the time of Moses and Joshua, then people would know and believe that the Kingdom of God was returning to earth. In short, this may have been a desperate plea for Jesus to return in power and glory.

How different was Theudas' attempt to that of Jesus on the Mount of Olives? Jesus expected God to fulfill the oracle of Zechariah by defeating the enemies of Israel. Theudas was simply following the examples of Moses and Joshua. Moses parted the Red Sea and Joshua led his followers into the promised land. Like other apocalyptical preachers of the time, these men trusted in the Scriptures. If God worked miracles in the past, then He could work miracles in the present. It never dawned upon them that the Old Testament Scriptures may have been exaggerated or were flat-out invented stories. Like Jesus, these miracle workers were true believers. So we should not judge them strictly on our knowledge but on what they truly believed.

The first unraveling of Luke's cover-up concerns the dating: if Theudas was killed between 44-46 AD, then how could Gamaliel have known about this in 35 AD, ten years prior? Talk about a prophet! In reality, Gamaliel could not have known about Theudas. But Luke knew about Theudas from the works of Josephus. *Antiquities* was written in 93 AD, so Luke's history was written after this date. This confusion between the author's knowledge and the character's knowledge is revealing: Luke was a horrible historian but a very capable fiction writer.

After noting that Theudas' efforts "came to nothing," Luke introduced Judas the Galilean, a rebel leader who appeared in the days of the census. Gamaliel would have known about Judas the Galilean, who led a tax revolt against Rome in 6 AD. This Judas was the most influential rabbi of the first century, so it is inconceivable that Gamaliel would have considered him a onetime wonder with no existing following. In fact, the Jewish war was started by Judas' later followers, sixty years after the census. Is it possible for a respected religious leader to be so out of touch with current events? Gamaliel would not have been so blatantly ignorant of current religious and political affairs.

According to Luke's convoluted history, this Judas came a short time <u>after</u> Theudas. This error by the author of Acts is simply shoddy history work. Most Christians refuse to believe that the Bible contains errors so they hopelessly try to find a Theudas that lived and died prior to 6 AD. Josephus must have forgotten about this Theudas, they "reason." But Josephus did not write about any other Theudas other than the one in 45 AD; so the hypothesis that an unknown Theudas roamed the countryside before the census is extremely unlikely.

In *Ant.* 20:101-102, Josephus followed the story of Theudas with the grim tale of Judas the Galilean's sons, who were crucified during the governorship of Tiberius Alexander, between 46-48 AD. Could Luke have confused Judas the Galilean with his sons? It certainly appears so. This at least restores the order of the passage. But again, we have the same problem: Gamaliel (35 AD) was foretelling the future (46-48 AD) and ascribing it to the past.

The Slavonic Josephus may hold the truth to the whole situation.

> But when those noble governors [Fadus and Alexander, 44-48 AD] saw the misleading of the people, they deliberated with the scribes to seize and put them [Jewish Christians] to death, for fear lest the little be not little if it have ended in the great. But they shrank back and were alarmed over the signs, saying: <u>"In the plain course such wonders do not occur. But if they do not issue from the counsel of God, they will quickly be convicted." And they gave them [the Christians] authority to act as they would</u>. But afterwards, becoming pestered by them, they had them sent away, some to the Emperor, but others to Antioch, others again to distant lands,—for the testing of the matter. But Claudius removed the two governors, [and] sent Cumanus [48-52 AD] (1) (emphasis mine)

This passage was inserted into the *War* after the death of Agrippa I (44 AD) and before the appointment of Agrippa II (49-93 AD) and the arrival of the new Roman governor, Cumanus. During the governorships of Fadus and Alexander, the Jewish Christians were causing problems for the ruling elites. There was talk of seizing the Christians and putting them to death. This no doubt happened as the sons of Judas the Galilean were captured and crucified as reported in the *Antiquities*. But after this period of persecution, the Pharisees used the same reasoning to spare the Christians as was reported in Acts 5:37-39. Essentially, if the wonders were not from God, then the Christians would be convicted. "And they gave them authority to act as they would," at least for a little while. The passage then suggests that the persecutions began anew after the arrival of Cumanus. In both Acts and the Slavonic Josephus, the Jewish Christians were given the benefit of the doubt for a short period of time. It seems quite obvious that Luke took his material from the same source as the Slavonic Josephus. But once again, the dating was between 44-48 AD. There is little doubt that the Gamaliel story was fictitious. The events did occur, but not in 35 AD.

Many religious scholars have recognized the impossible situation of the dating and have come up with a mediocre solution. As noted above, they simply argue that there was another Theudas who lived a short time before Judas the Galilean, approximately 1-5 AD. They claim that the silence of Josephus on such a figure does not prove that a Theudas did not live at that time. Thus, the Scriptures have been saved from error.

This scholarly explanation requires a stretch of the imagination. But even if it was true, then the description of Judas the Galilean can be shown to be maliciously misleading. According to Acts chapter 5, Judas was killed and his followers were scattered, and his movement failed because it was not from God. Is that what really happened?

Josephus wrote this about Judas the Galilean at the time of the census of Cyrenius:

> ...there was one Judas,...[who] became zealous to draw them to a revolt, [who] said that this taxation was no better than an introduction to slavery, and exhorted the nation to assert their liberty. [6 AD]...for Judas and Sadduc, who excited a fourth philosophic sect among us, and had a <u>great many followers</u> therein, filled our civil government with tumults at present, and laid the foundation of our future miseries, by this system of philosophy,...because the infection which spread thence among the <u>younger sort, who were zealous for it</u>, brought the public to destruction. [66-70 AD]. (*Ant.* 18.4-10) (emphasis mine)

This passage assures us that Judas the Galilean founded a new philosophy and this new teaching infected the nation for the next 60 years. In fact, this philosophy led the Jewish nation to war with Rome, the greatest power on earth. So it is obvious that the death of Judas (mysteriously missing from Josephus) did not stop or even slow his movement. Eerily, like the movement of Jesus, it flourished to a great extent after his death.

So why did the author of Acts feel it necessary to lie to the reader? The confusion or poor history concerning Theudas can be innocently explained away, but the unfair characterization of Judas the Galilean cannot. Luke purposely belittled Judas with the intent of minimizing him in the eyes of second-century Christians. He also wanted to forever cut the ties between Judas and the mythical Jesus. Surely, Jesus could never be associated with such an apparent loser. This misleading history has been working well to the present day.

However, the statement that the movement was scattered after Judas' death may have some truth to it. If the Romans captured Judas, then it would have been a prudent move to scatter or to hide. Eventually, these individuals reorganized as the Fourth Philosophy coalesced and expanded. But how was this scattering of Judas' movement any different from Jesus' disciples' reaction after the arrest and crucifixion of Jesus? After Jesus was arrested, "then everyone (all the disciples) deserted him and fled." (Mark 14:50 and Matt. 26:56) The non-canonical Gospel of Peter stated, "But we, the twelve disciples of the Lord, wept and grieved; and each one returned to his home, grieving for what had happened." (vs. 59) The disciples of Jesus fled from the scene of his arrest, denied Jesus when asked about him and hid in fear from the authorities. Jesus' followers acted exactly the same as Luke's portrayal of Judas' followers (Acts 5:37). It is interesting to note that Luke did not report that Jesus' followers fled, unlike Mark and Matthew. Instead, Luke reserved his scattering of disciples to the movement of Judas the Galilean. This, like so many other events, ties Jesus to Judas.

Judas the Galilean may have been the historical Jesus. The mythical Jesus of the Gospels was framed from the theology and life of Paul, and the historical Jewish Judas. The coincidences of Chapter Two illustrate how much of Judas' life was absorbed into the mythical Jesus. Therefore, it was necessary to color the history of Judas with failure. With one stroke of the pen, Christians and scholars alike have forfeited reason in favor of misguided faith. Unfortunately, Judas the Galilean has been long since forgotten. As of this writing, only one other book has been written about Judas the Galilean, and that book was penned by this author. (See Bibliography)

TIMELINE

Theudas Judas	Gamaliel	Theudas	Sons
Before the	(Acts 5:36)	(*Ant.* 20.97)	of
Census Galilean			Judas
???? (*Ant.* 18:1)			(*Ant.* 20.101)

```
|-----------|---------------------------|----------------|--------|--------|
 1 AD      6                           35              44       46      48
```

According to Gamaliel, Theudas preceded Judas the Galilean and both were "some time ago." We are given the impression that both individuals were one-hit wonders. And if they were insignificant footnotes to history, then would anyone even remember their names, thirty to thirty-five years after their deaths?

Josephus never mentioned a Theudas before Judas the Galilean. His only Theudas in *Antiquities* was beheaded during the governorship of Fadus, between 44-46 AD, some ten years after Gamaliel spoke of his death. If this was the Theudas, then Gamaliel was surely a prophet, predicting the future using past references such as "some time ago." After Theudas, Josephus wrote that the sons of Judas the Galilean were crucified.

Luke was a poor historian as he mistook the sons of Judas the Galilean for Judas the Galilean. In addition, Luke's treatment of Judas the Galilean is misleading, as Gamaliel supposedly said that Judas was killed and his followers scattered. Per Josephus, this minimizing of Judas and his movement was totally unjustified. In short, Luke lied about the whole episode.

One other important point should be noted. Theudas may have been an apostle. In the Gospels, there is a Judas (not Iscariot), a Thomas (twin) and a Thaddeus. It is likely that this Judas was a twin and nicknamed Thomas. The combination would yield Theudas or Thaddeus. There was a Judas Barsabbas in Acts 15:22, a leader in Jerusalem and a Joseph Barsabbas in Acts 1:23, also a main player in the early church. Could these two have been twins? (Jesus' sons (brothers) were Simon, James, Judas and Joseph). It may be that Theudas was a son of Judas the Galilean/Jesus. And considering that Simon and James were caught and crucified a few years later, three sons may have been lost in a short period of time. This would have been a painful time for the early church. (It also corresponds with the time of Paul's dismissal from the Jewish church and the reported attack by Paul on James, the brother of Jesus, in the Pseudoclementine *Recognitions*.) Could Paul have been behind this rash of persecutions? (See Chapters Eleven through Thirteen.)

11

HOW MANY GOSPELS?

When you attend church on Sunday mornings, you are not given the choice of which Gospel you would like to hear that day. But what if preachers practiced freedom of choice. Imagine your preacher or priest saying this: "today we will preach liberation theology and the sharing of wealth, because last week we preached the baptism of the Holy Spirit and tongues." Or, is it more likely that your church does pretty much the same thing, week in and week out? There are some slight differences in belief and practice among the myriad of churches. Some emphasize speaking in tongues, some adhere to a strict interpretation of the New Testament while others combine the Scriptures and tradition. But these are peripheral issues. In lockstep order, Christian churches today preach the same fundamental message: Jesus lived; he was crucified; he was resurrected; and he will come again. These are the essential tenets that were officially formulated in the Nicene Creed, and have been repeated unchanged for nearly two thousand years.

It is not unusual for Christians to believe that the Gospel has always been one uniform message. But in fact, in the very beginnings, there were two competing messages or Gospels, one for the conservative Jews and one for the Gentiles throughout the Roman Empire.

> I am astonished that you are so quickly deserting the one who called you by the grace of Christ and are turning to a different gospel—which is really no gospel at all. Evidently some people are throwing you into confusion and are trying to pervert the gospel of Christ. But even if we or an angel from heaven should preach a gospel other than the one we preached to you, let him be eternally condemned!…I want you to know, brothers, that the gospel I preached is not something that man made up. I did not receive it from any man, nor was I taught it; rather, <u>I received it by revelation from Jesus Christ</u>. (Galatians 1:6-12) (emphasis mine)

According to Paul, some people were preaching a gospel unlike his own. Is it possible to determine who these evil doers were? After all, Paul promised that these men would be eternally condemned, no matter how respected they were or how holy they behaved. The answer lies within Paul's letters to the Galatians and Corinthians. The one group that Paul detested and who hounded him at every turn was the circumcision group, led by James, the brother of Jesus, and by Cephas (Peter). This group certainly preached a different gospel as will be shown shortly. One point must be understood: these different gospels did not and could not coexist.

Certainly, the first gospel came from Jesus himself and would have been transmitted to the apostles while Jesus was still on earth, alive or resurrected. This gospel would have been given to the Pillar apostles, James, John and Cephas. James and John were the brothers of Jesus while it can be argued that Cephas was related as well. (Gal. 1:19; 2:9 and 1 Cor. 9:5) This firsthand personal knowledge of Jesus would have been a very effective tool in arguing about the supremacy of gospels. After all, the apostles did see Jesus feed the five thousand. Only they knew if Jesus suspended the laws of nature by producing matter out of thin air or simply taught his followers to share. Only these apostles were with Jesus when he was proclaimed Messiah, when he cleansed the Temple and when he was tortured and crucified by Rome. Their case for their gospel was strong indeed. It was a Gospel of firsthand information and experience, straight from the source, which was Jesus.

What did these Jewish apostles believe? They had a firm belief in one God, and to love that God was paramount in importance. To love God, one had to follow God's laws, which included circumcision, and to love thy neighbor as thyself. (Matt. 22:37-40) From this and Paul's writings, we know that the first Jewish Christians practiced circumcision and the whole law (dietary and all). They also practiced pure communism, the sharing of everything, so that no man was richer than his brother. This was to "love thy neighbor as thyself."

The only beliefs and practices which separated them from the other Jewish sects were the following: belief in Jesus' resurrection and hopeful return, their treatment of the Sabbath in the tradition of Judas Maccabee and their utter hatred of Roman occupation. This last difference has been effectively masked in the Gospel presentation of Jesus. Even though Jesus was crucified as a political enemy of Rome, most Christians throughout the ages have believed in a Jesus who was crucified for challenging Jewish laws. Nothing could be further from the truth. Jesus and his disciples were the most conservative of all Jewish groups, to the point of obsession.

Against this philosophy of Jesus stood Paul, the apostle to the Gentiles. He believed his own gospel was superior to that of James and Cephas, who followed in the footsteps of Jesus. Paul stated that his gospel was not invented by man or handed down from man, but came straight from the Risen Christ through <u>revelations</u>. Thus, we have the earthly Jesus battling the Risen Christ for control of his own church. Now, that is crazy!

Paul's gospel came from visions and revelations. Do you know what that means? The Christian message of today is comprised of dreams from a man who was unceremoniously excluded from the original Jewish Christian movement. In Gal. 2:11-13, Paul and Cephas (Peter) were in sharp disagreement over Paul's teachings. Even Paul noted in his one-sided account that Cephas won the argument and "the other Jews joined him in his hypocrisy, so that by their hypocrisy even Barnabas was led astray." At this point, Paul was forever on his own, outside of the true Jesus movement. Even his friend and coworker, Barnabas, could no longer support him.

What then did Paul teach which James and Cephas so vigorously opposed? It is unclear if James and Cephas knew the full extent of Paul's teachings. It seems as if Paul was very good at keeping these facts away from the Jewish leaders. As Paul stated in 1 Cor. 9:20-23, "To the Jews I became like a Jew, to win the Jews. To those under the law I became like one under the law (though I myself am not under the law), so as to win those under the law." In fact, Paul did not teach the law, the fundamental teaching of Jesus, James and Cephas. He purposely misled the Pillar apostles (James, John and Cephas), so that they would be unaware of his true teachings. Finally, Paul's teachings became known to the Jewish Christians, and at that point the Jews turned their backs upon him. Reread Galatians and Corinthians and note Paul's feelings for the Jewish Christians. As for the circumcision group, Paul said, "I wish they would go the whole way and emasculate themselves." (Gal. 5:12) And concerning the apostles he stated, "For such men are false apostles, deceitful workmen, masquerading as apostles of Christ. And no wonder, for Satan himself masquerades as an angel of light. It is not surprising, then, if his servants masquerade as servants of righteousness. Their end will be what their actions deserve." (2 Cor. 11:13-15) Paul's hatred for the Jewish leaders is quite obvious. This hatred is papered over by the book of Acts. In Acts, Paul did everything in his power to please the Jewish apostles. It was not until the final chapter that Paul said enough is enough; I will take my message to the Gentiles! In truth, Acts has little truth in it (See Chapter Fourteen). Paul and the early Jewish church split twenty years before this sanitized version of events in Rome.

If Paul did not teach the law, then what was this new gospel? The centerpiece of Paul's gospel was grace, the unconditional love of God, given as a gift to man. Man could not earn this gift by his own effort. Therefore, any attempt at works was a lost cause. But this philosophy was diametrically opposed to Jesus. When the rich young man asked Jesus what he needed to do, Jesus did not say, "Just believe in me." No, he said, "If you want to be perfect, go, sell your possessions and give to the poor, and you will have treasure in heaven. Then come, follow me." (Matt. 19.21)

Believe and be saved was Paul's fundamental message. His proof text for this revelation from the Risen Christ came from Romans 4:1-6.

> What then shall we say that Abraham, our forefather, discovered in this matter? If, in fact, Abraham was justified by works, he had something to boast about—but not before God. What does the Scripture say? "Abraham believed God and it was credited to him as righteousness." [Gen. 15:6] Now when a man works, his wages are not credited to him as a gift, but as an obligation. However, to the man who does not work but trusts God who justifies the wicked, his faith is credited as righteousness.

Paul believed there was nothing man could do to set himself right with God. No effort on the part of man could possibly bridge the gap between God and man. Therefore, following the Jewish Law and the Everlasting Covenant was utter nonsense as it could never reconcile one to God. Paul's contempt for Judaism peeked with his criticism of Moses and the veil which hid his face from the Jews. (2 Cor. 3:7-18) To Paul, Moses purposely hid the truth from the Jews, and these Jews had handed down the lies throughout the generations. This, of course, was totally at odds with Jesus and his original teachings.

James used the same passage from Genesis 15:6 to prove that works were necessary for a relationship to God. This is a complete rebuttal of the Pauline position on grace without works.

> You foolish man, do you want evidence that faith without deeds is useless? Was not our ancestor Abraham <u>considered righteous for what he did</u> when he offered his son Isaac on the alter? You see that his faith and his actions were working together, and his faith was made complete by what he did. And the scripture was fulfilled that says, "Abraham believed God, and it was credited to him as righteousness," [Gen. 15:6] and he was called God's friend. You see that a person is <u>justified by what he does and not by faith alone</u>. (James 2:20-24) (emphasis mine)

James even used the same passage in Genesis to prove his point that a person is justified by what he does and not by faith alone. This is consistent with the first "everlasting" covenant between God and man. God promised to protect and keep his nation of Israel in return for Israel's love and obedience. This love and obedience was perfectly displayed in Abraham's actions. Without the deeds, God would not have credited him with righteousness. If Abraham had refused to offer up Isaac, would he have truly believed, would he have been considered righteous?

Put another way, James laid out the perfect argument against Paul's personal theology. It also shows that not all interpretations of Scripture are accurate. Paul did not analyze Abraham's situation. Instead of recounting Abraham's obedience to God, Paul just included the part of the passage which supported his ideology. James, on the other hand, placed the passage in context. (It should be noted that today's churches now follow the gospel of Paul and often twist the Scriptures for their own purposes, whether good or bad).

> What good is it, my brothers, if a man claims to have faith but has no deeds? <u>Can such a faith save him?</u> Suppose a brother or sister is without clothes and daily food. If one of you says to him, "Go, I wish you well; keep warm and well fed," but does nothing about his physical needs, what good is it? In the same way, <u>faith by itself, if it is not accompanied by action, is dead.</u>
>
> But someone will say, "You have faith; I have deeds."
>
> Show me your faith without deeds, and I will show you my faith by what I do. You believe there is one God. Good! Even the demons believe that—and shudder. (James 2:14-19) (emphasis mine)

James' insistence on deeds is consistent with the teachings of Jesus. The Parable of the Sower describes four types of men who all receive the message of the Gospel, but only one type produces fruit. Those that do not understand the truth soon lose their way. Others who have no root, at first praise God, but soon lose interest. Some have too many worries in this life to pay attention to God's demands. So only the person who puts God's word into practice produces fruit. Only those who do God's bidding for a lifetime will be saved.

This interpretation does not cheapen God's mercy, but simply gives us a responsibility to do good in God's name. Paul's theology lacked this element of personal responsibility. In its place, he said the Holy Spirit would make you do right. However, this did not work in practice. Paul said this to his own prized converts in Corinth. "It is actually reported that there is sexual immorality among you, and of a kind that does not occur even among pagans: A man has his father's wife. And you are proud!" (1 Cor. 1-2) If Paul's theology was correct, then the

Holy Spirit would change the convert without any help from man. But this totally misses the point of repentance, which is a personal response to God, changing one's life from bad to good. Belief is fine, but God is not forcing anyone to change with the Holy Spirit. The change comes from man in response to his/her belief. This philosophy of faith without deeds produced horrible behavior then, as it does today. Is it any wonder that mankind has not morally progressed!

So which gospel was superior in nature? The Gospel of James and Cephas was patterned after the message of Jesus. They taught obedience to the law, which included circumcision as well as the dietary laws. Their attitude towards their fellow man was "Love thy neighbor as thyself," and was interpreted as a reason for their communistic behavior. "All the believers were together and had everything in common. Selling their possessions and goods, they gave to everyone as he had need." (Acts 2:44,45) To them, this was the Kingdom of God!

Paul's gospel focused upon faith, not deeds. His mystical promised Holy Spirit did not improve lives just as it does not today. Finally, Paul had to impose Christ's law upon his disciples, telling them to behave themselves. This faith without deeds was morally bankrupt two thousand years ago and is so today. Paul's error was based upon his own struggles in life. He never trusted God to forgive him. That is why he needed an intermediary. To the Jews, an intermediary was never necessary. They knew that following God was a daily struggle, but a quest that God could appreciate. God never expected us to be perfect, but he does expect us to try.

A passage which proves that being a good Jew was not overly difficult comes from Deuteronomy.

> The Lord your God will circumcise your hearts and the hearts of your descendants, so that you may love him with all your heart and with all your soul, and will live.... Now what I am commanding you today is <u>not too difficult for you or beyond your reach</u>. It is not in heaven, so that you have to ask, "Who will ascend into heaven to get it and proclaim it to us so we may obey it?"...No, the word is very near you; it is in your mouth and in your heart so you may obey it. (Deut. 30:6-14) (emphasis mine)

Unlike the pathetic moaning of Paul in Romans, the above passage said that the law was not difficult to follow and there was no need for an intermediary. All the believer had to do was follow God with an open heart and soul. With that comes salvation. There was never a need for the Pauline salvation cult. The Jews, led by James and Cephas, knew that they were already in a relationship with God. That was the same Everlasting Covenant which Jesus followed to his death.

But what about the Last Supper? Did not Jesus create a New Covenant? According to Paul, Jesus did initiate a New Covenant. But once again, this comes from the mind of Paul. His interpretation of the Last Supper came from revelations from the Risen Christ. The Gospel versions of that Last Supper were just following the story line as invented by Paul. By examining the actions of James and Cephas through the writings of Paul, they certainly did not acknowledge this New Covenant.

The argument between Cephas and Paul had a parallel in the writings of Josephus. An examination of this particular conflict will sharpen our understanding of Paul and Cephas, and will put the argument in an earlier time period than usually believed, 44 AD versus the traditional 54 AD. Around 44 AD, King Izates became enamored with the Jewish religion and wished to be circumcised. A Jewish teacher by the name of Ananias tried to dissuade Izates from circumcision.

> [Ananias] said, that he might worship God without being circumcised, even though he did resolve to follow the Jewish law entirely; which worship of God was of a superior nature to circumcision. He added, that God would forgive him, though he did not perform the operation, while it was omitted out of necessity, and for fear of his subjects. (*Ant.* 20.41,42) (emphasis mine)

Like Paul, Ananias was preaching a form of Judaism which excluded circumcision, as circumcision was unpopular to the peoples of the area and was not an easy sell to an adult male. Both Paul and Ananias taught that their message or gospel was superior to the other Jews, who pushed the whole law and circumcision. It is interesting that the book of Acts has Ananias instructing Paul shortly after Paul's conversion. (Acts 9:10-19) Now King Izates was persuaded by Ananias to forego circumcision until a certain Eleazar arrived on the scene.

> ...a certain other Jew that came out of Galilee, whose name was Eleazar, and who was esteemed very skillful in the learning of his country, persuaded him to do the thing [circumcision]; for as he entered into his palace to salute him, and found him reading the law of Moses, he said to him, "Thou dost not consider, O king, that thou unjustly break the principle of those laws, and art injurious to God himself, [by omitting to be circumcised]; for thou ought not only to read them, but chiefly to practice what they enjoin thee. How long will thou continue uncircumcised? But, if thou hast not yet read the law about circumcision, and does not know how great impiety thou art guilty of by neglecting it, read it now." (*Ant.* 20.43-45)

Perfectly consistent with the Galatians' story, where certain men came from James (the circumcision group from Galilee), Eleazar came out of Galilee to persuade King Izates to become a full Jew through circumcision. This Eleazar was "esteemed very skillful in the learning of his country," a compliment from Josephus, reminiscent of the description of Matthias and Judas. (*Ant.* 17.149 and *War* 1.648) Izates immediately was circumcised. It is likely that James and the Jewish church found out about Paul and his disciples' true teachings and began sending out emissaries to preach the conservative view on circumcision and the law. This occurred in 44 AD, a full ten years before the traditional dating. This time frame does not work with the traditional dating of Paul, as 44 AD minus approximately twenty years in the movement, would yield a conversion date of 24 AD for Paul. (In Galatians, Paul accounted for seventeen years in the movement. A few more years may have elapsed between the Council of Jerusalem and the excommunication at Antioch.) This earlier time frame, which takes into account the history recounted by Josephus, is only possible with my Judas the Galilean hypothesis.

Not only was Paul's message at odds with the Pillar apostles (Cephas, James and John), but the dating was much earlier than traditionally thought. Paul was removed from the movement in the mid 40's. This may explain the Pseudoclementine *Recognitions* (an alternative Acts) which state that Paul attacked and almost killed James in the 40's. Knowing what we do about King Izates and the date of his full conversion to Judaism, the attack on James may very well have occurred. (See Chapters Twelve and Thirteen for more startling revelations concerning the apostle Paul.)

So which gospel do you believe: the full law message taught by Cephas and James or the gospel of grace as preached by Paul? This book will point you in a direction not traveled before. Hopefully, this will help in bringing all to light. One contradiction does not destroy a religion, but a great volume of contradictions should give one pause to reflect. Could Paul have been very wrong and could the Gospel writers have been equally in error by promulgating Paul's message? The answer will be clearer with each page you read.

◆ ◆ ◆

It has been brought to my attention that the challenge to Traditional Christianity may demoralize some. Many people hold onto their Christian religion as security in an insecure and often cruel world. Believe me, it is not my intention to hurt people. Should we deny the truth so that some may live in ignorant bliss? The answer is no!

Although most churches believe in Paul's theology, the individuals comprising the church may hold differing belief systems. Some are good people who would do anything for anyone. Others are selfish brutes who use religion as a way of hurting others. This is true not only for religious organizations but for secular groups as well. A certain smaller percentage of the people are good, honest and likable folk. These people would be well respected and admired in any group situation. Aim to be like these people. Do not worry about the afterlife. God will settle the score, not us.

12

PAUL AND CAESAR

The subject of Paul the Apostle is a complex one, but even our study of Judas the Galilean and the Fourth Philosophy is impacted by his life and beliefs. For Paul was opposed to the basic tenets held by Judas and his followers: to teach and follow the Law, including circumcision. That is why there is so much confusion concerning the New Testament. In its pages, we see a primitive, law abiding Jesus and a Jesus following in Paul's footsteps. This New Testament Jesus is no doubt a composite character, combining much of the actual teachings of Jesus with preconceived notions about those teachings. For example, when Jesus criticized the Pharisees for holding onto the traditions of man over the laws of God (Mark 7:1-23), the New Testament added this Pauline touch, "In saying this, Jesus declared all foods 'clean.'" In reality, Jesus was defending the laws of God, which included clean and unclean foods. He was not declaring these purity laws null and void. So you see, nothing can be accepted at face value. It is up to us to sort out the real from the counterfeit. So it is necessary to better understand Paul in order to separate his beliefs from those of Judas/Jesus.

PAUL AND HEROD

The Fourth Philosophy was a reactionary movement patterned upon the Maccabees, with Herod the Great as the chief antagonist. Herod introduced foreign practices amongst the Jews just as Antiochus Epiphanes did some one-hundred and fifty years earlier. That Judas the Galilean simply opposed Herod is an understatement. The disciples of Judas were willing to give their very lives in order to stop the hellenizing tendencies of Herod. This fervor continued from the time of Matthias, through the death of John the Baptist to the murder of James, the brother of Jesus. Thus, if we can tie Paul to Herod, his credibility is severely damaged. In fact, if Paul was an Herodian, then our picture of Jesus is grossly distorted, because much of the New Testament Jesus comes from the life and teachings of Paul.

First, we will look to Paul's own writings for insights. In Romans 16:11, Paul said, "Greet Herodian the kinsman of me." The Greek word for kinsman is different than the word for brother. It is most likely that this kinsman would be a flesh and blood relative while brother could very well denote a spiritual relationship. This Herodian may be related by blood ties, but this by itself would still leave doubt. So Paul goes on and says, "Lucius and Jason and Sosipater the kinsmen of me." (Rom. 16:21). It is very possible that Paul had ties in Rome to several of his relatives who were Herodians. In all the other Epistles, Paul does not specifically mention any other relatives. So the case against Paul based upon his own writings is meager to be sure, but a possible tie to Herod is clearly present.

The Book of Acts, although historically flawed, may shed more light upon Paul's background. Saul, or Paul, was first mentioned in Acts 8:1, where he gave approval to the death of Stephen and to the general persecution of Christians. "But Saul began to destroy the church. Going from house to house, he dragged off men and women and put them in prison." (Acts 8:3) Saul intended to widen his search beyond Jerusalem so "he went to the high priest and asked him for letters to the synagogues in Damascus, so that if he found any there who belonged to the Way, he might take them as prisoners to Jerusalem." (Acts 9:2) Our focus should be upon Saul's influence at such a young age. Even though he was employed as a lowly thug by the Chief Priest, he did seem to have a certain pull with this particular priest. This does not prove that Saul was of Herodian descent, but the authority given him was extraordinary if he was from Tarsus and unrelated to those in power. In general, those who persecuted Jesus and the church were the Sadducees, High Priests and Herodians. Pharisees had a better feel for the people's pulse, and association with Rome and its policies was not at all popular. If Paul was really a Pharisee as he claimed, he would not have associated with the High Priest in this persecution. This persecution proves that Paul had no ties to the Pharisees.

In Damascus, Paul escaped the governor under King Aretas by being lowered by a basket from a window in the wall. (2 Cor. 11:32,33) This scene was obviously altered in Acts 9:23-25, where Paul was lowered from the wall to escape the Jews. Certainly, the letter of Paul should be trusted more than the sanitizing Acts. And if this is so, the enemy of Paul was King Aretas, the same king who opposed Antipas (Herod the Tetrarch) over the murder of John the Baptist. (*Ant.* 18.109-119) This apparent hatred of Saul (Paul) may have had more to do with his Herodian background than with his preaching.

In the church at Antioch, there was one Manaen, a member of the court of Herod the Tetrarch (Antipas). (Acts 13:1) Saul was mentioned right after him and a few others, as leaders of this particular church. Again, Saul is placed right next to an Herodian. Yet this association, though close, does not necessarily make Saul a member of the court as well.

Being a member of Herod's family had considerable advantages. For instance, they were given Roman citizenship at birth. Now in Acts 17:3, it is claimed that Paul and Silas were both Roman citizens. If Paul was a Pharisee, a Hebrew of Hebrews and a member of the tribe of Benjamin, it is doubtful that he would also have had Roman citizenship. Paul compared himself to the Jerusalem Apostles: "I was advancing in Judaism beyond many Jews of my own age and was extremely zealous for the traditions of my fathers." (Gal. 1:14) Here Paul used the term "zealous" for the law, placing himself at an equal or superior position vis-a-vis Cephas and James. If this was true, then Roman citizenship is unbelievable.

After being threatened by the Jewish Christians (Fourth Philosophy), Paul was arrested by the Roman guard, thus saving his life. (Acts 21:27-36) It is interesting that Paul's nephew was there to protect Paul after the arrest, supplying information to the Romans. This information undoubtedly came from a mole, for no self-respecting Jewish Christian would knowingly help Paul. The nephew may have been keeping a close watch upon the activities of Paul and his knowledge of the Fourth Philosophy might have come from the High Priest, an employee of the Herodians.

After escaping Jerusalem, Paul was sent to Caesarea (58 AD) to answer charges in front of the Roman Procurator, Felix (52-60 AD). From the narrative in Acts 24:22-26, we learn that Felix was married to Drusilla, the daughter of Agrippa I and sister of Agrippa II. Felix often spoke with Paul, listening to Paul's Gospel. The reason for this frequent discourse was the hope for a bribe, for Felix believed Paul possessed a large sum of money. That the friendly conversations occurred should not be doubted for Drusilla was a member of the Herodian family. This may indirectly indict Paul. And it is interesting to note that the bribe issue may relate to the sum of money sent by Paul's churches to the church in Jerusalem. (1 Cor. 16:1-4) Per this passage from Corinthians, Paul stated that he might accompany the money to Jerusalem. Obviously, the money never changed hands between Paul and Cephas.

In 60 AD, Felix was replaced by Porcius Festus. Felix never received his bribe for he left Paul in prison as a favor to the Jews. Festus convened a court, and it was decided that Paul should be sent to Rome to stand trial there. A few days later, King Agrippa II and his sister Bernice arrived in Caesarea to talk with Festus. (It should be noted that this Bernice later became the mistress of Titus, the Roman who destroyed Jerusalem. It was also rumored that she was having incestuous relations with her brother, Agrippa. (*Ant.* 20.145)) Festus informed Agrippa of Paul's case, and Paul was granted an audience. Paul made the most of his opportunity, praising the King with flattery upon flattery (Acts 26:2-3; 26:26-28). This action of Paul was opposite that of Jesus (based upon Simon and Agrippa I—*Ant.* 19.332-334) who was silent before Pilate. And consider Paul's attitude towards these Herodians, that of cordiality. The Fourth Philosophy, especially John the Baptist, would have vomited over this friendship.

The ties between Paul and the Herodians appear fairly secure, but Paul's teachings make it a certainty. In Romans 13:1-7, Paul wrote that the believers should pay their taxes to Rome and should also follow Caesar without reservation. From our analysis of Judas the Galilean, we know that his followers would rather die than be slaves to Rome. And it should be noted that Jesus was accused of teaching against the payment of taxes. However, since the Herodians were Rome's tax collectors, it is easy to see why Paul sided with the power of Rome. This may also explain the passage attributed to Jesus where he was a friend of tax collectors and sinners. This was Paul and <u>not</u> Jesus!

Knowing all this about Paul, the passages in Josephus become more provocative. Most scholars have minimized the importance of a Saul in the writings of Josephus because they have also overlooked Judas the Galilean and the Fourth Philosophy. But we know that Josephus centered much of his account of the times on the Fourth Philosophy (Jewish Christians). As such, the mention of a Saul who is opposed to the Fourth Philosophy should send off warning signals. In his letters, Paul was very critical of the circumcision group's teachings, from the dietary laws to circumcision. His hatred of this movement probably hit a zenith when the Jewish Christians turned their backs upon him and his gospel (Galatians). With this in mind, let us look at Josephus' accounts of Saul.

SAUL AND JOSEPHUS

Josephus mentioned a Saul four times in his writings. We will reproduce these and determine if this Saul was the New Testament Paul. Most scholars downplay any similarities between Josephus' Saul and the familiar Paul because such a connection would undermine the validity of the New Testament as well as Christianity. However, if Saul and Paul are one in the same, then we may be on our way to discovering the truth hidden beneath the surface of these writings.

Soon after the stoning of James in 62 AD (*Ant.* 20.200), Josephus introduced his readers to an unsavory character named Saul.

> Costobarus also, and Saulus, did themselves get together a multitude of wicked wretches, and this because <u>they were of the royal family</u>; and so they obtained favor among them, because of their kindred to Agrippa: but still they used violence with the people, and were very ready to <u>plunder those that were weaker than themselves</u>. And from that time it principally came to pass, that our city was greatly disordered, and that all things grew worse and worse among us. (*Ant.* 20.214.) (emphasis mine)

From the above passage, the following can be concluded about Saul. First, his rampage against the people came shortly after the stoning of James in 62 AD. This in itself is against the grain of Acts, where Paul was on his way to Rome in 62 AD. Second, Saul had ties to Agrippa and to other Herodians. This definitely jibes with our understanding of Paul's affiliations as represented by his letters. Third, his violence was against the people weaker than himself. These were the Jewish Christians, considered by Paul to be weak financially and in faith. (Romans 14:1—15:13) Finally, Saul worked with others in his rampage against the Christians. Paul's mode of operation always included coworkers, such as Timothy and Titus.

Is it possible that the author of Acts used this passage in his first mention of Paul? According to Paul in Galatians 1:13, he admitted to trying to destroy the church. "For you have heard of my previous way of life in Judaism, how intensely I persecuted the church of God and tried to destroy it." However, Paul never explained how he tried to destroy the church. In fact, this is the only passage which even mentions that former way of life in connection to the church.

The author of Acts may have placed the Josephus passage of Saul into the context of Paul's former life in which he tried to destroy the church. To determine if this is possible, we must examine the story of Paul's introduction in Acts chapters 7 and 8.

> While they were stoning him, Stephen prayed, "Lord Jesus, receive my spirit." Then he fell on his knees and cried out, "Lord, do not hold this sin against them." When he had said this, he fell asleep. And Saul was there, giving approval to his death.
>
> On that day a great persecution broke out against the church at Jerusalem, and all except the apostles were scattered throughout Judea and Samaria. Godly men buried Stephen and mourned deeply for him. <u>But Saul began to destroy the church. Going from house to house, he dragged off men and women and put them in prison</u>. (Acts 7:59—8:3) (emphasis mine)

This first mention of Saul (Paul) in the book of Acts occurred after the stoning of Stephen, the first recorded martyr of the church. It is interesting to note that the mention in Josephus was only a few passages after the account of the stoning of James, the brother of Jesus. Is it possible that the stoning of Stephen was really a reworking of the historical stoning of James? Robert Eisenman, in his work, *James the Brother of Jesus*, certainly thinks so. He claims that the speeches put into the mouth of Stephen were really attributed to James by early church historians. If this is so, then the positioning of Saul after Stephen has new implications.

The Saul of Josephus had a familial relationship with Agrippa, one of the Herodians. A similar tie between Paul and the Herodians is also detailed in the New Testament. In Romans 16:11, Paul said, "Greet Herodian the kinsman of me." He also was mentioned right after Manaen, a member of the court of Herod the Tetrarch (Antipas) (Acts 13:1). In addition, Paul's stance on taxation was Herodian in nature, not Jewish Christian (Rom. 13:1-7). In short, Paul was a member of the Herodians, just as Josephus depicted Saul.

In the Acts' description of Saul, he gave approval to Stephen's death and then went on a rampage against the people. This also is in accordance with the Josephus version where Saul and his buddies "used violence with the people." However, this one episode may be sheer coincidence. That is why we must examine the other references to Saul in Josephus.

Before analyzing the second Josephus passage, another version of Saul's persecution should be noted. In the Pseudoclementine *Recognitions* 1.70,71, an "Enemy" attacked James, throwing James from the "Pinnacle of the Temple," nearly killing him. This Enemy then went to the High Priest and promised to kill those who followed Jesus. Like the account in Acts, the Enemy set out for Damascus with his letters from the authorities. Clearly, this Enemy was Saul, as the accounts of Saul in Acts and the Enemy in the *Recognitions* have the exact same movements: persecution, letters from the authorities and then a trip to Damascus. The only difference concerns James. In the book of Acts, the attack on James is not mentioned. It is my contention that the Acts' account is a whitewash of this whole affair. Acts is combining two attacks by Saul (Paul) into this one account. In fact, there were a total of three attacks by Saul. The first persecution comes from Paul's own admission in Galatians 1:13. This happened before Paul's entry into the movement, approximately 25 AD. The second attack was the one mentioned by the *Recognitions*, where James was nearly killed. This occurred after Paul was removed from the movement, shortly after the time of Paul's collections and his trip to Jerusalem for the famine relief. This can be approximated at 45-47 AD. The third persecution occurred after the stoning of James in 62 AD.

Thus, the book of Acts is confusing the whole history of Saul (Paul). Only Paul knew about his pre-Christian persecution, but the author of Acts tries to combine two later attacks on the church into this pre-Christian persecution. By examining a few passages in James' and in Paul's letters, we can be totally assured that Paul was the Enemy.

> You adulterous people, don't you know that <u>friendship with the world</u> is hatred towards God? Anyone who chooses to be a friend of the world becomes an <u>enemy</u> of God. (James 4:4) (emphasis mine)

James is attacking the philosophy of Paul here. This is in context of the whole letter, where James used the same Bible passages as Paul to prove Paul wrong (James chapter 2) and chastised Paul for his tongue in chapter three and his boasting in chapter 4. This whole letter was a condemnation of Paul. In reply to this attack by James, Paul wrote the following to his disciples in defending himself.

> Have I now become your <u>enemy</u> by telling you the truth? (Gal. 4:16) (emphasis mine)

> I beg you that when I come I may not have to be as bold as I expect to be toward some people who think <u>we live by the standards of this world</u>. For though we live in this world, we do not wage war as the world does. (2 Cor. 10:2,3) (emphasis mine)

In both passages, Paul was condemning those elements as supported and directed by James. Note that in Galatians 2:12, James sent his messengers to tell Cephas to remove Paul from fellowship. From this point on, the war between James and Paul would rage. Thus, the attack on James in 45-47 AD makes perfect sense. Paul was simply repaying James for ruining his fund raising schemes.

The traditional dating for the Acts persecution is 35 AD. This would mean that this persecution was before Paul's conversion. But as can be seen from the above passages, an unhealthy hatred was present between James and Paul near the <u>end</u> of Paul's career in the movement. This was during the collection effort and before Paul's trip to Jerusalem around 45-47 AD for the famine relief. This trip to Jerusalem was recorded in Acts 11:29,30 but never mentioned by Paul in his letters. That is because the trip had not yet occurred. Thus, Paul's letters to the Romans, Corinthians and Galatians were written in the early 40's, not the mid 50's as claimed by the traditional dating.

The dating for all of Acts is suspect. In Acts 5, Theudas was beheaded in 44-46 AD and the sons of Judas the Galilean were crucified in 46-48 AD. Acts 8 records Phillip and the Eunuch, which can be dated at 44 AD (King Izates). Acts 10's account of Peter and Cornelius relates to the associated Simon/Agrippa story, dated at 43-44 AD. And the famine relief in Acts 11:29 was between 45-47 AD. Why then should we believe that Saul's attack on the Church in Acts 7 and 8 should be 35 AD? In context of all the events surrounding the attack, the dating must be in the middle 40's. This only makes sense under my dating throughout this book. The remaining passages by Josephus will further support my claims.

The second passage concerning Saul comes from the *Jewish War*, where Saul was a member of the Peace Party, around 66 AD.

> So seeing that the insurrection was now beyond their control and that the vengeance of Rome would fall upon them first, the most influential citizens determined to establish their own innocence and sent delegations to Florus and Agrippa, the former led by Simon, son of Ananias, the other distinguished by the inclusion of Saul, Antipas, and Costobar, kinsmen of the king. They begged both to come top the City [Jerusalem] with large forces and suppress the insurrection before it got beyond control. (*War* 2.418-419) (emphasis mine)

Once again, Saul was teamed up with Costobar and another relative named Antipas. They were sent to their kinsman, Agrippa, to petition for an army to be sent to Jerusalem to suppress the insurrection. This request had nothing to do with spiritual matters, but was simply an attempt to combat the more radical elements of the Fourth Philosophy. (Should Saul have worked against the Fourth Philosophy? From our viewpoint today, with our understanding of terrorism, the answer is yes. But that is because we identify with the occupying power, Rome. Like that ancient power, the U.S. does not tolerate anyone who opposes our way of doing business. However, to the rebels, Saul's actions were traitorous.)

In Acts 25:13—26:32, the author of Acts had Paul also meeting with Agrippa. In his account, Festus discussed Paul's case with Agrippa, and Agrippa agreed to hear Paul's plea. Instead of the above mentioned call for arms against the insurgents, Paul's defense before Agrippa recalled his conversion to the Way and his hope for Agrippa's acceptance of his version of Christianity. In the Acts' story, Agrippa said this to Festus, "This man is not doing anything that deserves death or imprisonment.... [He] could have been set free if he had not appealed to Caesar." (Acts 26:32,32)

Thus, the meeting with Agrippa was made into a spiritual discussion. It also set the stage for Paul's trip to Rome to meet with Caesar. Note that the author of Acts had to get Paul out of Jerusalem before 62 AD, so that there could not be any questions about Paul's role in the stoning of James, the brother of Jesus. This earlier dating also removed Paul from the politics of Jerusalem, right before the Jewish war began (66 AD). In fact, tradition has Paul and Peter being martyred in Rome around 66 AD. If one believes this propaganda, then one must disregard Josephus. This may be the reason why the church had Paul martyred in Rome. If he were dead, then he would not be associated with Josephus' evil Saul.

In another interesting story related by Josephus, the ambassadors that had been sent to Agrippa later returned to Jerusalem, where they were forced to flee from the insurgents, taking cover in the Upper Palace (*War* 2.425-429).

> After this calamity had befallen Cestius, many of the most eminent of the Jews swam away from the city, as from a ship when it was going to sink; Costobarus, therefore, and Saul, who were brethren, together with Philip, the son of Jacimus, whom was the commander of King Agrippa's forces, ran away from the city, and went to Cestius. But then how Antipas, who had been besieged with them in the king's palace, but would not fly away with them, was afterwards slain by the seditious. (*War* 2.556,557)

Saul and his brother escaped from Jerusalem with their lives while Antipas stayed and perished. That Saul was besieged by the Jews should not surprise us. He had never been with the insurrectionists (Fourth Philosophy). Saul's protector, after he fled the city, was the Roman commander Cestius. So in Josephus' version of events, Saul escaped the murderous Jews and found refuge with the Romans.

In the book of Acts, Paul had been mobbed at the Temple and sought protection from the Jews. The Jews listened to Paul until he gave his famous conversion story. That was too much! (It should be noted that the three conversion stories in Acts do not reconcile to Paul's own account in Galatians.) His ally in the escape was the Roman commander. It was here that the Roman commander learned that Paul was a Roman citizen. This citizenship got him away from the mob and into the arms of the Roman procurator, Felix (58-60 AD). It is interesting to note that Paul's nephew helped uncover an assassination plot against Paul (Acts 23:16). Two points tie this to Josephus' account. First, a family member is aiding Paul just as Costobarus did in the actual escape from Jerusalem. Second, an assassination would have been carried out by the Sicarii (assassins), members of the

Fourth Philosophy. These are the same people that killed Antipas and would have killed Saul and Costobarus if caught.

Note that both Saul and Paul escaped into the arms of the Romans. Josephus had Saul fleeing the Fourth Philosophy (Jewish Christians) from the Upper Palace, while Acts had Paul escaping from the Jews at the Temple. Luke always put a spiritual spin upon Paul's actions. The Acts' account never happened. First, Paul went to the Temple to assure James that he did not forsake the Jewish covenant. In fact, Paul had already been removed from the movement, and he vehemently opposed the Everlasting Covenant (See Galatians). James would have wanted nothing to do with him at this point in time. Second, according to Paul's own letters, the Temple no longer had any spiritual meaning. If Paul really did return to the Temple, then at best, he was being hypocritical.

As with the other stories, the writer of Acts was careful to place Paul in an earlier time frame. The 58 AD arrest was four years before the stoning of James and eight years before the start of the Jewish war. The escape written about by Josephus occurred in 66 AD.

The last mention of Saul by Josephus occurred in 66-67 AD. Saul was sent as an emissary to Caesar to shift blame from himself and his cronies to the Roman procurator, Florus.

> However, Cestius sent Saul and his friends, at their own desire, to Achia, to Nero, to inform him of the great distress they were in; and to lay the blame of their kindling the war upon Florus, as hoping to alleviate his own danger, by provoking his indignation against Florus. (*War* 2.558)

In this final passage about Saul, the following should be noted. Saul requested to see Nero in order to shift the blame from himself to Florus. This voluntary request was similar to Paul's appeal to Caesar in Acts 26:32. In both stories, Saul (Paul) wanted to lay his case before Caesar. In Acts, Paul was blamed for causing a disruption in Jerusalem because of his misunderstood gospel, which was antinomian. According to the Roman Governors and Agrippa, Paul was an innocent man. In Josephus, Saul also claimed his innocence to Nero concerning the kindling of the Jewish war.

It is paramount in importance to understand who Caesar was in 66-67 AD. The ruler of the world was none other than the madman, Nero. In 64 AD, a great fire consumed the city of Rome. Many claimed than Nero had started the fire, so that he could rebuild the city with his own architectural plans. Nero, however, knew that the politics of this was dangerous, so he made the Jewish Christians scapegoats, saying that they had started the fire. No one will ever know for sure who started the fire, but we do know that the punishments of the Jewish Christians included the following:

> Besides being put to death they were made to serve as objects of amusement; they were clad in the hides of beasts and torn to death by dogs; others were crucified, others set on fire to serve to illuminate the night when daylight failed. (Tacitus, *Annals*, xv.44)

Nero tortured these Jewish Christians to such an extent that the population felt sympathy for them. It is this Nero that Saul requested to meet. This meeting was not to chastise Nero for the slaughter, but rather to shift blame from himself to another, Florus. Saul was on the side of Rome; he had always been. The letter to the Romans stated:

> Everyone must submit himself to the governing authorities, for there is no authority except that which God has established. The authorities that exist have been established by God. Consequently, he who rebels against the authority is rebelling against what God has instituted, and those that do so will bring judgment on themselves.... This is also why you pay taxes, for the authorities are God's servants, who give their full time to governing. (Romans 13:1-7)

The apostle Paul said that all government was established by God and the authorities were God's servants. If this was written around 40 AD or after, then it would have coincided with the regime of Caligula, an equal to Nero in sadistic behavior. As it turned out, Paul's regard for justice and equality was nonexistent, in that he regarded both Caligula and Nero as God's servants. What a sick and perverted mentality!

From the above four stories concerning Saul in Josephus, we get a much different picture of the apostle to the Gentiles. This Saul sided with the authorities and was hell-bent on destroying the Fourth Philosophy (Jewish Christianity). The book of Acts was just a complete misrepresentation of the facts concerning Paul's life. The writer of Acts put Paul's later life in the 58-62 AD time frame in order to disavow the writings of Josephus. Yet, the real Saul (Paul) worked with the ruling authorities at the time of James' murder (62 AD). He also rubbed elbows with Agrippa and Nero, always working against the Jewish Christians (Fourth Philosophy).

Paul was never an honest man. His philosophy is best summed up by this admission in 1 Cor. 9:19-23, where he stated: "To the Jews I became like a Jew, to win the Jews…. To those not having the law I became like one not having the law, so as to win those not having the law…. I have become all things to all men so that by all possible means, I might save some."

This has been taught as a noble philosophy to help save people. Yet, we, as parents, would never teach our children to behave in such a way. There is no nobility in lying, and Paul's philosophy was the exaltation of the lie. The Jewish Christians called Paul a liar, this being deduced by Paul's insistence of his truthfulness. (Rom. 9:1; 2 Cor. 6:8; 2 Cor, 11:31; Gal. 1:20) When the Jewish Christians finally uncovered Paul's true teachings, they turned their backs on him (Galatians 2:11-13). Even at this point, the Jewish Christians knew of just a small percentage of Paul's real teachings. The split between the Jewish Christians, represented by Cephas (Peter) and James, and the Pauline Gentile congregations, may explain why Saul (Paul) hated the Jewish Christians so.

The deaths of the Jewish Christians may have been just desserts in Paul's twisted thinking. They had deserted him earlier in his career, and now he would stop at nothing to crush them. He personally persecuted them; he tried to get Agrippa to send an army to crush them and finally, he went to Nero to excuse himself from the kindling of the Jewish war. Was Saul responsible for the war? Probably not, but he was a player in this dark chapter of Jewish history.

FOR THE LOVE OF MONEY

According to Paul, he was a zealous Jew who tried to destroy the Jesus movement even though he was a young man. Now, if the Acts' version of Paul's early persecutions is not accurate, then is it possible to recreate the early persecutions described by Paul?

Concerning the year 19 AD, Josephus gave his reason why the Jews were expelled from Rome.

> There was a man who was a Jew, but had been driven away from his own country by an accusation laid against him for transgressing their laws, and by the fear he was under of punishment for the same; but in all respects a wicked man:—he then living at Rome, professed to instruct men in the wisdom of the laws of Moses. He procured also three other men, entirely of the same character with himself, to be his partners. These men persuaded Fulvia, a woman of great dignity, and one that had embraced the Jewish religion, to send purple and gold to the temple at Jerusalem; and, when they had gotten them, they

employed them for their own uses, and spent the money themselves. (*Ant.* 18.81-84)

When Tiberius heard of the swindle, he banished the Jews from Rome.

This passage has never been attributed to Paul because he has been viewed as a player of the late 30's and beyond. However, in Chapter Three, we have proved that the crucifixion of Judas/Jesus was shortly before this event in Rome. By moving the beginnings of the post-Jesus movement back in time by eleven to fourteen years (from 30-33 to 19 AD), the start of Paul's career could also be much earlier than previously thought.

It is interesting that Josephus did not name the Jew in the above story. He generally was quite adept at identifying individuals. It is possible that the name was deleted in the pious editing of Josephus as detailed in Chapter Three. Without the name Saul, we are left with similar behavior patterns, but we cannot place this action upon Paul with total certainty.

This Jew was driven from Judea because he had transgressed their laws. His flight from Judea was necessitated by the fear of punishment. This type of individual would never be able to openly mingle with the fanatical Jews again. After Paul's conversion, he traveled to Jerusalem twice by his own account (Gal. 1:18 and 2:1-2), but each time he only conversed privately with the leaders. Obviously, Paul knew of the dangers lurking in Jerusalem.

The unnamed Jew went to Rome to make a living. Even though he had been forced to leave Judea for transgressing the law, he professed to "instruct men in the wisdom of the laws of Moses." This seems quite unusual. If a man knows the Law in Rome, he should know the same Law in Jerusalem. However, this pattern fits perfectly with Paul. Paul was always criticized by the circumcision (those from James, the brother of Jesus), but he claimed to have a superior knowledge of the Law to his own followers. These followers were generally Jewish converts, and later, simply Gentiles. These converts would know no better. They generally took Paul at his word, even though the circumcision called him a liar. In the Josephus passage, the unnamed Jew had convinced Fulvia, a rich Jewish convert, of his qualifications.

With the help of three other men, the unnamed Jew convinced Fulvia to contribute a vast sum to the Temple in Jerusalem. First, the unnamed Jew worked his scam with others. In the four passages about Saul in Josephus, this Saul was always accompanied by others, namely Costobarus, Antipas and hired hands. Note that Josephus called the followers of Saul "wicked wretches" (*Ant.* 20.214) just as he called the unnamed Jew a "wicked man" and his friends "of the same character as himself."

The scam concerned the contribution of purple and gold to the Temple in Jerusalem. This wealth never left the unnamed Jew's possession. Compare these actions to those of Paul.

> Now about the collection for God's people: do what I told the Galatian churches to do. On the first day of the week, each one of you should set aside a sum of money in keeping with his income, saving it up, so that when I come no collections will have to be made. Then, when I arrive, I will give letters of introduction to the men you approve and send them with your gift <u>to Jerusalem. If it seems advisable for me to go also, they will accompany me</u>. (1 Cor. 16:1-4) (emphasis mine)

Like the unnamed Jew, Paul collected money from his converts to be sent to Jerusalem. Paul also made sure that he would accompany the funds to the city. He was quite sure that no one would object to his plan.

The above instructions were for the Galatians and Corinthians. However, it seems as though Paul's credibility was being challenged by the Jews. It is possible that Paul's history of deceit had made him a target of the unrelenting James and his Jewish Christian disciples. 1 and 2 Corinthians as well as Galatians are merely documents which defend Paul's honesty and hard work. With the faith of a television evangelist, Paul stated:

> Remember this: whoever sows sparingly will also reap sparingly, and whoever sows generously will also reap generously. Each man should give what he has decided in his heart to give, not reluctantly or under compulsion, for God loves a cheerful giver....This service that you perform is not only supplying the needs of God's people [Jews in Jerusalem] but is also overflowing in many expressions of thanks to God. (2 Cor. 9:6-12)

After calling the Jewish Apostles "deceitful workmen, masquerading as apostles of Christ" (2 Cor. 11:13), Paul repeated his claims of personal sacrifice and suffering (2 Cor. 11:16-33). He then topped his sales pitch with a boast that he was called up to heaven (2 Cor. 12:1-10). This all leads to the passage: "Now I am ready to visit you for the third time, and I will not be a burden to you, because what I want is <u>not your possessions but you</u>." (2 Cor. 12:14) (emphasis mine) However, I am sure that Paul accepted the possessions with open arms. These possessions never made it to the Jewish Christians in Jerusalem.

One last tie between Paul and the unnamed Jew is the city of Rome. The unnamed Jew's con game caused quite an uproar in Rome, to the extent that all Jews were punished. Surely, this unnamed Jew could never show his face in Rome again. Is it just coincidence that Paul never traveled to Rome as attested by himself (Rom. 1:8-15)? In his letter to the Romans, Paul claimed he wanted to visit Rome but other factors always prevented the trip. Also, the book of Acts only had Paul going to Rome to visit Nero in 62 AD (Acts 28:11-31). This entire history of Paul is fiction as Saul's meeting with Nero actually occurred at Achia in 66-67 AD (*War* 2.558). With Paul's unmatched ego, it seems incredible that he would never visit the greatest city of his day, the seat of ancient power, Rome. One would think that Rome would have been his base of operation. The unnamed Jew incident may explain why only letters went to Rome. Paul knew he could not safely show his face in that great city.

Although the above explanation about the unnamed Jew is conjecture, it should be noted that Saul met with Nero at his <u>own</u> wish in 66-67 AD. (*War* 2.556-558) This was the same Nero who tortured the Jewish Christians in Rome after the Great Fire of 64 AD. The Jewish Christians were crucified, set ablaze and torn apart by wild animals, all to satisfy the cruelty of Nero. I cannot imagine that Judas/Jesus would have freely consented to such a meeting. Only the most cynical, self-centered man would have met with Nero under these circumstances. Considering what we now know about Paul, such a meeting should not surprise us; he hated the Jewish Christians with a passion.

If this new history of Paul is correct, then the traditional time frame of his life must be wrong. In orthodoxy, Paul converted a few years after the crucifixion of Jesus, approximately 35 AD. By his own account of time in Galatians, Paul's participation in the Jewish Christian movement lasted from his conversion to his excommunication in Antioch, or about twenty years. This would have placed the year at 55 AD. He later went to Jerusalem, where he was captured and imprisoned. The year for this act would have been 58 AD, the dating for the Egyptian.

Of the above, the only verifiable dating is the twenty years in which Paul was a member of the Jewish Christian movement. If Judas/Jesus died in 19 AD, and Saul was a player in Rome at that time, his conversion may have been in the early 20's AD. Thus, his participation as a Jewish Christian may have been from 20-40 AD or a few years later. This may help explain a passage from the Pseudoclementine *Recognitions* 1.70, where the Enemy (Paul) attacked James and almost killed him. The dating for this attack was in the 40's, per Eisenman.(1) This could not have happened per the traditional dating, for Paul would have been a member of the Way during the 40's. However, if Paul had been excommunicated in the early 40's, then the motive for the attack on James would be evident.

A comparison of visits to Jerusalem between Acts and Paul's own account in Galatians should help solve the whole affair. Paul mentioned two visits to Jerusalem: the first, three years after his conversion and the second, fourteen years later. The book of Acts detailed four visits: the first, at Paul's conversion; the second, at the famine (44 AD); the third, at the Council of Jerusalem (53 AD); the fourth, at Paul's arrest and imprisonment. Obviously, Galatians would have been written before the fourth visit. But what about the second visit at the time of the famine? Is it possible that Paul did not write about this visit because it had not yet happened? Remember that Paul was collecting money for the poor in Jerusalem. This is the same activity that Josephus described in his account of Queen Helena and King Izates. (*Ant.* 20.49-53) They also were sending money and food to Jerusalem during the famine. If Paul's collection activity was tied to the famine, then this solves the mystery of why Paul does not relate this famine-related visit in the letter to the Galatians. In Galatians, Corinthians and Romans, Paul did everything possible to convince his followers that he was trustworthy. This was done so that the collection could go on.

In connection with the famine collection, Josephus also wrote about clashes between Pauline Christians and Jewish Christians; those who insisted upon circumcision and those who taught against it. (*Ant.* 20.34-48) This was no different than the excommunication of Paul in Galatians. If the Josephus account was in the early 40's, then it follows that the Antioch disagreement between Paul and Cephas would have been in the 40's as well. This earlier dating of Paul explains the unexplainable. The attack on James in the 40's and the visit to Jerusalem at the famine now fit into the time frame of Paul.

So what happened to the money that Paul had collected from those dear souls in Corinth and Galatia? Surely, the Jewish Christians did not receive any assistance from Paul. Most likely, Paul used the money to further his own agenda and those goals of his Herodian friends and family. In the 60's, Saul had the resources to hire men to attack the church. It is possible that he used the money in the 40's to stir up trouble for James and Cephas. In the 40's, the Fourth Philosophy came under attack; Theudas was beheaded and the sons of Judas the Galilean were crucified. Could Paul have had a hand in this persecution? The answer will never be known. However, we do know that Paul persecuted the Church in the 20's, the 40's and the 60's. It is not too much of a stretch to assign him credit for fingering the sons of Judas the Galilean. In this, Paul may have been much like the mythical Judas Iscariot.

In all likelihood, the glowing account of Paul in the book of Acts is a total sham. To the very early church, Paul would have been an embarrassment, for his life was so unlike Judas/Jesus. The Gospels and Acts were designed to place the beliefs of the Gentile church onto Jesus and to make Paul the hero in the post-Jesus world. This post-Jesus world was not Jewish, but rather, Roman. Thus, Paul's harsh words and condemnations of Cephas and James were smoothed over, and it was the evil circumcision group who hounded the godly Paul. The reality was much different.

NOT ONE BUT THREE

According to the traditional story of Paul, he persecuted the church once, right after the stoning of Stephen. This occurred some short time after the crucifixion of Jesus, probably around 35 AD. After Paul's conversion on the road to Damascus, we are led to believe that Paul served the church well, for the rest of his life. His departure for Rome in 61-62 AD would calculate to approximately 27 years of service.

But according to Paul, Josephus and the Pseudoclementine *Recognitions*, there were three persecutions. The first persecution was hinted at by Paul in Galatians. As a young man, he persecuted the church, but later repented, and like Moses and Jesus, spent time in Arabia organizing his thoughts. He later returned to Damascus. This early persecution may relate to the unnamed Jew who caused great carnage to the Jews in Israel and in Rome, so much that he could not safely show his face in Jerusalem or in Rome. This persecution was shortly after the crucifixion of Judas/Jesus in 19 AD. The subsequent conversion was approximately 22-25 AD.

After spending approximately 20 years in the Jewish Christian movement, Paul was removed from fellowship at Antioch (Galatians) around 44 AD. With the monies collected from the churches in Galatia and Corinth, Paul traveled to Jerusalem. This is a trip not mentioned by Paul in his letters, the famine relief effort, as detailed in Acts 11:27-30. While in Jerusalem, Paul attacked James (*Recognitions* 1.70,71), almost killing him. He received letters from the High Priest to hunt down other leaders of the movement. Around this time, the two sons of Judas the Galilean were captured and crucified. Whether they were handed over (betrayed) to the High Priest by Paul, we will never know. Regardless, this persecution in Jerusalem was the second persecution.

It should be stressed that the "Enemy" as described in the *Recognitions* was not a young man but one who had a long history with James and Peter. This alone points towards the end of Paul's career with the church. There are several other passages from the Pseudoclementine literature which underscore the bitter fight between Paul and the Jewish Christians.

> For some among the Gentiles have rejected my [Peter] lawful preaching and have preferred a lawless and absurd doctrine of the man who is my enemy. And indeed some have attempted, whilst I am still alive, to distort my words by interpretations of many sorts, as if I taught the dissolution of the law and, although I was of this opinion, did not express it openly. But that may God forbid!" (*Letter of Peter to James* 2.3,4)

> "Following up this disposition it would be possible to recognize where Simon [Paul] belongs, who as first and before me [Peter] went to the Gentiles, and where I [Peter] belong, I who came after him and followed him as the light follows darkness, knowledge ignorance and healing sickness." (*Homilies of Clement* 2.17.3)

> "Thus he who does what haters do finds love; the enemy is received as a friend; people long for him who is death as a bringer of salvation; although he is fire, he is regarded as light; although he is a cheat, he obtains a hearing as a proclaimed of truth...." (*Homilies of Clement* 2.18.2)

Obviously, those who used this literature in the second century believed Paul to be the "Enemy." Like the letter of Galatians suggests, Peter traveled throughout Paul's territory, proclaiming a different message than Paul, "as the light follows darkness." This confirms that the persecution as described in the *Recognitions* was at the <u>end</u> of Paul's career with the Jewish Christians. And this happened around 45 AD.

But what did Paul do between 45 and 62 AD? This may be answered by two passages in Acts. In Acts 18:5,6, Paul proclaimed, "I am clear of my responsibility. From now on I will go to the Gentiles." This sentiment is once again put forward in Acts 28:23,29, where an exasperated Paul said to the Jews, "Salvation has been sent to the Gentiles and they will listen." These two passages may not be historical, but they do represent what Paul did in the years after his removal from the movement. Paul went his own way without heeding any direction from James or Peter. Peter may have tried to undo Paul's damage but in this he failed. (Paul's communities outlived the Jewish Christian communities, and that was the beginning of our modern day Christian church.) At some point, Paul returned to Jerusalem and teamed up with his brother and other Herodian friends.

The third persecution was recorded by Josephus. Shortly after the stoning of James, the brother of Jesus, Saul gathered up henchmen and attacked the poor, or the church. This occurred in 62 AD. (*Ant.* 20.197-214) Saul's later actions as recorded by Josephus were also directed against the Fourth Philosophy.

The genius of Acts chapters 7,8 and 9 is the melding of three persecutions into one. Thus, Paul persecuted the Church before his conversion but never afterwards. In the history described in this chapter, Saul persecuted the church once before his conversion and twice afterwards. The author of Acts used the mention of Damascus cleverly in his revised history, claiming that Paul was converted to Jesus on his way to Damascus, thus co-opting Paul's account of his conversion in Galatians and the account in the *Recognitions* where Saul was given letters by the High Priest to arrest the leaders in Damascus. This Damascus cover was continued when Paul was lowered in a basket by the disciples to escape the Jews (Acts 9:25). Paul wrote about such an event in 2 Cor.11:32,33, but that escape was from King Aretas, not from the Jews. This escape from King Aretas was due to the quarrel between the Herodians and the King. Aretas blamed the Herodians for the death of John the Baptist in 35-36 AD. Since Aretas died in 40 AD, the event described by Paul had to have happened between 36-40 AD, a few years after the traditional conversion.

In addition, the third persecution was absorbed into the one persecution by the story of Stephen and his death. The real stoning occurred in 62 AD and the person being stoned was none other than James, the brother of Jesus. This is the same James who hounded Paul throughout his career within the movement. Like the book of Acts, where Saul approved of Stephen's death, Josephus introduces us to Saul right after James' death.

The combination of three persecutions into one persecution has worked wonderfully for two thousand years. Scholars have never seriously questioned why the Pseudoclementine *Recognitions'* persecution by Paul would be dated in the 40's. Such a date could not be reconciled to traditional history. Also, since scholars have never been bold enough to doubt the last years of Paul, the passages by Josephus have been ignored. In effect, there has never been a proper analysis of Paul's life. Hopefully, my effort will help fuel renewed interest in finding the truth.

THE PROBLEM OF PAUL

Acts (1)

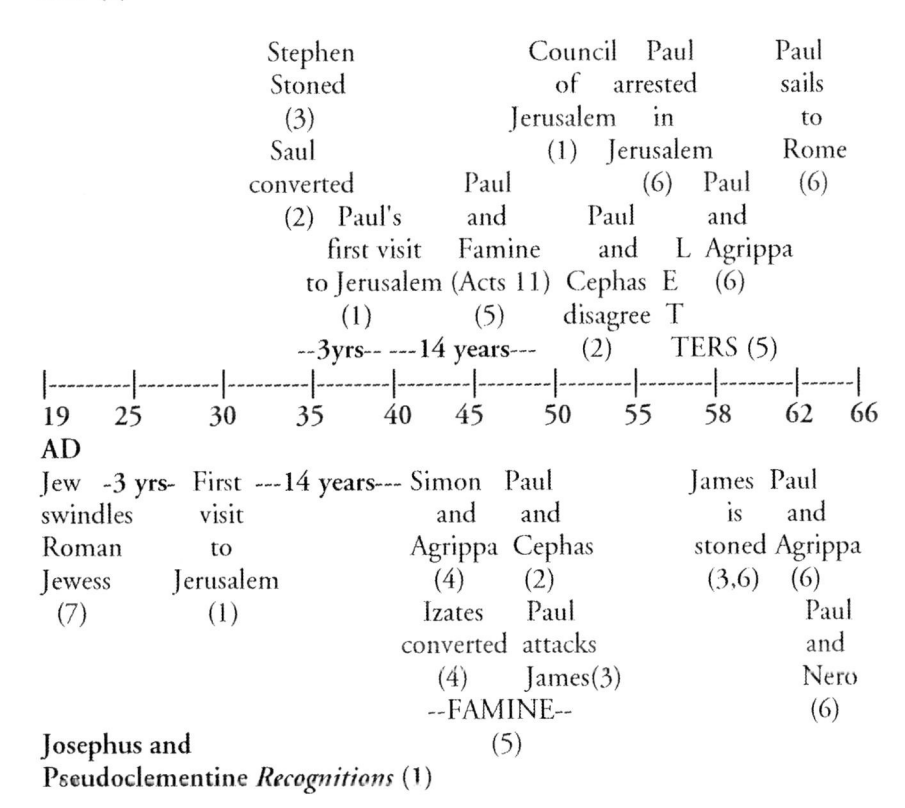

```
              Stephen              Council   Paul          Paul
              Stoned               of        arrested      sails
                (3)                Jerusalem in            to
              Saul                   (1)     Jerusalem     Rome
              converted   Paul              (6)   Paul     (6)
                (2) Paul's  and             Paul    and
                    first visit Famine      and   L Agrippa
                    to Jerusalem (Acts 11) Cephas E  (6)
                        (1)        (5)     disagree T
                      --3yrs-- ---14 years---  (2)    TERS (5)
|---------|---------|---------|--------|--------|--------|--------|--------|--------|------|
19        25        30        35       40       45       50       55       58       62     66
AD
Jew    -3 yrs- First ---14 years--- Simon   Paul          James    Paul
swindles       visit                and     and           is       and
Roman          to                   Agrippa Cephas        stoned   Agrippa
Jewess         Jerusalem            (4)     (2)           (3,6)    (6)
(7)            (1)                  Izates  Paul                   Paul
                                    converted attacks              and
                                    (4)     James(3)               Nero
                                        --FAMINE--                 (6)
Josephus and                         (5)
Pseudoclementine Recognitions (1)
```

1. Both the New Testament and Josephus timelines incorporate the two meetings in Jerusalem as detailed by Paul in Galatians: 3 years after his conversion and then 14 years later. Note that Paul never mentioned a visit to Jerusalem during the famine. This is due to the fact that the letters to the Corinthians, Galatians and Romans <u>preceded</u> his eventual trip to Jerusalem for the famine relief.

2. Since the actual crucifixion of Jesus occurred 14 years earlier than traditionally thought (19 AD vs. 33 AD), the beginning story of the church would have also been 14 years earlier. Thus, it is possible that Paul persecuted the church in 19 AD and converted to the faith in 20-24 AD. If this scenario is true, then Paul would have been excommunicated by Cephas and James around 40-44 AD.

3. The Book of Acts claims that Saul persecuted the early church and approved of Stephen's stoning around 35 AD. In Josephus, Saul persecuted those weaker than himself after the stoning of James, around 62-64 AD. This description of Saul was used by Luke to invent his own version of history. Also, the Pseudoclementine *Recognitions* claims that Paul attacked James in Jerusalem in the 40's. This could not have occurred based upon the chronology of Acts, but it does fit with the earlier positioning of Paul within the movement.

4. The two passages from Josephus concerning Simon and Agrippa as well as King Izates, Ananias and Eleazar, show that a struggle was underway for the hearts and minds of Jewish <u>converts</u>. In the early 40's, Jewish Christians were being sent out from Galilee to ensure converts were accepting full conversion, which included circumcision. This is the exact argument described by Paul in Galatians. This helps prove that Paul's career with the Fourth Philosophy (Jewish Christians) was nearing an end by 40-45 AD.

5. Scholars date 1 and 2 Corinthians, Galatians and Romans at 57 AD, based upon the chronology of Acts (which is absolutely useless in dating events). According to the early placement of Paul within the movement, these letters were written shortly after Paul's excommunication (early 40's). Note that Paul was collecting monies for those in Jerusalem. This effort probably related to the famine which Josephus placed between 44-48 AD. If Paul traveled to Jerusalem at the time of the famine, he may have come in contact with James, and a struggle may have ensued (Ps. *Rec*.). In any event, the monies probably went into the Herodian coffers and not to the Fourth Philosophy (Jewish Christians).

6. The story of Paul's later career in Jerusalem is dated a few years earlier in Acts than in Josephus. This earlier dating of Acts (58-62 AD) helps to distance Paul from the following: the stoning of James in 62 AD; Saul's petition for an army from Agrippa in 66 AD; and Saul's appeal to Nero in 66-67 AD, two years <u>after</u> Nero massacred Jewish Christians in Rome. In short, Acts sent Paul to Rome before the Saul of Josephus could do his dirty deeds in Jerusalem and beyond. This being the case, the entire ending chronology of Paul's life is bogus. It is therefore possible to shift Paul's career with the Fourth Philosophy to an earlier time.

7. In full circle, the beginnings of Paul's career may be traced back to an unnamed Jew who extorted money from a wealthy Jewess in 19 AD Rome. This

unnamed Jew worked with others, professed to be knowledgeable in the Law and convinced converted Jews to send monies to Jerusalem. All this fits in nicely with Paul's methods as described by himself in Galatians, Corinthians and Romans. Paul's anti-Law attitude may have actually preceded his "conversion" to Jewish Christianity. The "conversion" for Paul was the synthesis of anti-Law teachings with the death and resurrection of Jesus. It was through this "grace" that Paul could soothe his own conscience.

13

NOT ONE PERSECUTION, BUT THREE

In the preceding chapter, I proposed that Paul persecuted the church three times, once before his conversion and twice after his removal from the movement. This is a very radical departure from the traditional viewpoint of the apostle Paul. However, the Judas the Galilean hypothesis allows for this new interpretation of Paul since the history of the church can be pushed back fourteen years, from 33 AD to 19 AD. In this chapter, I will outline three different timelines, two from the New Testament and one from the writings of Josephus. There are two timelines from the New Testament because Paul's own writings are different from the account of Paul's life as recounted in the book of Acts. After each timeline, difficulties, in relation to other sources, will be examined.

THE TRADITIONAL PAUL

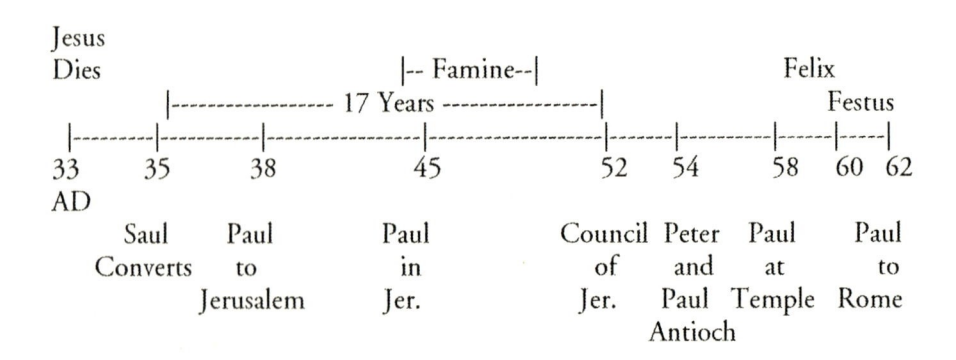

```
Jesus
Dies                    |-- Famine--|              Felix
        |---------------- 17 Years ----------------|    Festus
|-------|-----------|-----------------|----------------|-------|----------|------|-----|
33      35          38                45               52      54         58     60   62
AD
        Saul        Paul              Paul             Council Peter      Paul   Paul
        Converts    to                in               of      and        at     to
                    Jerusalem         Jer.             Jer.    Paul       Temple Rome
                                                              Antioch
```

The traditional timeline for Paul begins with the crucifixion of Jesus at 33 AD. This, of course, is totally dependent on Luke's dating of John the Baptist. In

Chapter Five, the traditional dating of John's ministry has been proved to be wrong in beginning, ending and duration.

If Jesus died in 33 AD, then it follows that Paul persecuted the church shortly thereafter and then converted on the road to Damascus, or approximately 35 AD. (Some traditional timelines have Jesus dying in 30 AD and Paul converting around 32 AD). In Galatians, Paul described two trips to Jerusalem, one three years after his conversion (38 AD) and one fourteen years later at the Council of Jerusalem (52 AD). Paul never mentioned his trip to Jerusalem for famine relief (45 AD), although this trip is detailed in Acts 11:27-30.

A few years after the Council of Jerusalem, Peter visited Paul in Antioch, and an argument ensued. According to Paul's version, Peter was clearly in the wrong even though all the Jews, including Barnabas, sided with Peter. After a few more years, Paul once again headed to Jerusalem in order to set things right with the Jerusalem church (58 AD). This can be accurately dated at 58 AD, as Luke mentioned an individual named "The Egyptian." This Egyptian can be dated by the writings of Josephus.

Once in Jerusalem, James ordered Paul to undergo rituals at the Temple. Paul complied with the request, but was identified by Jews from the province of Asia as one who taught against the law. The Jews tried to kill Paul, but he was saved by the Romans. Because Paul was a Roman citizen, he was sent to Felix from 58-60 AD, where he languished in prison. When Felix died, Festus replaced him as procurator. Before Festus and Agrippa, Paul pleaded his case and gospel. He was then sent to Rome to plead his case before Caesar.

Before we get into the difficulties of this account, we must appreciate the skill of Luke in ironing out any differences between Paul and the Jerusalem church. To this day, most Christians believe that the Christian church was one seamless movement.

1. With all of Luke's inconsistencies concerning dating, scholars have nevertheless used his timeline in dating Paul's letters. Romans, 1 & 2 Corinthians and Galatians were written after the Council of Jerusalem, which can be dated at approximately 52 AD. This date is arrived at by adding 17 years to the year in which Paul converted (35 AD). However, this whole chronology is dependent on Luke's history of John the Baptist. If the Baptist dates are erroneous, then so are the dates for Paul. Per Chapter Five, it was proved that Luke's beginning and ending dates for John's ministry were wrong. If that is so, then the dating of Paul should be reassessed.

To ascertain the dating for Paul's letters to the Romans, Corinthians and Galatians, we must examine the internal evidence of those letters. Three important pieces of information should be considered. First, the argument with Peter in Antioch is traditionally given a date at around 53-55 AD, shortly after the Council of Jerusalem. However, according to Josephus, a similar type of argument occurred between Ananias and Eleazar. Ananias taught King Izates that he could become a Jew without circumcision (Paul's view) while Eleazar, who was sent by his superiors in Galilee, insisted upon circumcision (Peter's view). This altercation occurred in 44 AD. (*Ant.* 20.34-46) Note that individuals were being sent from Galilee (or from James) in order to combat Pauline teachings. In Antioch, the Jews turned their backs upon Paul. It is very likely that the Antioch confrontation between Peter and Paul occurred in the same time frame as Ananias and Eleazar, or approximately, 44 AD.

Second, scholars have never properly addressed the visits to Jerusalem as enumerated by Paul and by the book of Acts. Paul mentioned two visits to Jerusalem, one three years after his conversion and the second, fourteen years later (Council of Jerusalem). The book of Acts mentioned four visits to Jerusalem: one soon after Paul's conversion, a second at the time of the famine, a third at the Council of Jerusalem and a fourth near the end of Paul's career. It is understandable that Paul would not have mentioned the fourth visit, as that visit was in the future. But what about the famine-related visit? Why did Paul withhold this important visit from his audience (Galatians)? I believe Paul never mentioned this visit because it had not yet taken place. Paul was in the midst of collecting a great sum of money from his disciples in Corinth and Galatia. This money was being collected to help the poor in Jerusalem, during the famine. This famine stretched on from 44-48 AD. It is my contention that Paul's letters to the Romans, Corinthians and Galatians were near the beginning of this famine or around 44 AD. This would push back the Council of Jerusalem to 42 AD and Paul's conversion to 25 AD, give or take a few years. Of course, this only works if my Judas the Galilean hypothesis is correct.

Third, any mention of John the Baptist or to his baptism is more and more unlikely, the further one moves away from his year of death. According to the Gospels, John's short ministry ended around 31 AD. And it follows that John's disciples would have joined with the disciples of Jesus as John supported the Messianic role of Jesus. If this was the case, then why would John's influence still be felt in 55 AD or twenty-four years after his death? This seems incredibly unlikely. However, in Chapter Five, it was definitively proven that John did not die until 35-36 AD, and he had a huge following at this time. John's baptism and influence may have been felt for many years after his death. If Paul was writing his letters in the early 40's, then a conflict with John's teaching was a real possibility (Apollos).

2. The traditional dating has Paul being sent to Rome in 60-62 AD. This conveniently removes Paul from Jerusalem before Josephus' several mentions of a Saul. This Saul can be easily identified with Paul. (See Chapter Twelve—Paul and Caesar.) Thus, the fourth mention of a Jerusalem trip in the book of Acts may be totally fictional. Paul no doubt returned to Jerusalem, but not as described by the book of Acts.

3. According to Acts 7:38, during the stoning of Stephen, "the witnesses laid their clothes at the feet of a young man named Saul." The New Testament claims that Saul was a young man when he first decided to persecute the church. And it follows that the converted Saul (Acts Chapter Nine) was also a young man. This contradicts the Pseudoclementine literature, where the enemy (Paul) was an established foe. In the *Recognitions* and *Homilies of Clement*, this enemy was constantly being hounded by Peter. This may refer to the Antioch meeting and all subsequent clashes between Peter and Paul. Thus, the picture as painted by Acts may be totally wrong.

ACTS—CHAPTERS FIVE THROUGH TWELVE

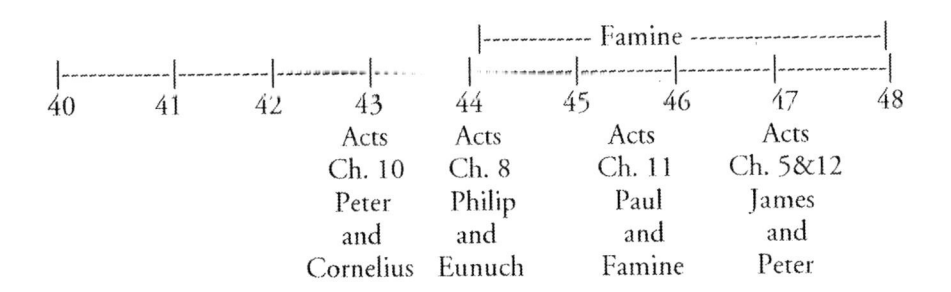

```
                          |----------- Famine -----------------|
|-----------|----------|----------|..  |..........|----------|----------|----------|
40         41         42        43    44         45         46         47         48
                                Acts  Acts       Acts       Acts
                                Ch. 10 Ch. 8     Ch. 11     Ch. 5&12
                                Peter  Philip    Paul       James
                                and    and       and        and
                                Cornelius Eunuch Famine     Peter
```

The book of Acts is interesting literature, but its chronology of events is confused and downright misleading. The above references surround the persecution by Saul (Acts 8) and the conversion of Paul (Acts 9). All of the surrounding events occurred in the mid to late 40's. If that is the case, then how could the persecution and conversion of Saul be in 35 AD? Would it not follow that the persecution of Paul would be in 44-45 AD? But if that is the case, then the Council of Jerusalem would not be until 61-62 AD. That is impossible.

1. Acts chapter 5 refers to Theudas and Judas the Galilean. Luke was taking material from *Ant.* 20.97-102, where Josephus described the deaths of Theudas and the sons of Judas the Galilean. Theudas was beheaded during the governorship of Fadus (44-46 AD) and the sons were crucified during the reign of Alexander (46-48 AD).

The story of James and Simon (Peter) being imprisoned in Acts chapter 12 also comes from the story of the sons of Judas the Galilean. The sons were named James and Simon and were crucified.

2. In Acts chapter 10, Peter traveled to Caesarea to meet a Gentile named Cornelius. This is a story of inclusion as Peter accepted Cornelius into the movement. This story was taken from *Ant.* 19.332-334, where Simon was taken to Caesarea to meet with Agrippa for preaching exclusion from the Temple. This story can be dated to 43 AD.

3. In Acts chapter 8, Philip converted a eunuch to Christ. Much of this fabricated event can be attributed to the King Izates story, found in *Ant.* 20.34-46. This can be dated to 44 AD.

4. In Acts chapter 11:27-30, Paul was sent to Jerusalem with money for famine relief. This famine occurred between 44-48 AD. Paul never mentioned this trip in his letters, signifying that such a trip had not yet occurred.

In essence, the book of Acts' timeline is confused and misleading. (See Chapter Fourteen—Acts—A Misleading Account). However, the confusion concerning this timeline has been ignored by scholars. They blindly believe these above events all happened in the mid to late 30's. In their defense, if these events happened in the 40's, then Christianity as we know it today is a complete sham. The following timeline will prove this statement.

THREE PERSECUTIONS, NOT ONE

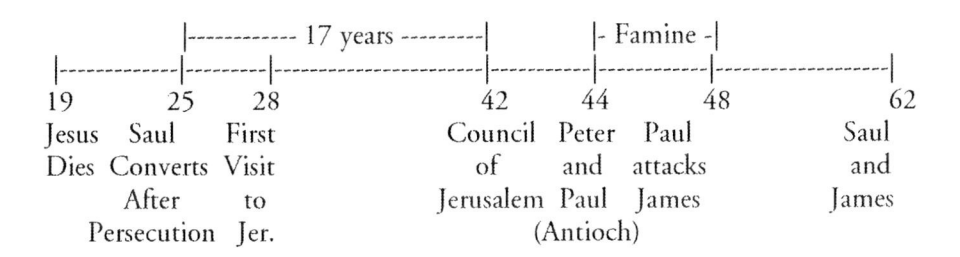

```
            |------------ 17 years ---------|      |- Famine -|
|------------|---------|-----------------------|-----------|-----------|------------------|
19          25        28                      42          44          48                 62
Jesus       Saul      First                   Council     Peter       Paul               Saul
Dies        Converts  Visit                   of          and         attacks            and
                      After                   to          Jerusalem   Paul    James      James
                      Persecution Jer.                    (Antioch)
```

The first persecution of the church by Saul occurred in the early 20's, somewhere between 22-25 AD. This is a decade earlier than traditionally believed, and is based upon Jesus being crucified under Pilate in 19 AD. (See Chapter Three—Pilate's Reign). This persecution is not the one reported in Acts chapters 7 and 8. In this first persecution, Saul not only enraged the Jews in Judea, but managed to have the Jews persecuted in Rome as well. This is the reason why Paul only traveled to Jerusalem in cover of night. And it explains why Paul <u>never</u> visited Rome, even though this was the center of power, the one place a person like Paul would have considered the jewel to his little empire. This persecution is detailed by Josephus in *Ant.* 18.81-84. Saul's attitude towards the Jews and the Jewish Christians in particular may have been negative for an extended period of time, from 19-25 AD. In Acts, the conversion is overnight on the road to Damascus, but Paul's own account in Galatians only says in "my previous way of life in Judaism, how intensely I persecuted the church of God and tried to destroy it." This sounds more like a ongoing effort as compared to the weekend version in Acts.

The earlier dating for Saul is consistent with John the Baptist introducing Judas the Galilean in 6 AD and with Judas/Jesus' crucifixion in 19 AD. These earlier dates pose grave problems for traditional Christianity, in that the seventeen years in the movement as described by Paul (Gal. 1:18—2:5) places the Council of Jerusalem at approximately 42 AD. This is near the end of Paul's career with the Jewish Christian movement.

The argument between Peter and Paul in Antioch is detailed in the letter to the Galatians. Paul claimed to have won the argument, but even he has to admit that all the Jews, including Barnabas, sided with Cephas (Peter). It is at this point that the Jews turned their backs upon Paul and his gospel. Keep this in mind when reading Galatians and 2 Corinthians. Paul's hatred for James cannot be controlled. He called the Jewish apostles "deceitful workman, masquerading as apostles of Christ." He even went as far as calling them servants of Satan. Ouch!

The letters to the Galatians and Corinthians were efforts by Paul to defend himself against the claims of Cephas (Peter) and James. Paul did everything in his power to describe his worthiness, making claims about his life that were quite amazing. (2 Cor. 11:22-12:13) Paul even claimed to have been "caught up to the third heaven," hearing things "that man is not permitted to tell." The reason for this effort is quite clear: Paul was in the middle of a great collection for the saints in Jerusalem. He needed to stay relevant. Even though he had been removed from the Jewish Christian movement, Paul now claimed superiority over that movement. From this point on, Paul had no ties with Cephas or James.

In the *Recognitions of Clement* 1.70,71, the "Enemy" attacked James at the Temple, nearly killing James. This "Enemy" then received letters from the High Priest and proceeded to go to Damascus, to where he thought Peter had escaped. This scenario for the enemy is inserted into the Acts' chapter 8 persecution by the young man named Saul. However, this cannot be! Surely, a young man with limited experience could not be named as the "Enemy." The Pseudoclementine "Enemy" was the older Paul, the man who had once been part of the Jewish Christian movement. In this literature, Peter traveled all over the world to combat the teachings of the Enemy. This is consistent with the account in Galatians and is also supported by the King Izates story in *Ant.* 20.34-46. In both accounts, representatives were sent from Galilee to combat the teachings of Paul in favor of a strict interpretation of the Law, which insisted upon circumcision. This can be dated to 44 AD.

When Paul arrived in Jerusalem with his hoard of collected money, he did not give said money to James and the church. Instead, a fight broke out where James was nearly killed. No one will ever know what Paul did with the money which had been collected. Maybe he used part of it to bribe the High Priest in assisting his aims in persecuting the Christians. This may explain a puzzling question left by the traditional view: how could a young man named Saul be given such power by the High Priest? In reality, the older Paul had plenty of money to buy support.

It should also be noted that the sons of Judas the Galilean were captured and crucified around this visit by Paul, between 46-48 AD. Could part of the second persecution have included James and Simon, the sons of Judas/Jesus? Paul knew the Fourth Philosophy well and could have easily been instrumental in the capture of some of the movement's leaders. Could this have been the genesis of the betrayal story, later assigned to the mythical Judas Iscariot? Clearly, in the eyes of the early Jewish Christian church, Paul was the "Enemy," the "Liar" and a betrayer of Jesus.

After the second persecution, Paul no doubt went back to his Gentile flocks. Never would he consciously confront the Jews again. This is supported from Acts 18:6, where Paul tells the Jews, "Your blood be on your own heads! I am clear of my own responsibility. From now on I will go to the Gentiles." So for a very long time, Paul traveled and preached his evolving gospel of grace, based upon revelation after revelation. And there was nothing or anyone to stop him. This may have occurred between 48-62 AD.

In 62 AD, James was captured by Annas (the son of the former High Priest Annas—7-15 AD). He was illegally tried and stoned to death. (*Ant.* 20.197-203) This is the basis for the Stephen story in Acts chapter 7. It is interesting that the young Saul was introduced right after Stephen's death. In *Ant.* 20.214, Saul is mentioned right after James' death. In both versions, Saul persecuted those weaker than himself, namely the church. In reality, this was Saul's third persecution of the church. The book of Acts cleverly combined the second and third persecutions and disguised these as the first and only persecution by Saul (Paul).

This no doubt explains why the later church did everything in its power to distance Jesus from Judas the Galilean and the earlier time frame. If it is understood that Saul converted in the early twenties, then the three persecution scenario can be easily understood. This is the reason why the 20's have been excluded not only from the book of Acts but from Josephus as well. Josephus has an 18 year period, from 19-37 AD, where everything has been expunged. The early Gentile church of Paul removed all information which could possibly tie Paul to the literature which condemned him as the "Enemy."

CONCLUSION

This three persecution scenario may seem incredible to most Bible students, but it is the only explanation which takes into account all relevant information. The writings of Josephus have been ignored by traditional Christianity. How can we possibly ignore the Saul who was introduced right after the stoning of James? The Pseudoclementine literature has also been totally discounted by traditional Christianity. This literature claimed that Paul was the "Enemy" of the early church. Many early Jewish Christians believed this to be true. How can we ignore such a strong picture of those early days?

Throughout this book, I have endeavored to introduce material which presents a totally different picture of early Jewish Christianity. From John the Baptist to Judas the Galilean, the history of Jewish Christianity was really the history of the Fourth Philosophy as described by Josephus. Saul's place in the story can only be discovered by understanding the events that went on before.

Was Paul an evil man? Was there any good in him? This was answered by James: "Anyone who chooses to be a friend of the world becomes an enemy of God." (James 4:4) This is a simplistic viewpoint, but one held by the early Jewish Christian church. Paul argued against this interpretation: there are "some people who think that we live by the standards of this world. For though we live in this world, we do not wage war as the world does." (2 Cor. 10:2,3) Paul saw his struggle against the powers of darkness, while James saw the practical consequences of disobeying God. Who do you believe? That is the important question today.

14

ACTS—A MISLEADING ACCOUNT

The story of Acts supposedly chronicled the historical actions of the Apostles after the crucifixion of Jesus. In this account, the Twelve were introduced and minimized as the true hero of the story emerged. Paul became the focus of Acts as Peter and James slowly drifted into oblivion. Was this chain of events true or simply a jumble of half truths and flat-out falsifications?

I will list nineteen accounts in Acts which have a different parallel passage in Josephus or in Paul's writings. Then each disputed section will be separately analyzed. In this way, the full extent of the historical tampering will become evident. This is important because the sheer number of contradictions helps support my Judas the Galilean hypothesis. When combined with the Judas and Jesus similarities as enumerated in Chapter Two, the New Testament becomes a purposeful misrepresentation of facts mixed with utter fiction.

1. Acts 1:12-26—Judas Iscariot is replaced by Matthias, an unknown disciple.

2. Acts 2:1-4—The Twelve speak in tongues on Pentecost, drawing attention to themselves.

3. Acts 2-5—No other information is available from Josephus.

4. Acts 5:36-39—Theudas and Judas the Galilean are examples of grand failure.

5. Acts 6:8-7:60—Stephen is stoned to death, becoming the first church martyr.

6. Acts 8:1-3—Saul approves the death of Stephen and then persecutes the church with blind rage.

7. Acts 8:26-40—Philip baptizes the Ethiopian eunuch.

8. Acts 9:1-19—Saul converts on the road to Damascus and is instructed by Ananias in the new faith.

9. Acts 9:23-25—Paul escapes from Damascus, evading the murderous Jews.

10. Acts 10-11:18—Peter brings the Gospel to Cornelius, a Roman centurion.

11. Acts 11:27-30—Paul and Barnabas are sent with collection monies to Jerusalem for famine relief.

12. Acts 12:1-19—Peter and James are imprisoned. James is beheaded while Peter miraculously escapes.

13. Acts 15:1-35—The Council at Jerusalem certifies Paul's mission to the Gentiles.

14. Acts 15:36-41—Paul and Barnabas part company after a sharp disagreement over John Mark.

15. Acts 21:27-22:29—Paul escapes the Jews at the Temple and finds refuge with the Roman guard.

16. Acts 25:23-26:32—Paul speaks to Agrippa and Bernice in defense of the Gospel.

17. Acts 26:32—Paul appeals the Jewish charges against him to Caesar.

18. Acts 27 and 28—In Acts chapter 27, Paul sails to Rome. On the way, he is shipwrecked on Malta. In Chapter 28, Paul arrives in Rome where he meets with the Jews before his meeting with Nero.

19. Acts 16:10—In this verse, the telling of Acts changes from third to first person. It is assumed that Luke joins Paul at this point in the narrative.

These nineteen areas of concern are not the whole story. Corroboration for most of Paul's actions are not recorded in Josephus and the only confirmation comes from the writings of Paul. For example, Paul stated that he suffered more than all others. In context, Paul was comparing himself to the Jewish apostles, specifically Cephas and James, and wished to convince the Corinthians that he surpassed those "super apostles" both in faith and in action.

> Five times I received from the Jews the forty lashes minus one. Three times I was beaten by rods, once I was stoned, three times I was shipwrecked, I spent a night and a day in the open sea. I have been constantly on the move. I have been in danger from rivers, in danger from bandits, in danger from my own countrymen, in danger from Gentiles; in danger in the city, in danger in the country, in danger at sea; and in danger from false brothers. (2 Cor. 11:24-26)

This extensive listing of dangers provided the author of Acts with the opportunity to include these in his narrative. The dangers were specific but Paul gave them no context. Why was he stoned? Most stonings resulted in death, examples being Stephen and James, the brother of Jesus. Why did he receive the thirty-nine lashes? According to Mel Gibson's recent movie, the lashes themselves could kill. Could anyone survive this torture five times? Where and when was he shipwrecked? Not only did Paul claim to have survived three separate shipwrecks, he spent a night and a day in the open sea. Paul's travels are detailed in Acts 13 and 14 and later in Acts 16 through 21. Did all these events really happen as we read them? Could any one person have survived all these perils as claimed by Paul? Could he have exaggerated? And is it possible that Acts created a colorful history for Paul with his self proclaimed dangers as support? This will remain forever unanswered. However, after the nineteen areas of historical manipulation are explored, you may find the travel history concerning Paul hard to believe as well.

1. In Acts chapter 1, Judas Iscariot was replaced by the unknown disciple named Matthias. According to Paul, Jesus was "delivered up," translated as a betrayal (1 Cor. 11:23); but it could not have been a member of the Twelve, for he wrote that the resurrected Jesus appeared first to Peter and then to the Twelve (1 Cor. 15:3-5). The Gospels and Acts had Jesus meeting with the Eleven, not the Twelve (Mark 16:14; Acts 1:3 and Acts 1:12-13). It must be remembered that Paul wrote his account at least fifty years before Acts. In this lengthy span of time, the story of Jesus' capture may have evolved to include a betrayal. The Gospels and Acts created a fictional character named Judas Iscariot, who became this betrayer. This Judas represented all that was evil: his name Judas stood for Judah or the Jews and Iscariot was a garbling of sicarios, those rebels aligned against Rome, who used assassinations as their weapon of choice. Like Josephus' description of the Fourth Philosophy as bandits, Judas was portrayed as a thief, and this

Judas committed suicide, just as the Sicarii had done at Masada. The leader at Masada was named Eleazar, and he was the grandson of Judas the Galilean.

In short, the death of a Judas Iscariot never occurred. On the other hand, a Judas was dead. Judas the Galilean, known by his title Jesus, was crucified by the Romans for his stance on taxes and his claim of kingship. This Judas had to be replaced. A movement cannot continue without leadership. Therefore, it was imperative to install a new leader.

The purpose of Acts chapter 1 was to diminish the importance of James, the brother of Jesus. James was the one who actually replaced Jesus as the unquestionable head of the movement. This fact is verified by Paul who recounted his meetings with the Pillar apostles in Jerusalem (Galatians 2). The author of Acts refused to give any credit to James, but instead made Matthias one of the Twelve.

This Matthias was an unknown, never to be heard from again. Was he a real person or a literary device to confuse the reader? The only Matthias in the Judas the Galilean/Jesus tradition was the co-teacher with Judas in 4 BC at the Golden Eagle Temple Cleansing. This Matthias was burnt alive by Herod the Great and his leadership role was assumed by Judas the Galilean. Did the book of Acts playfully misuse this story? Judas replaced Matthias in 4 BC as leader of the rebel movement. Was the name Matthias used as a not so subtle joke to replace Judas/Jesus? In my opinion, that is the case.

2. It is amazing that the Twelve Apostles were made to speak in tongues as proof of the Holy Spirit. Throughout the Gospels, Jesus downplayed the miracles, hoping that people would follow his teachings, not just an occasional miracle. That is not to say that the Twelve could not or would not perform miracles. These were not scientific people. Any healing, whether natural or not, was seen as an act of God. However, speaking in tongues was not a part of the Jewish Christian movement. Jesus did not speak in tongues and nowhere does Josephus mention this practice amongst the Jews.

The Gentile churches founded by Paul practiced speaking in tongues and the interpretation of these ramblings. In fact, the church in Corinth was fascinated by the gift of tongues. This caused confusion and an unruly worship. Paul tried to curb the excesses of the "Holy Spirit," even though he claimed that this was a gift from God.

> Follow the way of love and eagerly desire spiritual gifts, especially the gift of prophecy. For anyone who speaks in a tongue does not speak to men but to God. <u>Indeed, no one understands him; he utters mysteries with his spirit.</u> But

everyone who prophesies speaks to men for their strengthening, encouragement and comfort. He who speaks in a tongue edifies himself, but he who prophesies edifies the church. I would like everyone of you to speak in tongues, but I would rather have you prophesy. He who prophesies is greater than one who speaks in tongues, unless he interprets, so that the church may be edified. (1 Cor. 14:1-5) (emphasis mine)

In Paul's Gentile churches, speaking in tongues was a gift of the Holy Spirit, except his version of tongues was unlike that of Acts chapter 2. The Twelve spoke in various languages so that others could understand. Why then did the Holy Spirit refuse to do this same trick among the Gentiles? Paul stated that the gift of tongues did not speak to men but to God. So, in essence, the babbling was the language of God. This supposed gift of tongues was an attention grabbing device. Do people really have another voice within themselves or do they want others to believe so? Is this not similar to the Pharisees who loved attention? Jesus condemned these men as hypocrites.

The Twelve also grabbed the attention of foreigners in the area. But why would they be going after foreigners when thousands of their own were waiting to hear from them? Maybe this whole chapter was meant to undo the Tower of Babel episode where arrogant men were separated by God by language. This undoubtedly was part of the answer to the tongues. The Gospel would unite the world as language had once separated it. But we should never forget Paul's teachings. His emphasis on tongues made the whole episode possible.

3. From Acts chapter 2 to most of chapter 5, there is no corresponding information from the pen of Josephus. From the year 19 to 37 AD, all of his colorful history was erased. This is similar to the twelve minute gap in the Nixon tapes, but even more devastating. Had we been able to view these missing years, we could have identified the death of Judas the Galilean, and could have proven with certainty his claim to kingship among the early Jews. We also could have been privy to the first acts of the apostles from an historian, not just from the fertile minds of much later disciples.

This lack of information from Josephus does not disprove this section of Acts, but it should give us pause. Why would later Christians desire to doctor the pages of Josephus? Why did they move Pilate's governorship from 18 to 26 AD? (See Chapter Three) Was this done to shift Jesus' death to a later time? Why was the death of Judas the Galilean, the most influential rabbi of first-century Israel, omitted by Josephus? Could it be because Judas was crucified? After all, his claim to be Messiah and his opposition to Roman taxation would have been punishable by crucifixion. This would have been a crucial piece of information for Christians to destroy if they had wanted to hide Jesus' true background. And why would Christians want to delete the years from 19 to 37 AD, covering the first generation of post-Jesus disciples? This period corresponds to the Acts' chapters in question. Did Josephus have relevant things to say about Peter and James, the brother of Jesus? If so, then this would have been reason to destroy the documents because James was summarily written out of the first fourteen chapters of Acts.

4. Acts 5:36-39 introduced us to Theudas and Judas the Galilean. The New Testament account had Gamaliel in 35 AD referring to an event in the future, the death of Theudas (45 AD), and then to the death of Judas the Galilean (6 AD). Judas was said to be <u>after</u> Theudas according to Acts. This confused order may follow the account in Josephus where the <u>sons</u> of Judas the Galilean were crucified (46-48 AD) after the death of Theudas.

The passage in Acts also discredited Judas the Galilean, saying his movement failed after his death and that it was not from God. From Josephus, we know that Judas' Fourth Philosophy consumed the nation for over fifty years after his death, from 19 AD to 73 AD. Why would Acts misrepresent the facts about Judas the Galilean? To destroy the legacy of Judas was paramount in importance, to forever distance Jesus from Judas. The smear campaign worked wonderfully, to such an extent that modern day scholars dismiss Judas even though Josephus portrayed him as one of the most important figures of first-century Israel. For more information concerning Theudas and Judas the Galilean, see Chapter Ten.

5. According to Acts, the first martyr of the post-Jesus Christian era was Stephen. This Stephen was not one of the Twelve, but represented those who were in charge of the Greek speaking Jews in Jerusalem. It is interesting that Acts bypassed the Aramaic speaking Jews for the Greek speaking Jews in awarding this singular praise. This Stephen was "full of faith and of the Holy Spirit.... A man full of God's grace and power, [who] did great wonders and miraculous signs among the people." (Acts 6:5-8) In fact, this mention of the Holy Spirit is remarkably similar to Paul's preaching concerning the Holy Spirit. That Stephen became the first martyr has much to do with this connection.

In *Ant.* 20:200, James, the brother of Jesus, was stoned to death. This form of death is identical to how Stephen died. Was Stephen a mythical stand-in for the historical James? According to *Ant* 20:214, after the stoning of James, Saul gathered together a group of "wretches" and did violence to the people. This Saul was none other than Paul. It is interesting to note that Saul also attacked the people after the stoning of Stephen. Is this pure coincidence or is something sinister happening?

The Acts' version of Stephen is a whitewashed version of the stoning of James, without giving James credit for being a martyr. The identification of Saul after Stephen and James is a dead giveaway as to the method being employed by Acts: take a few facts and twist them into an acceptable pro-Pauline message.

6. As mentioned above, Saul persecuted the church after the deaths of Stephen and James. The accounts are as follows:

> And Saul was there, giving approval to his [Stephen's] death. On that day a great persecution broke out against the church at Jerusalem, and all except the apostles were scattered throughout Judea and Samaria. Godly men buried Stephen and mourned deeply for him. But Saul began to destroy the church. Going from house to house, he dragged off men and women and put them in prison. (Acts 8:1-3)

> [After the death of James] Costobarus also, and Saulus, did themselves get together a multitude of wicked wretches, and this because they were of the royal family; and so they obtained favor among them, because of their kindred to Agrippa: but still they used violence with the people, and they were ready to plunder those that were weaker than themselves. And from that time it principally came to pass, that our city was greatly disordered, and that all things grew worse and worse among us. (*Ant.* 20.214)

The similarities between the two passages are startling. Both accounts happened shortly after the stoning of a religious follower of Jesus, Stephen and James, respectively. It is instructive that the Acts' version said that Saul gave approval to Stephen's death. This is not explicitly stated in Josephus, but the actions of Saul after the stoning of James point in the same direction. Did Saul approve of the stoning of James, the brother of Jesus? The answer is a resounding yes! (According to the Pseudoclementine *Recognitions* 1.70-71, Paul also attacked James in the 40's. Certainly, a history of distrust and hatred was present in their strained relationship.)

In both passages quoted above, chaos broke out after Saul's persecution. In Acts, disciples were scattered throughout Judea and Samaria while Josephus said that the city was greatly disordered. The Acts' version may have used the scattering to Samaria as a way to segue to the next topic of Philip in Samaria.

In Acts, Saul had the power to imprison disciples. Most scholars believe he had some connection to those in power. Josephus plainly stated that Saul was an

Herodian, related to Agrippa. That explains why Saul could persecute and imprison with impunity. This tie to the Herodians is present in Paul's writings and in his gospel. His stand on taxation, for example, was pro-Herodian.

The New Testament's version of events had Saul persecuting Christians, or the church. Josephus only said that Saul persecuted those weaker than himself, probably referring to Jesus' movement. This police action against the poor demonstrated Paul's aversion to Jesus' gospel concerning the poor. "Blessed are you who are poor, for yours is the kingdom of God." (Luke 6:20)

The only real difference between the two accounts concerns the dating. In Acts, the persecution occurred shortly after the death of Jesus, around 35 AD. In Josephus, Saul's rampage happened after the death of James, in 62 AD. Like the earlier Theudas and Judas the Galilean passage, the Acts author had no qualms about shifting events in history to make his story appear genuine. To make Saul attack the early church as opposed to the later church was not altogether wrong. Saul did attack the early church. However, it appears as if Saul also attacked the later church as well.

In Galatians 1:13, Paul stated, "For you have heard of my previous way of life in Judaism, how intensely I persecuted the church of God and tried to destroy it." Surely, the writer of Acts knew that Saul had opposed the church before his conversion. The passage from Josephus was taken and placed in this earlier time frame to explain the wickedness of the young Saul.

That Saul persecuted the early church is not in question. The question is: did Saul attack the later church (62 AD)? There is no doubt that he did. He even met with Nero, the same madman who had massacred the Jewish Christians after the Great Fire of Rome (64 AD). Only a hater of the Jewish Christian movement would have done such a thing. (See Paul and Caesar—Chapter Twelve).

7. Anytime a Bible story has a supernatural event at its core, we should be careful in analysis. Like the present day, the laws of nature were in effect in the time of the early church; people do not disappear in the twinkling of an eye as Philip did after baptizing the eunuch (Acts 8:39). This godly act was just a literary device to transport Philip to another time and place. (If such a story were told about a current day preacher, we would all scoff. But for some reason, Christians today assume God worked differently in the past.)

The story of Philip and the eunuch is familiar to most Bible students and goes something like this. Philip was instructed by an angel of the Lord to go from Jerusalem, where he encountered a eunuch on the road. This eunuch was reading the Scriptures, which he did not fully understand. Philip seized the opportunity to explain the Scriptures concerning Jesus. When the eunuch saw water, he said, "Look, here is water. Why shouldn't I be baptized?" So Philip baptized the eunuch. Then in a flash, God miraculously whisked Philip away to another adventure.

Could this story have really happened? Probably not, but there is a parallel passage in Josephus that has all the above elements. This historical account detailed the spiritual enlightenment of King Izates. King Izates was not a Jew by birth but was brought to that religion by a man named Ananias, a Jewish merchant who taught the king's harem to follow God according to the Jewish religion. This Ananias (eunuch) gained access to King Izates and taught the King "that he might worship God without being circumcised, even though he did resolve to follow the Jewish law entirely; which worship of God was of a superior nature to circumcision." (*Ant* 20.41) Thus, we have a Pauline conversion of the King. Ananias preached Judaism without circumcision. This is comparable to Paul's teachings as noted in Galatians.

Not long after, another Jew by the name of Eleazar arrived, being sent from his leaders in Galilee.

> [Eleazar] was esteemed very skillful in the learning of his country, persuaded him to do the thing [circumcision]; for as he entered into his palace to salute him, and found him reading the law of Moses, he said to him,... "How long will thou continue uncircumcised? But, if thou hast not yet read the law about circumcision, and does not know how great impiety thou art guilty of by neglecting it, read it now." (*Ant.* 20.44, 45)

When King Izates was confronted by what Eleazar said concerning the law and circumcision, he did not hesitate to be circumcised. Thus, he became a true Jew, part of the covenant between man and God.

The parallels between Acts and Josephus are as follows: both stories involved a eunuch or one who infiltrated the king's harem; the eunuch and the King both were reading the Scriptures but did not fully understand; Philip instructed the eunuch while Eleazar performed the same task for the King; the eunuch was taught to be baptized and immediately went into the water while the King was instructed in circumcision and immediately had his surgeon perform the operation.

The New Testament story imitated the story of King Izates. This was done so that the Pauline gospel could be placed back into history, to 33-35 AD. Remember, this supposedly occurred before the conversion of Paul. In actuality, this King Izates conversion was similar to the argument detailed by Paul in Galatians.

Per Josephus, the dating of Izates' conversion was approximately 44 AD. There is no good historical reason to assume the Galatians account was later than Josephus' story.

In Galatians, certain men were sent from Galilee, from James. These messengers convinced Cephas to withdraw fellowship from Paul. In Josephus, Eleazar was also sent by those from Galilee. In both cases, the Jews carried the day, and Paul and Ananias were discredited. However, after the Jewish war with Rome, very few Jews followed Jesus. In the end, therefore, Paul and his gospel of "grace" won the day. And Acts made certain of that.

8. Saul's conversion in Acts chapter 9 was much different than Paul's own account in Galatians.

> But when God, who set me apart from birth and called me by his grace, was pleased to reveal his Son in me so that I might preach him among the Gentiles, I did not consult any man, nor did I go up to Jerusalem to see those who were apostles before I was, but I went immediately into Arabia and later returned to Damascus. (Gal. 1:15-17)

The following can be gleaned from the above passage. First, Paul was trying to impress his listeners. From the context of Galatians, much harm had been done to Paul's ministry by his unfortunate falling out with Cephas. The Jews had all abandoned him. Now he was doing his best to keep hold of the Gentiles. Paul said that the Son was revealed to him so that he could preach to the Gentiles. And from that moment on, his attack on those represented by James (the circumcision) would be ongoing. He even wished they would emasculate themselves (Gal. 5:12).

Secondly, Paul stated that he did not consult with any man. The gospel he taught came directly from the Risen Christ. This differs from Acts where Ananais (remember him from King Izates) placed his hands upon Saul, whereby Saul received the gift of the Holy Spirit.

Thirdly, Paul claimed that he went immediately into Arabia and later returned to Damascus. The Acts' version had Paul being led by the hand directly to Damascus. What happened to Arabia? The answer is clear. Acts tried to alter the facts to fabricate a new story concerning Paul. According to Acts, Paul was now a member of an ongoing concern, Christianity, and it was God who was calling the shots. It made Paul out to be a humble servant, where Paul's account was self centered and arrogant. Paul stated that his gospel was not received from any man but through the Risen Christ. Paul insisted that human intervention had <u>not</u> resulted in his gospel.

9. While in Damascus, Paul angered the Jews by his teaching about Jesus and escaped their wrath by being lowered in a basket through an opening in the wall. (Acts 9:25) Paul was the hero and the Jews played the villains!

The parallel version according to Paul was much different.

> In Damascus the governor under King Aretas had the city of the Damascenes guarded in order to arrest me. But I was lowered in a basket from a window in the wall and slipped through his hands. (2 Cor. 11:32, 33)

Paul was still making himself the hero of the story, but the adversary was not the Jews but King Aretas. King Aretas had a very good reason to capture Paul. He held all Herodians responsible for the death of John the Baptist. (*Ant.* 18.109-119) From his letters and his teachings, Paul was an Herodian. Josephus confirms this in his passages about Saul (See Paul and Caesar—Chapter Twelve).

Once again, Acts altered Paul's account to place blame for an action upon the Jews. It would not have looked good to reveal the true reason for the escape: Paul had ties with the Herodians who engineered the death of John the Baptist. This would have occurred in Paul's later "Christian" years (post 37 AD) and not at his conversion in the mid 20's.

A pattern has been established. The book of Acts took information from Josephus and from Paul and molded them into one misleading narrative. The purpose was to denigrate the Jews, including the main leaders of the Jewish Christian movement: Judas the Galilean (the historical Jesus), James, the brother of Jesus and Cephas, James' second-in-command. Acts eventually made them all subservient to Paul's gospel.

10. The story of Peter and Cornelius is an event which bridged the gap between Jew and Gentile. Without this meeting, the Jews would not have accepted Paul's message, his gospel. In fact, the meeting between Peter and Cornelius preceded the majority of Paul's travels. This means that God was working through both Peter and Paul to include Gentiles into the fold.

The Acts' story goes like this. Cornelius had a vision which prompted him to send two servants and one soldier to Joppa to bring back Peter to Caesarea. As they were approaching Joppa, Peter had a vision which said, "Do not call anything impure that God has made clean." While Peter pondered over this dream, the servants of Cornelius arrived at his house and convinced Peter to go back to Caesarea with them. When Peter arrived in Caesarea, he went to Cornelius' house, where he met Cornelius and concluded that God had included both Jews and Gentiles into the church. Then the Holy Spirit came upon the Gentiles, and they began speaking in tongues. Peter then had them baptized in the name of Jesus Christ. Thus, the Kingdom of God was opened to the Gentiles.

Before comparing this story to a parallel passage in Josephus, we must note two things. First, both Cornelius and Peter had visions which helped bring them together. It would seem as though the subject of Gentile inclusion had never occurred to Peter. In all his years conversing with Jesus, they had never discussed the Gentiles. How unlikely is that? Dreams and visions are more in line with the Pauline movement, where everything was based upon revelation from the Risen Christ. That is why Paul was branded as a liar by the Jewish Christians. To think that Peter would also fall into this category is beyond naïve.

Secondly, the baptism of the Holy Spirit and the speaking in tongues was also associated with the teachings of Paul. Remember, the true teachings of Jesus focused upon actions, living a life which never wavered from the goal of God's kingdom. This included the sharing of all property. Of course, in the story, Cornelius was accepted as worthy without any period of testing. This, indeed, was Pauline theology placed upon Peter. The <u>inclusion</u> of Cornelius by Peter helped Paul win the day at the Council of Jerusalem in Acts chapter 15.

The parallel passage by Josephus will be reproduced below.

> However, there was a certain man of the Jewish nation at Jerusalem, who appeared to be very accurate in the knowledge of the law. His name was <u>Simon</u>. This man got together an assembly, while the king was absent at <u>Caesarea</u>, and had the insolence to accuse him as not living holily, and that he might be <u>excluded</u> out of the temple, since it belonged only to native Jews. But the general of Agrippa's army informed him, that Simon had made such a speech to the people. So the <u>king sent for him</u>; and, as he was then sitting in the theatre, he bade him sit down by him, and said to him with a low and gentile voice, "What is there done in this place that is contrary to the law?" But he had nothing to say for himself, but begged his pardon. (*Ant.* 19.332-334) (emphasis mine)

In the above account, Simon preached that those who did not live holy lives should be excluded from the temple. This included the Herodians (Agrippa) and certainly all Gentiles. When Agrippa heard of this, he sent his soldiers to Jerusalem and brought Simon back to Caesarea. Simon knew that his life was in danger so he said nothing to Agrippa. This silence was similar to how Jesus responded to Pilate. This was probably a standard operating procedure: do not give up information on yourself or your compatriots.

The similarities between Josephus and Acts are as follows. In Acts, the holy man was Simon Peter while Josephus just mentioned Simon. (Peter was a nickname used by members of the movement, not by outsiders.) This Simon was brought to Caesarea by soldiers in both stories: in Acts it was for the inclusion of Gentiles, while in Josephus it was for the exclusion of Herodians and Gentiles. This change from exclusion to inclusion is incredible. In reality, the Jewish Christian movement was very exclusionary. This fact is reinforced by the book of Galatians, where Simon Peter and all the Jews turned their backs upon Paul when they understood what he was teaching. (Paul had deceived them into thinking he was teaching Moses. Paul actually taught against the law and circumcision, the very sign of the Everlasting Covenant.)

Changing Simon into a pro-Pauline figure was pure genius by the author of Acts. This revelation to Peter after the death of Jesus negated everything the apostles had learned while Jesus was still on earth. This then confirmed the gospel of Paul.

> I want you to know, brothers, that the gospel I preached is not something that man made up. I did not receive it from any man, nor was I taught it; rather, I received it by revelation from Jesus Christ. (Gal. 1:11,12)

Revelations from God were present in the construction of Paul's gospel and in the Acts' story of Peter and Cornelius. If Peter preached from these revelations, then Paul's revelations must also be accepted. In reality, Simon never followed revelations but rather followed the teachings of the earthly Jesus (Judas the Galilean), not the Risen Christ.

11. The journey of Paul to Jerusalem in Acts 11:27-30 may have occurred, but not according to the traditional timeline of Paul's career. In Paul's letter to the Galatians, a trip to Jerusalem at the time of the famine was never mentioned.

> [After converting] I [Paul] went immediately into Arabia and later returned to Damascus. Then after three years, I went up to Jerusalem to get acquainted with Peter and stayed with him fifteen days.... Fourteen years later I went up again to Jerusalem, this time with Barnabas. (Gal. 1:17-2:1)

According to traditional dating, Paul converted around 35 AD. The above 17 years would make it 52 AD. Since the famine occurred in the 40's, during the reign of Fadus (44-46 AD) and Tiberius Alexander (46-48 AD) (*Ant.* 20.101), it seems as if Paul omitted a very important trip. In fact, mentioning a famine relief mission would have been fantastic public relations, the very art where Paul excelled. Therefore, it is my opinion that the famine relief had not yet happened. Paul could not have mentioned an event which happened in the future.

But if this is true, then the whole timeline for the church must be adjusted. The chapter on Pilate made it clear that Pilate came to Judea in 18 AD. If Judas the Galilean/Jesus was crucified in 19 AD, then the conversion of Paul could have been in the early 20's. If Paul converted in 22-25 AD, then the 17 years puts the council of Jerusalem at 39-42 AD. This would be consistent with the King Izates episode. The same struggle between Paul and Peter (Galatians) was also going on with Ananias and Eleazar (44 AD) (*Ant.* 20.7-47). After the conversion of Izates, he and his mother sent money to Jerusalem to aid in the famine relief (*Ant.* 20.50).

If the council of Jerusalem occurred in 39-42 AD, then it preceded the famine. Two items must be noted. First, Paul's letters to the Romans, Corinthians and Galatians have been misdated. Instead of being from the early to mid 50's, they would have been from the early 40's (post-council but pre-famine). In Corinthians and Galatians, Paul defended his record against all others because he was attempting to win back his disciples. This was necessary, not because of their souls, but because a collection was underway.

So if Paul did go to Jerusalem with a large cache of money, he did so after the collections were complete. This would have been in the mid 40's. According to the Pseudoclementine *Recognitions*, Paul attacked James in Jerusalem in the 40's. This dating corresponds to my revised history of Paul. Also note that Paul hated James at this point and would have done just about anything. (In 62 AD, Saul was mentioned right after the stoning of James. Could Paul have been involved in this murder?)

If one disagrees with my earlier time frame concerning Paul, then it must be explained why Paul did not mention the famine relief. It must have slipped his mind, some will say. How convenient!

12. These two events happened at the same time, around 46-48 AD: in Acts chapter 12, Simon Peter and James were captured and imprisoned; in *Ant.* 20.102, the sons of Judas the Galilean, Simon and James, were captured and cru-

cified. The timing for these events is remarkable as are the identical names, James and Simon.

In reality, the sons of Judas the Galilean/Jesus underwent the same tortures as their famous father, crucifixion. (See Chapter Nine—You Will Indeed Drink From My Cup). The Acts' version was simply a way to take a familiar story and turn it into a diversionary device. The deaths of James and Simon helped remove a fictional character from the history of Acts. In the Gospels and Acts, James and John, the sons of Zebedee, were part of the main three apostles, along with Peter. But according to Paul, the three Pillars were Cephas (Peter), and the brothers of Jesus, James and John. The Gospels and Acts downplayed the actual brothers of Jesus to destroy any familial relationships. Therefore, the fictional sons of Zebedee took the place of Jesus' brothers. Again, this was just one more way to diminish the Jewish ties between Jesus and his family. Also note that Acts never mentioned James, the brother of Jesus, until chapter 15, even though we know from the writings of Paul that he and Cephas were heading the church from the very beginning.

The sons of Judas the Galilean, or rather, the sons of Jesus were omitted from the Gospels because Jesus never married in the sanitized accounts. Even though all the apostles had wives (1 Cor. 9:5), we are to believe that their leader, Jesus, was celibate. This single lifestyle was patterned after Paul and not the Jewish model as represented by Abraham, Moses, David and Solomon. The sons of Jesus were hidden in the apostle lists. James the Younger was the son of Jesus while James, son of Zebedee, was really Jesus' brother. Simon the Zealot was undoubtedly Simon the offspring of Judas the Galilean/Jesus. Writing the sons out of the Gospels was necessary for several reasons. First, Jesus had to be celibate, for the Gentile Christian God could not be sullied by sex. Second, if Jesus had fully grown children by the 40's, then he would be much older than thirty during his ministry. Third, any mention of children would tie Jesus to Judas the Galilean and the Fourth Philosophy. Like the rest of Acts, this mangling of the deaths of Simon and James distance Jesus from his true legacy.

So why was the event even recorded by Luke? It is very likely that the story was already woven into the rich tapestry of church history by the time Acts was written. Instead of denying the story, Luke simply changed a detail here and a detail there. In Chapter Nine, it was already shown that the two brothers who drank of the same cup were Simon and James, the sons of Judas/Jesus. Not only did the Gospel writers invent the cup story and insert James and John in the sons' stead, but now the crucifixions of James and Simon were replaced by a mythical imprisonment of Peter and James, the son of Zebedee. Submerged beneath the lies of the Gospels and Acts were the martyrs of the Fourth Philosophy, the sons of Judas/Jesus, James and Simon.(1)

13. The Council at Jerusalem has been fully analyzed in my earlier book, *Judas the Galilean*. In that book, I compared Acts chapter 15 to Paul's account in Galatians. All discrepancies were disclosed, and it was determined that the Council as reported in Acts never occurred, or at least not as reported.

Paul verified that a meeting did take place in Jerusalem (Gal. 2:1-10).

> Fourteen years later I went up again to Jerusalem, this time with Barnabas. I took Titus along also. I went in response to a revelation and set before them the gospel that I preach among the Gentiles. But I did this privately to those who seemed to be leaders, for fear that I was running or had run my race in vain. Yet not even Titus, who was with me, was compelled to be circumcised, even though he was a Greek. This matter arose because some false brothers had infiltrated our ranks to spy on the freedom we have in Christ Jesus and to make us slaves. We did not give in to them for a moment, so that the truth of the gospel may remain with you. As for those who seemed to be important—whatever they were makes no difference to me; God does not judge by external appearances—those men added nothing to my message. On the contrary, they saw that I had been given the task of preaching the gospel to the Gentiles, just as Peter had been given the task of preaching the gospel to the Jews.... James, Peter and John, those reputed to be pillars, gave me and Barnabas the right hand of fellowship when they recognized the grace given to me. They agreed that we should go to the Gentiles, and they to the Jews. All they asked was that we should continue to remember the poor, the very thing I was eager to do.

The following are major points of interest. Paul stated that he, Barnabas and Titus met privately with the Pillar apostles. This in itself is in conflict with the Acts' version, where everything was brought out into the open. In addition, Paul's version relied upon a revelation (from the Risen Christ) while Acts said Paul was sent by the church to ascertain the proper teachings in regards to the circumcision question.

It is interesting to note that the beginning of Acts 15 is timed differently from Galatians.

> Some men came down from Judea to Antioch and were teaching the brothers: unless you are circumcised, according to the custom taught by Moses, you cannot be saved. This brought Paul and Barnabas into sharp dispute and debate with them. So Paul and Barnabas were appointed along with some

other believers, to go up to Jerusalem to see the apostles and elders about this question. (Acts 15:1-2)

This supposed meeting in Antioch happened <u>before</u> the Council according to Acts. In fact, it was the reason for the Council. Note that Paul and Barnabas successfully disputed the circumcision group at Antioch. This whitewashed history is at complete odds with Paul's version. In his account, Paul said the confrontation at Antioch occurred <u>after</u> the Council. And it should be fully noted that Barnabas was won over by the arguments of the circumcision. Acts' history simply made the Antioch confrontation go away. In reality (according to Galatians), Paul was removed from fellowship, and all the Jews turned their backs upon him, even Barnabas. (Gal. 2:11-13) In addition, Paul's attacks on the Jewish Christians were quite savage in the letter to the Galatians. A very unhealthy hatred was simmering in Paul's heart.

As mentioned in the famine episode, this Council at Jerusalem probably came before the famine, in that Paul never acknowledged a famine-related trip to Jerusalem. The purpose of Acts was simple: make Paul the hero and bend the Pillar apostles in his direction. Placing the Council after the Antioch fight made for a harmonious church where the Jewish Apostles slowly but surely came to Paul's point of view. By knowing that the Council pre-dated the split, we can be assured that the two sides never really reconciled. And if this is true, then all of modern day Christianity follows the teachings of a man who was removed from fellowship; removed from Jesus.

So why did Paul even mention the Antioch confrontation in his letter to the Galatians? Word must have spread that Paul was rebuked by the Jerusalem leaders for his gospel, which de-emphasized the law and circumcision. Paul had to try and convince his Gentile followers that he was correct, not James and Peter. Therefore, he belittled James and Peter throughout this letter, saying such things as: those who appeared to be the leaders and that they (Peter and James) added nothing to his message. He then called Peter a hypocrite and finished the letter by once again trashing the law of Moses. This one-sided history was necessary as Paul was in the midst of a huge collection. He could collect no money if his Gentile followers believed him to be an outcast from the movement. His plea was simple: my message is from the Risen Christ, not from one of those so-called leaders. We assume that Paul was successful in his pleas to the Gentile churches, but this is not certain. If he was successful, then he gained a huge sum of money. If he was not, then his career as an evangelist to the Gentiles was over. I believe he persuaded the Gentiles for a little while, long enough to get his money. But from

Josephus, we know that Paul's career ended with his living comfortably with his Herodian friends and rubbing elbows with Nero.

One other point must be made. In Acts, the leaders of the Jewish church did not insist the Gentiles had to become full Jews. It was definitely encouraged but like other Jewish sects, Gentiles could accept the moral precepts without following the whole law. These Gentiles were "God Fearers." To be or not to be "a Jew" was the great question for the Gentiles. This is the same question that King Izates had to answer. Should I be circumcised or not? King Izates chose to become a full Jew and be circumcised. James was offering the same choice to all Gentiles. Moses should be preached to them, and they could decide if they wished to be full converts or God Fearing Gentiles. Paul, on the other hand, did not follow this agenda. He threw out the possibility of circumcision, saying it had nothing to do with his gospel. This was definitely beyond the bounds of the historical meeting. James and Cephas would have wanted every Gentile to convert. That they were willing to accept God Fearing Gentiles in their movement was misconstrued (dishonestly) by Paul, and the Antioch confrontation was proof of Paul's perverted interpretation of this meeting. For Paul always accepted personal revelations over human contact, even if he had to lie and cheat.

14. An obvious contradiction between Paul and Acts concerns Barnabas, Paul's traveling companion. Barnabas may have been more than a co-worker with Paul; he may have been a monitor. In Acts 14:12, Barnabas was called Zeus by the Lycaonians while Paul was referred to as Hermes, the chief speaker. Could Barnabas have had more of a role than just sidekick? Could he have been appointed by James and Peter to watch Paul's activities? After all, Paul had persecuted the church. Regardless, Barnabas was an important figure in Paul's mission.

In Galatians 2:13, Paul wrote that all the Jews turned their backs upon him, and that included his traveling companion, Barnabas. In fact, this argument between Paul and Peter forever separated Paul and Barnabas. Thus, the <u>reason for the separation was the law</u>. Barnabas followed Cephas (Peter) and James, whose teachings supported the law and circumcision, even for Gentiles. On the opposing side stood Paul, discredited in the eyes of all Jews. Paul was removed from the movement, but his writings in Galatians and Corinthians made it clear that he (Paul) was in the right and deserved the support of all Gentiles. After all, he was the self-proclaimed apostle to the Gentiles.

Acts 15:36-40 portrayed the breakup between Paul and Barnabas in a quite different manner. In fact, the real reason was not part of the discussion.

> Some time later Paul said to Barnabas, "Let us go back and visit the brothers in all the towns where we preached the word of the Lord and see how they are doing." <u>Barnabas wanted to take John, also called Mark, with them</u>, but Paul did not think it wise to take him, because he had deserted them in Pamphylia and had not continued with them in the work. <u>They had such a sharp disagreement that they parted company</u>. Barnabas took Mark and sailed for Cyprus, but Paul chose Silas and left, commended by the brothers to the grace of the Lord. (emphasis mine)

The breakup in Acts was due to a petty difference over traveling partners. This seems so ridiculous that we assume that even great apostles have unlimited pride. However, after comparing this to Galatians, it should be clear that Acts simply papered over the real reasons for the split. The split was due to the law and circumcision, of which Paul was not properly teaching, at least according to the Pillar apostles, Cephas, James and John. These three Pillars were also the central three in the ministry of Jesus. Barnabas had good reason to leave Paul. Who would you follow: the men who had worked next to Jesus throughout his life and who were the first to report of the resurrected Christ, or Paul, a man who had no firsthand knowledge of Jesus? The answer was obvious to Barnabas. Thus, the reason for the Acts' story is clear. Paul must always appear to be the winner of each and every disagreement and the other apostles must eventually see Paul's wisdom and grace.

15. The book of Acts had Paul travel to Jerusalem one last time, at the end of his long career. This was not recorded in any of Paul's writings because his letters all predated this trip. However, Josephus does record Saul's adventures in Jerusalem. The writings of Josephus and the book of Acts both had Paul in Jerusalem, but they differ in time. However, the parallels are obvious. According to Acts, Paul traveled to Jerusalem between 58-60 AD, two to four years <u>before the stoning of James</u>. Josephus mentioned Saul in Jerusalem between 62-66 AD, right <u>after the stoning of James</u>. (See Chapter Twelve—Paul and Caesar for a full description of these parallels.)

One important piece of information is provided by Acts even if it is an invented story. James, the brother of Jesus, was portrayed as a leader in Jerusalem. And his followers were described as "zealous for the law." (Acts 21:20) Now if the followers were zealous for the law, then the leaders were as well. Thus, the story as related by Paul in Galatians rings true: Cephas and James were zealous upholders of the law and circumcision.

The misleading part of the Acts' narrative concerns Paul's position in the movement at 58-60 AD. As discussed earlier, Paul had been removed from the Jewish Christian movement in the early to mid 40's. There was no way that James would have had anything to do with him. The purpose of the story was to keep Paul in the movement, even as a central figure.

In reality, Josephus' version had Saul escaping the Jews in 66 AD. The attack on him occurred at a palace and not at the Temple. In addition, Saul was saved by the Romans in both Josephus and in Acts. Thus, Acts is a fabrication, pure and simple. Paul never met with James, and he was not considered part of the Jewish Christian movement. Acts shaped events so that Paul could still be in control of Christian history.

16. Paul met with Agrippa in Acts and in the writings of Josephus. In Acts, the meeting occurred in 60-62 AD, and the topic was Paul's faith in Christ Jesus. Josephus had Saul meeting with Agrippa in 66 AD, and the discussion had nothing to do with spiritual matters: Saul wanted Agrippa to send an army to Jerusalem to put down the Jewish Christians (Fourth Philosophy). (See Chapter Twelve—Paul and Caesar.)

As a side note, Agrippa's sister Bernice was present at the supposed discussion. This Bernice was rumored to be having an incestuous relationship with Agrippa. John the Baptist was put to death for criticizing the unwholesome relationship between Herod the tetrarch and Herodias, his brother's wife. Unlike John, Paul made no smart remarks about the couple and so received their blessings. One last note should be made about Paul's favorable relationship with Agrippa and Bernice. This same Bernice became the mistress of Titus, the future Roman emperor who destroyed Jerusalem and tore down the Temple. Great company!

17. The meeting with Nero was totally whitewashed by Acts. Paul appealed to Rome so that he could defend himself against the Jews. This was in 60-62 AD. In Josephus, Saul traveled on his own accord in 66-67 AD to meet with Nero, to defend himself against any fault concerning the Jewish war. It should be noted that this conference with Nero happened after Nero had murdered his mother, wife and unborn child. In addition, Nero had slaughtered the Jewish Christians in 64 AD, after the Great Fire. There was good reason to hide the real history of Paul concerning this meeting with Caesar. (See Chapter Twelve—Paul and Caesar).

18. Knowing that Paul's appeal to Caesar did not really happen as reported in Acts, the final two chapters must be sheer fiction. The author of Acts described the dangerous trip from Jerusalem to Rome, where Paul's ship was grounded on the island of Malta after surviving two weeks of storms and low spirits. But it was Paul who encouraged the crew and who ultimately saved the day. Paul's inspiration for his calm demeanor came in the form of an Angel from God, who said, "Have no fear Paul; you must stand before Caesar; and lo, God has granted you all those who are sailing with you."

This trip to Rome served several purposes for the author of Acts. First, Paul had to be transported away from Jerusalem, away from the spot where James would soon be murdered. Second, in this story, the Roman centurion treated Paul compassionately, in the same manner as the Roman centurion in the time of Jesus, who said, "Surely he was the Son of God." (Matt.27:54) Third, the dangers that had been enumerated by Paul in 2 Corinthians 11:24-26 could be used once more. Paul had stated that he had been in three shipwrecks. What was one more! Fourth, through the power of God (an Angelic vision or visit), Paul saved all souls upon the ship. Certainly God was concerned for the Gentiles on board as no Jews were among the passengers.

When the weary travelers had been brought to shore, the natives showed them kindness and lit a bonfire to warm the bones from the wind and cold. Paul placed a bundle of sticks upon the fire, and a viper escaped the flames and attached to Paul's hand. The natives assumed that Paul was an evil man for the poisonous snake would take his life even after surviving a shipwreck. But to their surprise, Paul shook off the snake and suffered no ill effects. The natives, seeing that he was unharmed, praised him as a god. This little story has one major flaw. According to the Christian commentator, William Barclay, there are no poisonous snakes in Malta today, and in Paul's time, the snake that resembled a viper was quite harmless.(2) If that was the case, then there are lies within the lies. The <u>natives</u> would have known full well that there were no poisonous snakes on the island. Once again, Acts conned the readers, who knew and know nothing about Malta.

When Paul finally arrived in Rome, he was allowed to see visitors with minimum supervision. The Jews of the area came to see him, assuring him that they had heard nothing bad about him. (This seems hard to believe in that James and Cephas were busy preaching against Paul's gospel.) When Paul sensed that he had an impartial audience, he preached his gospel, arguing long and hard. Some of the Jews believed, but most did not. At the Jews stubbornness of heart, Paul said, "For this people's heart has become calloused; they hardly hear with their ears and they have closed their eyes…. Therefore, I want you to know that God's salvation has been sent to the Gentiles, and they will listen." And with that, the early history of the church had ended. In one last utterance, Paul took his gospel away from the Jews and stated that the Gentiles were worthy and would believe. This is the only true part of the story. The Jews would never believe in Paul's gospel because it destroyed the importance of their covenant with God, their Everlasting Covenant. The author of Acts was simply rephrasing Paul's arguments in Galatians and Corinthians, where the Jews were demonized since they would not follow his gospel.

19. The "we" passages begin in Acts 16:10 and are repeated throughout the rest of the book. Most scholars believe that Luke joined Paul's traveling companions here and stayed with the apostle, just as Dr. Watson accompanied Sherlock Holmes. This homey touch gives Acts a greater sense of reality, or at least, the scholars say so.

It should be noted that most of Acts has already been proved false or misleading. Therefore, the "we" passages should also be viewed skeptically. The most important information concerning the question of the "we" passages is the dating of Paul and the dating of Acts. Traditional dating has chapter 16 occurring after the council of Jerusalem, approximately 52-55 AD. Those that preach this date in regards to Paul also believe Acts was written shortly after the Jewish war, anywhere from 75-90 AD. If Luke was thirty years old in Acts 16, then he would have been 50-65 years old at the writing of Acts. If this dating is accurate then there is no problem.

I have dated Paul's removal from the Jewish Christian movement at approximately 45 AD. (See Chapter Twelve—Paul and Caesar.) If a Luke traveled with Paul, it would have been before the split. Per my earlier book, *Judas the Galilean*, the writings of Matthew and Luke were estimated at approximately 105-125 AD.(3) This dating is due to Luke's heavy dependence on the writings of Josephus. (Josephus wrote *Antiquities* in 93 AD.) If my dating is correct, then Luke would have been between 90 and 110 years old when Acts was written. This appears incredibly unlikely as few men survived to this age in that time in history, due to poor nutrition and ineffective medicines. Few men last that long today. In my opinion, the "we" passages are just one more example of Acts twisting the truth. These "eyewitness" accounts fill in the mythical story of Paul, using his own list of dangers quoted earlier in this chapter. But like the rest of Acts, we can be assured that little is really as it seems.

It should be fairly clear that the book of Acts was used as a propaganda tool by Gentile Christians to minimize the impact of Jewish Christians on the movement. At every turn, the Jews were either persecuting Paul or were made to change their positions to Paul's gospel. This is sheer nonsense. The Jewish Christian movement, led by Cephas and James, preached the law and circumcision to Jew and Gentile alike. They may have accepted uncircumcised Gentiles as half brothers, but they certainly preferred full participation. They never accepted Paul's teachings, and Paul's own letter to the Galatians confirms this. Paul was removed from the movement in the 40's, and he later returned to Jerusalem to once again persecute the church. The book of Acts had to hide this all, but there are too many pieces of evidence against its sanitized version of church history. Acts should be read as literature, but not history. The real history was destroyed by the Romans; the Jewish Christians were mostly extinguished during the Jewish war. Only the Gentiles remained. Only their fictional history was recorded in Acts.

15

JAMES, THE SADDUC

In traditional Christianity, Peter (Cephas) was Jesus' number one follower, his second-in-command. This has been a safe assumption, as the Gospels clearly show such a relationship between Jesus and Peter. The Gospels paint a picture of Twelve Apostles, who formed the core of Jesus' disciples. Of these twelve, three were closest with Jesus: Peter, James and John. And of these three, Peter was number one behind the master, Jesus.

The Twelve Apostle scheme has been argued about amongst scholars for years. Did Jesus really have twelve main disciples? This will never be known with one hundred percent certainty, but the number twelve is significant. According to the Old Testament, Israel was comprised of twelve tribes as it escaped Egypt in the time of Moses. Without a doubt, Jesus would have grasped the importance of this number in building his organization. There may have been many apostles or close disciples with heavy responsibilities, but the Twelve were symbolic. The Twelve would help usher in the Kingdom of God.

As for the Three, there were three Priests in addition to the twelve within the teachings of the Dead Sea Scrolls.(1)

> In the Council of the Community there shall be twelve men and three Priests, perfectly versed in all that is revealed of the Law, whose works shall be truth, righteousness, justice, loving-kindness and humility. They shall preserve the faith in the Land with steadfastness and meekness and <u>shall atone for sin by the practice of justice</u> and by suffering the sorrows of affliction. (emphasis mine)

Again, it is reasonable to assume that the number three had significance to Jesus. According to the Gospels, these three were Peter, James and John, all unrelated to Jesus. However, according to Paul's description of the Three, referred to as the Pillars, at least James was the brother of Jesus. (Galatians 1:18—2:10) We also know from 1 Corinthians 9:5, that Jesus had multiple brothers who were very active in the movement. It is my belief that James and John were the brothers of Jesus and that Cephas, if not a brother, was a close relative. This familial relationship between Jesus and the Three was written out of the Gospels in order to distance Jesus from his true past. The close relationship between physical brothers was too much like the Maccabees, those band of brothers who drove the Greeks out of Israel and from the Temple in the second century BC.

Per the above passage, the three Priests were to "atone for sin by the practice of justice." James, the brother of Jesus, was known as James the "Just." This designation, "Just," meant Righteous One or Just One. It should also be noted that Jewish Christianity was known by the disciples as the Way of Righteousness. (Josephus referred to this group as the Fourth Philosophy.) James the Just was a leader of the group during the lifetime of Judas/Jesus and was the number one leader after the death of Judas/Jesus.

The Gospels simply ignored the historical Three in favor of a mythical Three. James and John, the brothers of Jesus, were transformed into James and John, the sons of Zebedee. In this way, Jesus could be separated from his true family and his true disciples. The same can be said for Peter. Paul referred to this Peter as Cephas, and both names translate to Rock. According to Eisenman, there is much in the early history of the church to associate this Cephas with relations of Jesus. If this is the case, then the core of Jesus' apostles were family members and his movement was much like that of the Maccabees. It should be noted that Judas the Galilean's movement was also based upon the Maccabean movement. According to the Slavonic Josephus, a direct tie to the Maccabees is detailed.

> "Come, men of Judea, now is the time for men to behave like men, to show what reverence we have for the Law of Moses. Let not our race be shamed, let us not bring disgrace upon our Law-giver. Let us take as a model for [our] exploits Eleazar first and the seven Maccabee brothers and the mother who made men [of them]. For, when Antiochus had conquered and subjugated our land and was ruling over us, he was defeated by these 7 youths and [their] old teacher and an old woman. Let us also be worthy of them, let us not prove weaker than a woman. But even if we are to be tortured for our zeal for God, a greater wreath has been plaited for us. And if they kill us, our soul as it leaves [this] dark abode will return to [our] forefathers, where Abraham and his offspring [dwell]." (2)

The beginnings of the Fourth Philosophy had everything to do with the Maccabees. This is why the Gospels tried so hard to eliminate the brothers' influence in Jesus' ministry as well as their leadership role in the early church. To admit to the brothers was tantamount to proclaiming Jesus to be a member of the Fourth Philosophy; and not only a member, but the leader, or Judas the Galilean.

This being understood, the relationship between Jesus and Peter should be questioned. Was Peter the real leader of the church after Jesus' death? The Catholic Church believes so, and quotes this Scripture as proof.

> "But what about you?" he [Jesus] asked. "Who do you say I am?"
> Simon Peter answered, "You are the Christ, the Son of the living God."
> Jesus replied, "Blessed are you, Simon son of Jonah, for this was not revealed to you by man, but by my Father in heaven. And I tell you that you are Peter, and on this rock I will build my church, and the gates of Hades will not overcome it. I will give you the keys to the kingdom of heaven; whatever you bind on earth will be bound in heaven, and whatever you loose on earth will be loosed in heaven." (Matt. 16:15-19)

This passage certainly makes a strong case for Peter being the main man. There are, however, two points which may question the passage as a whole. First, Peter gave a description of Jesus that was certainly post resurrection, "the Son of the living God." Perhaps the disciples felt strongly about Jesus, but this description came before he was even considered Messiah by his own followers. Second, Peter's revelation did not come from man but from God. This is exactly what Paul said in Galatians about his own gospel. "I want you to know, brothers, that the gospel I preached is not something that man made up. I did not receive it from any man, nor was I taught it; rather, I received it by revelation from Jesus Christ." (Gal. 1:11,12) These revelations from "God" seem too much alike. Perhaps the Peter episode was invented as a way to show that man could not figure out God on his own, and that Peter, like Paul, had been chosen by God to lead. This invention of history will become evident as we look at the life of James, the true leader of the post-Jesus movement.

JAMES

Was James the real successor to Jesus? To determine this, we must go back to the oldest known document concerning James. That document is the letter to the Galatians, written approximately 45 AD by Paul. In that letter, Paul stated that three years after his conversion, he met privately in Jerusalem with Cephas and James, the brother of the Lord. Fourteen years later, Paul once again traveled to Jerusalem and there met with the Pillar apostles, James Cephas and John. From this, we know that James was in the top three. In an earlier letter to the Corinthians, Paul said that the resurrected Jesus appeared to Cephas, the Twelve and then to James. All this proves is that James was important, not necessarily the leader.

However, after discussing the Jerusalem Council, Paul revealed the true score in relation to James' role in the church.

> When Peter came to Antioch, I opposed him to his face, because he was in the wrong. Before <u>certain men came from James</u>, he used to eat with the Gentiles. But when they arrived, he began to draw back and separate himself from the Gentiles because he was afraid of those who belonged to the circumcision group. The other Jews joined him in his hypocrisy, so that by their hypocrisy even Barnabas was led astray. (Gal. 2:11-13) (emphasis mine)

Paul's take on this event may be very skewed. He called Peter a hypocrite and a coward because he followed the instructions of James. First of all, the instructions of James must have included information about Paul's true teachings, of which Peter was unaware. Peter and all the other Jews accepted the message from James without question, as all turned their backs upon Paul. Second, James was calling the shots from back home, in either Jerusalem or Galilee. A similar event was told by Josephus, where Eleazar was sent from Galilee in 44 AD to correct the teachings of Ananias. (*Ant.* 20:43) Eleazar was no doubt also sent by James.

In fact, James also certified who was to teach and who was not to teach. Paul bitterly complained about this certification in 2 Cor. 3:1-3:

> Are we beginning to commend ourselves again? Or do we need, like some people, letters of recommendation to you or from you? You yourselves are our letter, written on our hearts, known and read by everyone. You show that you are a letter from Christ, the result of our ministry, written not with ink but with the Spirit of the living God, not on tablets of stone but on tablets of human hearts.

Paul had a way of buttering up his audience. He told his congregation that they were his letter from Christ. Therefore, he did not need a letter from the Jerusalem Church, or from James. The Corinthians may have bought this line, but the Jerusalem apostles would not have approved.

James' role in the early church is somewhat hidden in the book of Acts, but even Acts has to admit his preeminence. In the Jerusalem Council, after hearing all the facts, it was James, not Peter, who decided the issue concerning the Gentiles.

> "It is my [James] judgment, therefore, that we should not make it difficult for the Gentiles who are turning to God." (Acts 15:19)

James was shown to be the leader in the Jerusalem Church in Acts Chapter 15, but he was not even introduced until Chapter 12. Robert Eisenman convincingly proves that James was actually written out of the earlier chapters. The election of Matthias to replace the mythical Judas Iscariot was really James replacing Jesus (Judas the Galilean). The stoning of Stephen was actually a worked over version of the stoning of James. (Note that Saul was mentioned right after Stephen in Acts and was in action shortly after the stoning of James, per *Ant.* 20.214.) In addition, the early chapters of Acts had Peter and John preaching at the Temple, but never mentioned James. In short, the book of Acts was a very successful attempt to minimize the role of James in the early church. However, by reading between the lines, James' preeminence is assured.

There are also many other early documents which point towards the leadership of James. Robert Eisenman presents a compelling case for the supremacy of James in his book, *James, the Brother of Jesus*. A few of his proofs will be reproduced below. The first comes from Eusebius, who quotes Hegesippus, an early church historian who lived from 90-180 AD.

> But James, the brother of the Lord, who, as there were many of this name, was surnamed the Just by all from the days of our Lord until now, received the Government of the Church with [from] the Apostles. (3)

Eusebius then quotes Clement of Alexandria, who lived from 150-215 AD.

> Peter, James and John after the Ascension of the Savior, did not contend for the Glory, even though they had previously been honored by the Savior, but chose James the Just as Bishop of Jerusalem. (4)

From these early Christian historians, it was known that James occupied the most important position in the early church. They do seem to imply that the office was voted upon by the Apostles as opposed to have been given by the earthly Jesus. However, the following passage from the Gospel of Thomas overtly states that Jesus directly honored James with the leadership role.

> The Disciples said to Jesus: "We know that you will depart from us. Who is it that shall be great over us [after you are gone]?"

Jesus replied to them: "In the place where you are to go [Jerusalem], go to James the Just for whose sake Heaven and Earth came into existence." (Logion 12)

From the Gospel of Thomas, Jesus directly appointed James. Regardless of whether James was directly appointed by Jesus or was voted upon by the Apostles, the point is clear: James was the undisputed leader of the early church. This is very important as James was the brother of Jesus. Like the Maccabean dynasty, brothers served after brothers. In this respect, the Jesus movement mirrored the Maccabees. And it should be noted, the Fourth Philosophy also had relatives of Judas in important positions. Judas' own two sons (Simon and James) were crucified and another son, Menahem, marched into Jerusalem as a Messiah and cleansed the Temple. His grandson, Eleazar, led the Sicarii in their last stand against Rome at Masada. The only question is: was the Sadduc, the second-in-command to Judas, also his brother?

THE SADDUC

> Yet there was one Judas, a Gaulonite, of a city whose name was Gamala, who taking with him Sadduc, a Pharisee, became zealous to draw them to a revolt, who both said that this taxation was no better than an introduction to slavery, and exhorted the nation to assert their liberty.... For Judas and Sadduc, who excited a fourth philosophic sect among us, and had a great many followers therein, filled our civil government with tumults at present, and laid the foundation of our future miseries, by this system of philosophy, which we were before unacquainted withal; concerning which I shall discourse a little, and this the rather, because the infection which spread thence among the younger sort, who were zealous for it, brought the public to destruction. (*Ant.* 18.4,9-10) (emphasis mine)

In my Judas the Galilean hypothesis, I have linked Judas and Jesus in a myriad of activities, as enumerated in Chapter Two. In addition, the ministry of John the Baptist was shown to have started in 6 AD, right before the census of Cyrenius and the nationwide introduction of Judas the Galilean. The only piece of the puzzle missing is the Sadduc, the second-in-command to Judas. Unlike my previous book, *Judas the Galilean*, where I equated the Sadduc with Cephas (Peter), I now strongly believe that the Sadduc was a title for James, the brother of Jesus.

It has already been shown that James was the leader of the church after the death of Jesus. This succession of brothers is similar to that of the Maccabees where Judas was followed by his brothers Jonathan, Simon and then John. As already noted earlier, the Fourth Philosophy, championed by Matthias and Judas, patterned their movement after the Maccabee brothers. Therefore, it is very likely that the Sadduc was a relation to Judas, most probably a brother. Josephus lists later generations who were leaders in the Fourth Philosophy. Simon and James, the sons of Judas the Galilean, were crucified between 46-48 AD. Another son, Menahem, marched on Jerusalem as Messiah in 66 AD and cleansed the Temple. And a grandson, Eleazar, led the Sicarii at Masada. In short, the sons and grandsons were in positions of power a generation or two after Judas' death. At the time of Judas, it is logical to expect his brothers to have been in leadership positions.

Before we attempt to tie James to the Sadduc, it is necessary to further examine the above passage concerning the Sadduc. The followers of Judas and Sadduc were said to be "infected" with the Fourth Philosophy. This derogatory statement by Josephus is similar to other negative comments about the early Christians. Tacitus wrote the following concerning the fire at Rome in 64 AD.

> Nero set up as the culprits and punished with the utmost refinement of cruelty a class hated for their <u>abominations</u>, who are commonly called Christians. Christus, from whom their name is derived, was executed at the hands of the procurator Pontius Pilate in the reign of Tiberius. Checked for the moment, this <u>pernicious superstition</u> again broke out, not only in Judaea, the source of the evil, but even in Rome.... (*Annals*, xv. 44) (emphasis mine)

This sentiment from Tacitus is supported by Suetonius, who wrote that the Jews who followed "Chrestus" caused disturbances in the city of Rome. This was dated around 50 AD. Thus, the Jewish Christians were reviled by a large section of the Gentile population in Rome. This revulsion of Jewish Christianity was not limited to just Judea and Rome. Pliny the Younger wrote about the Jewish Christians in Bithynia, around the year 112 AD.

> The contagion of this <u>superstition</u> has spread not only in the cities, but in the villages and rural districts as well; yet it seems capable of being checked and set right. (Plin. Epp. X (ad Traj.), xcvi) (emphasis mine)

This infection ascribed to the Fourth Philosophy was mirrored in the descriptions of the early Jewish Christians in Rome and beyond. And it should be noted that both Tacitus and Pliny commented on how the Christians would undergo torture as opposed to betraying God. This same virtue was also attached to the Fourth Philosophy.

Josephus also said that the infection had spread to the younger generation who were zealous for it. This passage may have been used by the author of Acts to describe the followers of James.

> Then they [James and the elders] said to Paul: "You see, brother, how many thousands of Jews have believed, and <u>all of them are zealous for the law.</u> They have been informed that you [Paul] teach all the Jews who live among the Gentiles to turn away from Moses, telling them not to circumcise their children or live according to our customs." (Acts 21:20,21) (emphasis mine)

In an earlier chapter, it was noted that this event never happened, as Paul was no longer in the Jewish Christian movement. Luke simply substituted this Temple attack by the Jews for the historical attack of Saul and his brother in Jerusalem, around 66 AD. However, by using material from Josephus, Luke may have tied the Sadduc to James. Both holy men had a great number of followers, zealous for the law. Luke does try to give the impression that James was not in control of the masses, but the exact opposite was true: the disciples mimicked the actions of James. James was zealous for the law!

From the letter of James, this zealous attitude was revealed in James' attack on the rich. Like the Sadduc, James defended the poor at every turn, saying that the rich had "lived on earth in luxury and self-indulgence…[and had] fattened [themselves] in the day of slaughter." (James 5:5) This class warfare was also a staple of the Fourth Philosophy as taught by Judas and Sadduc.

In tying James to Sadduc, we have listed the brother connection, the similarity between the negative comments of the historians concerning the Jewish Christians and the Fourth Philosophy, the zealous behavior of the disciples and the exaltation of the poor over the rich. We now need to examine the term Sadduc for any other clues which may tie Sadduc with James.

According to Eisenman, Sadduc or Saddok is a "term linguistically related both to the word 'Sadducee' in Greek and the 'Zaddik' in Hebrew."(5) This Zaddik terminology is associated with the idea of Righteousness.

> 'Kabbalah' means that which is received, the received tradition. It is the Jewish mystical tradition. One of its better known tenets is the idea of 'the Zaddik' or 'the Righteous One'. James is known in almost all early Christian texts as 'the Just' or 'Just One', and this eponym is, in fact, equivalent to that of the 'Zaddik' in Jewish Kabbalah. (6)

Not only does Eisenman connect the Just terminology to the Zaddik but goes on to do the same with Paul's Pillar language.(7) In Galatians, Paul stated that James, Cephas and John were reputed to be the Pillars of the church. So there is a real convergence of these various terms and their meaning of Righteous One: Sadduc, Zaddik, Just, and Pillar. In addition, Zaddik was also assigned to the "Righteous Teacher" in the Dead Sea Scrolls.(8)

In fact, Eisenman makes a strong case that James was the Righteous Teacher, noted in the Dead Sea Scrolls. His claim is based upon the internal content of the Scrolls. Critics argue that his claim ignores the external data such as carbon dating and paleography. These external considerations are not in line with a 30-60 AD James. For example, the paleography tests suggest a time frame of 5 BC–5 AD. However, the beginnings of James' career may have been 4 BC, along with the rise of Judas the Galilean. Qumran had its greatest numbers from 4 BC to 68 AD, per the coins left behind which date the various periods. James could have been the Righteous Teacher of the Dead Sea Scrolls and united with his brother, Judas (Jesus), for the nationwide revolt against Rome in 6 AD. If this was the case, then the riddle of the Sadduc is solved. James was the Sadduc and the Righteous Teacher. (It is possible that Judas/Jesus was the Righteous Teacher, but in any event, the Righteous Teacher would have supported the Fourth Philosophy just as the Holy men supported Judas Maccabee.)

There may have been a succession of Teachers of Righteousness, as the community filled its main office with the most qualified of individuals.(9) Jesus may have been the Righteous Teacher until his crucifixion. After the crucifixion, James would have succeeded Jesus in this office. James could have been the High Priest of the post-Jesus movement, just as Jesus was the High Priest in heaven (see Hebrews 4:14—5:10). In the same way, there may have been more than one Evil Priest and Liar. Paul was referred to as the Liar. Although he was not the original Liar of the Dead Sea Scrolls, he was considered the Liar by the early Jewish Christian church.

It is surprising that Josephus never mentioned the Sadduc again after ascribing the fall of Israel to him and Judas the Galilean. Judas was noted later in the *War* and *Antiquities* but always after Josephus described his sons (Simon, James and Menahem) or his grandson (Eleazar). This generational effect kept Judas within the scope of Josephus' history. Is it possible that the Sadduc had no children? Perhaps this is the reason why Josephus did not write about Sadduc's influence relating to later years. According to a fourth-century church historian, Epiphanius, James died a virgin.(10) This may be an exaggeration considering Paul claimed that the Lord's brothers had wives (1 Cor. 9:5). However, this fourth-century virgin claim might well be a distorted history of James' family reality. In all probabilities, James and his wife were childless. This condition happens to people today as it has throughout the ages. So it is possible that the Sadduc and James also shared this barren family history.

One other point must be made regarding James. According to Epiphanius, James died at the age of ninety-six in 62 AD. This would bring his birth date to 35 BC. By the time the Sadduc joined Judas the Galilean in 6 AD (maybe earlier), James would have been forty years old. This is certainly old enough to be taken as a Righteous Teacher or Holy man. His legendary status in the Jewish church may have stemmed from his extended leadership role. Judas the Galilean started his career in 4 BC and probably survived until 19 AD, an amazing twenty-two years. By comparison, John the Baptist preached from 6 AD to 36 AD or thirty years. And James' ministry covered an incredible time span, from 6 AD to 62 AD or fifty-six years.

This early dating of James is supported by the Slavonic Josephus. According to that tradition, Persian astrologers visited Herod the Great between 27-22 BC. These astrologers had been following a star for nearly two years, pushing the date of Jesus' birth to somewhere between 29-24 BC.(11) (This may be the source for Matthew's birth narrative.) This dating has a close proximity to Epiphanius' claim that James died at the age of ninety-six in 62 AD. Even if this is a slight exaggeration of ten years (note his virgin exaggeration above), James would have been born somewhere between 35-25 BC, within a year or so of Jesus (Judas). In any event, James was definitely an old man at his death.

This also calls into question the Gospel designations concerning James: the Less and the Younger. James, the brother of Jesus, was not below any individual in status, except Judas/Jesus. And as for age, the Younger could not have described the aged James, reputed to be ninety-six years old in 62 AD. I believe that James the Less and James the Younger were nicknames for James, the son of Judas the Galilean. Consider the story in the Gospels, where Mary and her children were following Jesus, circa 30 AD. If James the Just was one of these children, as is claimed, then he would have been tagging along with mom at the age of sixty-four, a real mama's boy. And Mary, the mother of Jesus, would have been at least eighty. How unlikely! This story really relates to the story of Judas/Jesus' wife and children; and James, the Younger, was one of these children

Josephus stated that the Sadduc was a integral part of the census uprising of 6 AD, but the Sadduc (or James) may have been an important part of Judas the Galilean's movement prior to 6 AD. The 6 AD milestone recounts the census of Cyrenius and Josephus' mention of the Sadduc in *Antiquities*. It is most likely that the Sadduc was in close contact with Matthias and Judas at the time of the Golden Eagle Temple Cleansing. Since the movement of Matthias and Judas was patterned after the brother revolution of the Maccabees, it follows that the Sadduc (or James) was also involved. Perhaps when Matthias and Judas were teaching in Jerusalem, James was in the Qumran area, teaching righteousness to his students. After all, earliest Christianity was known as the Way of Righteousness.

16

THE FOURTH PHILOSOPHY

This chapter will outline the Fourth Philosophy of Judas the Galilean by using timelines. These timelines have been taken from my earlier book, *Judas the Galilean*, and will highlight the main phases of the movement and events within each phase. In addition, a timeline of the life of Paul will also be included. This will compare the traditional view of Paul to our revised history.

The Fourth Philosophy had four phases:

1. The Beginnings—Its philosophy reached back to the Maccabees, while the first mention of its birth dated to 25 BC. The impetus for the movement was foreign or unholy occupation. In the very beginnings, the unwanted power to be overthrown was Herod the Great. Later, the Romans assumed control with the help of the Herodians.

2. The Kingdom of Heaven—This was a time of great joy for the disciples, when Judas the Galilean or Jesus preached his gospel while on earth. This period lasted from 4 BC to 19 AD, the date of Judas/Jesus' crucifixion. The nationwide movement began at the census of Cyrenius, in 6 AD. According to the Slavonic Josephus, John the Baptist's ministry preceded the tax revolt by Judas/Jesus.

3. The Imminent Return of Jesus—This era was ushered in by John the Baptist and the apostles of Jesus. Its intent was to prepare the Jews for Jesus' return by preaching repentance. Only when the Jews were ready would Jesus return. This period began in 19 AD and ended around 50 AD. During these thirty years, the Fourth Philosophy took a wait and see approach. They generally reacted to events rather than stirring up trouble. They were content to wait for the return of Jesus.

4. Disintegration—When the followers of Jesus were either killed or died of old age, many started to doubt the imminent return of Jesus. This activist wing of the movement still had nationalistic goals, but they would no longer wait for Jesus. Splinter groups such as the Zealots, the Sicarii and the miracle workers began to promise the people victory over Rome, with or without Jesus' help. This phase slowly developed in the 50's and 60's. With the death of James, the brother of

Jesus, in 62 AD, the splinter groups became much more powerful as James was the last link to the historical Judas/Jesus. The wait and see approach had ended and all hell broke loose. Jerusalem was eventually destroyed along with the Temple in 70 AD. In 73 AD, the Romans surrounded Masada, and the Sicarii committed its last act of rebellion, mass suicide.

While this movement evolved within the Jewish confines, Paul was preaching a different gospel to his Gentile followers. This new gospel of grace flourished at the same time the Jewish Christians became splintered and utterly destroyed. That is why the gospel of Paul now dominates all Christian thinking. Later Pauline writers placed this new gospel upon Jesus and his apostles in many subtle and not so subtle ways. Jesus supposedly held Pauline views, while the apostles, slow as they were, eventually adopted Paul's philosophy. Of course, this is not true, as the preceding chapters have proved.

THE FOUR PHILOSOPHIES
(The Beginnings)

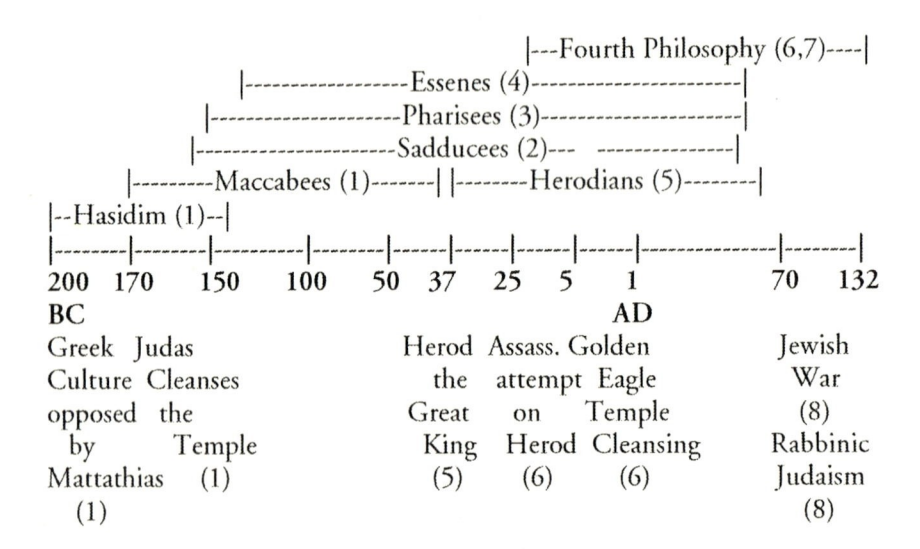

```
                                        |---Fourth Philosophy (6,7)----|
             |------------------Essenes (4)---------------------|
             |------------------Pharisees (3)--------------------|
             |------------------Sadducees (2)---  --------------|
     |---------Maccabees (1)-------| |--------Herodians (5)--------|
|--Hasidim (1)--|
|--------|----------|----------|---------|------|------|------|------|---------------|--------|
 200    170       150       100       50    37    25     5      1              70     132
 BC                                                            AD
 Greek  Judas                         Herod Assass. Golden                    Jewish
 Culture Cleanses                      the  attempt Eagle                     War
 opposed the                          Great   on   Temple                     (8)
   by    Temple                       King  Herod Cleansing                   Rabbinic
 Mattathias  (1)                       (5)   (6)    (6)                       Judaism
   (1)                                                                          (8)
```

1. From 196-142 BC, Israel was occupied in varying degrees by the Seleucid Kingdom. They were Greek in culture and ruled as absolute monarchs. The most famous of their kings was Antiochus Epiphanes, who in 167 BC established an idol in the Temple and desired all Jews to follow Greek customs. Mattathias organized a resistance movement to this Greek presence, and he and his five sons were successful in eventually driving the Greeks out of Israel. Mattathias' five

sons were named Judas, Simon, John, Jonathan and Eleazar. The most famous of these sons was Judas Maccabee, the one who cleansed the Temple and who is still celebrated by Jews today in the Jewish feast of Hanukkah. The Maccabean rule lasted until 37 BC, the year that Herod the Great assumed power.

The holy men of that time, the Hasidim (meaning godly), supported the movement led by Mattathias. "Many of those attracted to the cause came from the poorer elements of society, so that the rebellion assumed the aspect of class warfare."(1) This aspect of revolt was repeated during the days of Judas the Galilean.

2. The Sadducees were a small group of aristocratic priests who originally opposed the Maccabean rule. This group was much more comfortable with the Greek rulers before Judas Maccabee. However, in time, the Sadducees aligned themselves with the Maccabean movement, where they could better influence policy.(2) In the time of Judas/Jesus, the Sadducees sided with Rome and the Herodians, those invested with power. Needless to say, they were very much against the popular movement of Judas/Jesus and were instrumental in having him crucified.

3. The Pharisees represented the masses and were opposed to the Sadducees. They were of middle class origins, and their rise dates from the Hasidim's break with the "Hasmonaean regime because of its secular character."(3) Pharisees believed in an evolving relationship between God and man and were much more likely to be nationalistic. They were also the social critics of the time. Many of the early Jewish Christians came from the ranks of the Pharisees. Jesus criticized a number of Pharisees for being self-righteous. As critics of the ruling elites, they could only perform their jobs if they concentrated on the will of God. Jesus only lashed out at those who loved themselves more than their fellow man.

4. The Essenes may have been a reactionary group opposed to Jonathan, who ruled after Judas Maccabee, from 160-143 BC. Many Dead Sea Scroll scholars claim that the Essenes framed this Jonathan as the Wicked Priest. There may be some truth in this as Jonathan was constantly making alliances with different kings and may have been untrustworthy to a number of people. Even if this is true, I believe the purpose of the Essenes was to place Israel on the right path before God, back to the good old days of Mattathias and Judas Maccabee.

They also were an offshoot of the Hasidim and had contempt for Hellenization and worldly Sadducees. They felt that they were the true representatives of the high-priestly tradition.(4) Their method was the pursuit of righteousness. Just as the Essenes desired to go back to the ideals of Mattathias and Judas, later Essenes saw this same spark in Matthias and Judas the Galilean. That is why there seems to be so much in common between Essenes and followers of the Fourth Philosophy (Jewish Christians). According to Josephus, there were two types of Essenes: those who married and those who practiced a chaste lifestyle. Judas and his movement would have been closely associated with those who married; after all, to marry and have children was the will of God as told by Genesis.

5. The Herodians came into power in 37 BC and replaced the Maccabeans. Their first king was Herod the Great. According to Josephus, Herod introduced foreign (Greek) ways to Israel and was vehemently opposed by the more Law abiding citizens. In a sense, the whole Maccabean movement was swept aside by Herod. The Maccabees had been successful in stemming the Greek culture from overtaking Judaism; now Herod was intent on reintroducing Greek culture to the Jews. An important symbol of this Hellenization was the Golden Eagle, which was placed in the Temple. This act was reminiscent of Antiochus Epiphanes, who had placed an idol in the Temple some 150 years earlier.

6. In 25 BC, a group of ten men attempted to assassinate Herod using short swords hidden in their tunics. They were found out and executed. This may have been the first act against Herod and was followed twenty years later by the Temple Cleansing of Matthias and Judas. This Temple Cleansing marked the beginnings of the Fourth Philosophy. This movement had the same aim as the Maccabees: to overthrow the foreign invaders. The beauty of Judas' genius was his ability to take the best from the Essenes and Pharisees and fuse them together with extreme nationalism, creating a movement of fanatics. The majority of these members were slaughtered in the Jewish war.

7. The nationalism of the Fourth Philosophy survived even though the Jamesian wing had been discredited. After 70 AD, nationalists were drawn to other rabbis and this eventually led to a second Jewish war, led by Bar Kochba in 132 AD. Rome also won this second war. The remnants of the Jamesian wing of the Fourth Philosophy became known as the Ebionites or the Poor. This group was excluded from both Judaism and Gentile Christianity and was eventually lost to history.

8. After 70 AD, the Jewish nation was destroyed. The Sadducees, Pharisees and Essenes perished from view, to be replaced by a unified Rabbinic Judaism. Prior to the destruction of Jerusalem, a Pharisee named Johanan Ben Zakkai escaped the siege by being smuggled out to the Romans. He later received permission to create a synod at Jamnia which eventually replaced the Sanhedrin. This Rabbinic Judaism was pro-Roman and discouraged further attempts to find the "Messiah." In fact, to this day, the books of the Maccabees (rebels from authority) are absent from the Jewish Scriptures.

THE FOURTH PHILOSOPHY
(The Kingdom of Heaven)

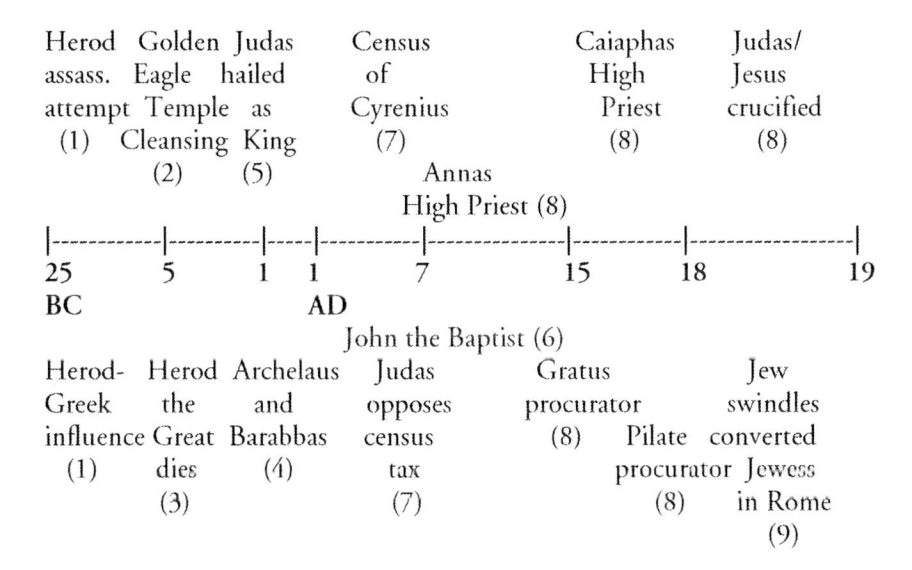

```
Herod   Golden  Judas     Census              Caiaphas    Judas/
assass. Eagle   hailed    of                  High        Jesus
attempt Temple  as        Cyrenius            Priest      crucified
  (1)   Cleansing King     (7)                 (8)         (8)
          (2)    (5)               Annas
                              High Priest (8)
|-----------|----------|-----|-----------|---------------|------------|-----------------|
25          5          1     1           7              15          18                19
BC                          AD
                              John the Baptist (6)
Herod-  Herod   Archelaus Judas               Gratus                  Jew
Greek   the     and       opposes             procurator              swindles
influence Great Barabbas  census               (8)     Pilate         converted
  (1)    dies    (4)      tax                          procurator     Jewess
          (3)             (7)                             (8)         in Rome
                                                                        (9)
```

1. Herod the Great was a successful king in that he rebuilt the Temple and accomplished other fine works. He admired the Greek culture, and he desired to pull Judea into that world. To many, this was progress towards a better life. But to a growing number, this accommodation to the Greek world was a step backwards. Ten of these fanatics attempted an assassination, using a technique later employed by the Sicarii (hiding small swords under their garments). The attempt failed, and the ten were put to death.

2. Twenty years after the failed assassination attempt, Matthias and Judas persuaded their young students to pull down the Golden Eagle from the Temple.

This cleansing of the Temple was a direct affront to Herod, who had adorned the Temple with this "gift," as an honor to Caesar. Herod had the young men arrested, along with Matthias and Judas. Matthias and a number of their young followers were burnt to death while Judas sat in prison awaiting his fate at the hands of Herod.

3. Shortly after the Temple Cleansing, Herod died (4 BC). Before his death, Herod ordered his subordinates to execute all prisoners to coincide with his own death. In that way, there would be mourning all over Israel at his death. Luckily for Judas and the other prisoners, this insane plan was never implemented.

4. Archelaus, the son of Herod, assumed power after his father's death. Sensing his weakness, the mob insisted that he lower taxes and release prisoners to them. Archelaus agreed to their wishes and released Herod's prisoners (4 BC). Some, like Judas, had been imprisoned by Herod for their part in the Golden Eagle Temple Cleansing (insurrection in the city).

5. After escaping the death penalty, Judas and his followers headed to Sepphoris in Galilee. In dire need of weapons, they bravely stormed the armory at Sepphoris and equipped themselves for the fight against Archelaus. What came against them was the power of Rome; the city of Sepphoris was destroyed. Judas learned his lesson; all fights against Rome and the Herodian hirelings must be attempted only through the power of God. Judas instituted his Kingdom of God, and was hailed as King or Messiah.

6. According to the Slavonic Josephus, a wild man began baptizing people in the Jordan during the reign of Archelaus (6 AD). This wild man was John the Baptist, and he held the same political views attributed to Judas the Galilean and the Fourth Philosophy. The introduction of John was right before Josephus described the ministry of Judas the Galilean, a rabbi unlike "the rest of those their leaders." (*War* 2.118) John's ministry may have been coordinated with the nationwide tax revolt of Judas. Judas was a "clever rabbi," and this Messianic forerunner (John) would have been consistent with his modus operandi. For example, when Jesus entered Jerusalem, he did so on a donkey. This was a Messianic statement. So it is very likely that Judas/Jesus sent out John to prepare the way. However, this occurred in 6 AD, not in 30 AD as the Gospels declare.

7. In 6-7 AD, Coponius became procurator of Judea and helped institute the census of Cyrenius. The High Priest, Joazar, helped convince the masses to accept this odious taxation. In opposition to Rome and the census tax stood Judas the Galilean. Judas had spent the previous ten years building his power base in Galilee. The census tax issue brought him nationwide attention, not only from the masses but from the Romans as well.

8. From 7-15 AD, Annas presided as High Priest, a tool of the Roman procurator. Judas the Galilean was a thorn in his flesh, opposing the tax and Rome at every turn. In 15 AD, Gratus became procurator and replaced Annas with annually appointed High Priests. His last appointment was Caiaphas, the son-in-law of Annas. In 18 AD, Pontius Pilate replaced Gratus as procurator. His first acts were especially heinous to the followers of Judas: he brought Roman standards into the city, and he used the Temple money for a building project. This disregard for the Jewish sensibilities brought Judas the Galilean to Jerusalem. His entry into Jerusalem must have caused quite a stir. The Romans had him cornered; he was arrested, brought before his old nemesis Annas and was finally crucified.

9. While the drama played out in Jerusalem, another event occurred in Rome which may have introduced the world to Saul, the eventual apostle to the Gentiles. The unnamed Jew swindled a converted Roman Jewess; he convinced her to send funds to the Temple in Jerusalem and absconded with said money. The unnamed Jew had the same modus operandi as Paul: he claimed to be a learned teacher of the Jewish people; he worked with others in the scam; his victims were naive converts to Judaism; and he promised them the grace of God if they would only help those in Jerusalem, the seat of God's holy Temple. This scam provided ammunition for Tiberius and the Senate to expel the Jews from Rome. This may explain why Paul never visited Rome again.

THE FOURTH PHILOSOPHY
(The Imminent Return of Jesus)

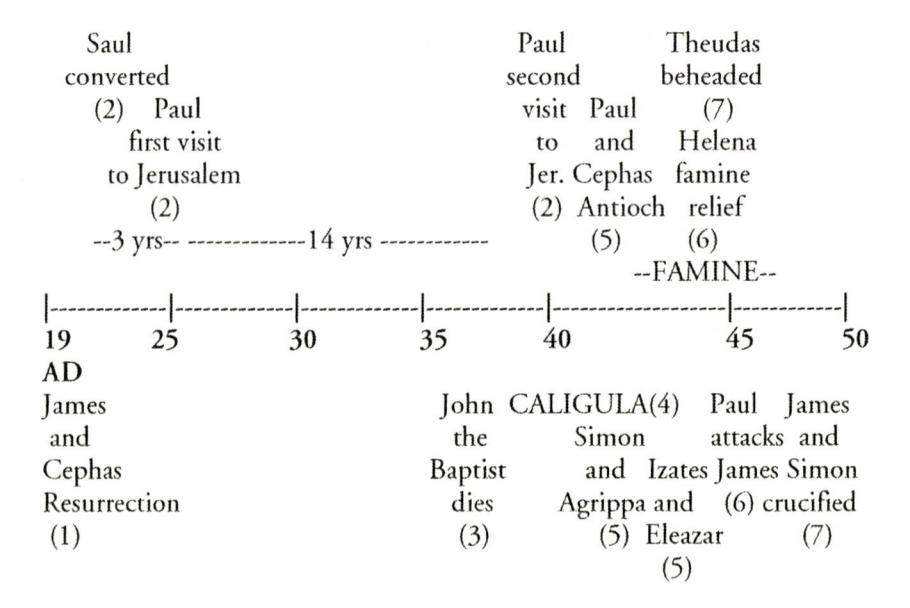

```
    Saul                          Paul        Theudas
  converted                      second       beheaded
   (2)  Paul                     visit Paul     (7)
        first visit               to   and    Helena
        to Jerusalem              Jer. Cephas famine
           (2)                    (2)  Antioch relief
   --3 yrs-- -------------14 yrs ------------  (5)    (6)
                                                --FAMINE--
|-------------|-------------|-------------|--------------------|------------|
19           25            30            35            40            45           50
AD
James                                   John  CALIGULA(4)   Paul      James
and                                     the     Simon                attacks and
Cephas                                  Baptist and   Izates James Simon
Resurrection                            dies    Agrippa and   (6) crucified
(1)                                     (3)     (5) Eleazar            (7)
                                                    (5)
```

1. The resurrection of Judas/Jesus may have been the idea of Cephas and James who first reported the event to the disciples (1 Cor. 15:3-8). Or this may have been the brainchild of Judas/Jesus as a fall back position if the fight with Rome did not succeed on the Mount of Olives. Josephus did call Judas/Jesus a "clever rabbi." Either way, the belief in the resurrection and immediate return of Jesus helped keep the movement strong and vibrant. As the years rolled along, this position was increasingly attacked by those in the movement who desired action instead of waiting.

2. A few years after the crucifixion of Judas/Jesus, Saul "converted" to the Fourth Philosophy. In Galatians, Paul stated that he went to Jerusalem three years after his conversion experience. Then fourteen years later, he returned to Jerusalem to privately discuss his work among the Gentiles with Cephas, James and John, the Pillars of the church. Paul's concept of grace and his antinomian attitude may have developed before his conversion to the Way of Righteousness. The unnamed Jew who started the uproar in Rome (19 AD) also claimed to know God's will, but had earlier been forced to leave Judea for teaching against the Law.

3. In 35-36 AD, John the Baptist was killed by the Herodians for criticizing their behavior, niece marriage (incest). John championed the cause of repentance. Only repentance and the practice of righteousness would prepare the way for the Lord. In this sense, John was preparing the way for Jesus. But this was for the return of the conquering Jesus, not the introduction of the earthly Jesus. Note that the message of repentance was the same as being preached by the Twelve <u>after</u> the crucifixion. In addition, John's description of Jesus corresponded to the Jesus portrayed in Revelation, not an earthly being.

John did introduce the earthly Jesus, but this was way back in 6 AD, per the Slavonic Josephus. John's career lasted an amazing thirty years, from 6-36 AD. In this period of time, John built quite a following. The Pseudoclementine *Recognitions* even claim that some of John's disciples considered John the Messiah, not Jesus. This sentiment is confirmed by Josephus. According to Josephus, Herod Antipas had John put to death because he was afraid of John's influence over the people. (*Ant.* 18.118)

4. Caligula was Emperor from 37-41 AD. He planned to have a statue of himself placed in the Temple, to be worshipped as a God. This would have started the Jewish war with Rome in the 40's. Luckily, Caligula was assassinated and no statue was placed in the Temple. This event caused the Fourth Philosophy to examine its policy towards outsiders. After this, the movement became even more exclusionary.

5. Three recorded events illustrate this exclusionary mentality. First, Simon preached that only native Jews should worship at the Temple. This enraged Agrippa, who sent for Simon to appear before him in Caesarea. Second, King Izates was schooled in Judaism by a "Pauline Jew" (Ananias) who preached that circumcision was not necessary. Later, a Jew named Eleazar, sent from Galilee, persuaded Izates to accept full Judaism and be circumcised. Third, the argument between Paul and Cephas was of the same order. Messengers from James told Cephas to withhold fellowship from the Pauline converts as they were not full Jews (circumcised). It is at this point that the Fourth Philosophy turned its back upon Paul. This excommunication enraged the apostle to the Gentiles, and his anger is evident in his letters to the Romans, Corinthians and Galatians.

6. According to Josephus, the great famine raged in Judea from 44-48 AD. Queen Helena and King Izates sent money and food to lessen the suffering in

Jerusalem. This same fund-collecting activity was also occurring within the communities of Paul. Paul had started raising money for famine relief before his excommunication by Cephas. The letters to the Romans, Corinthians and Galatians are defenses against the charges brought against him. In the center of this defense was his desire to continue the collection for God's elect in Jerusalem. There is no doubt that Paul brought money to Jerusalem (see Acts 11:27-30), but the money did not go to the Fourth Philosophy but rather to the Herodians (Paul's family). This mismanagement of funds may have caused the fight between Paul and James, where James was seriously injured.

7. Shortly after Paul gained revenge against James, other prominent members of the Fourth Philosophy became targets of Rome. Theudas, basing his revolt on the miracle working methodology of Judas/Jesus, led a band into the desert and was eventually seized and beheaded. This Theudas may have been the son of Judas the Galilean. He may have also been represented in the Gospels as Judas Thomas or Thaddaeus. The second significant arrest of Fourth Philosophy leaders concerned Judas' two sons, James and Simon. These two may have been known as the Sons of Thunder, per the Gospels. These two drank of the same cup as Judas/Jesus; they were crucified.

THE FOURTH PHILOSOPHY
(Disintegration)

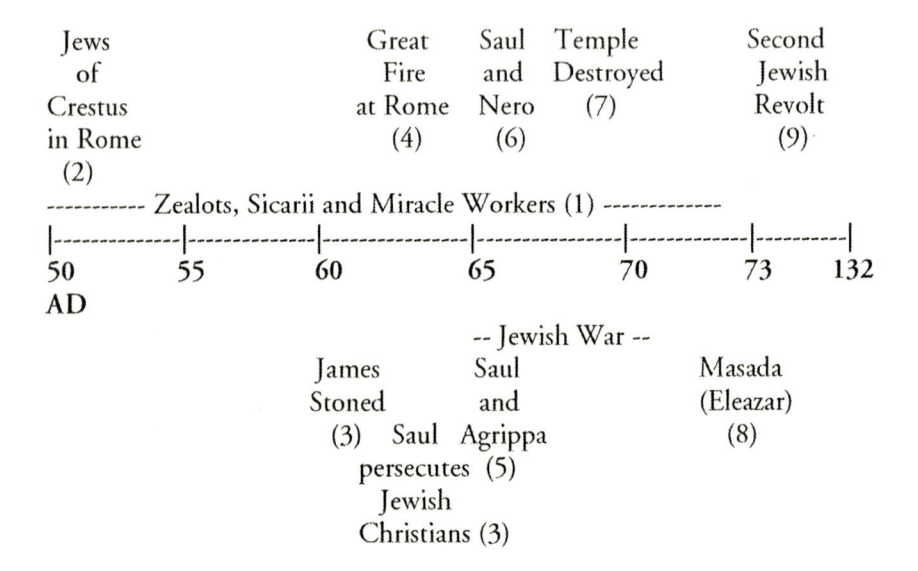

```
  Jews                Great    Saul  Temple         Second
   of                 Fire     and   Destroyed      Jewish
 Crestus            at Rome    Nero    (7)          Revolt
 in Rome              (4)      (6)                   (9)
   (2)
---------- Zealots, Sicarii and Miracle Workers (1) -------------
|-------------|--------------|----------------|----------------|--------------|----------|
50            55             60               65               70             73        132
AD
                                        -- Jewish War --
                                James      Saul              Masada
                               Stoned       and             (Eleazar)
                                (3)   Saul  Agrippa            (8)
                                    persecutes (5)
                                      Jewish
                                   Christians (3)
```

1. A clear sign of disintegration within the Fourth Philosophy was the creation of splinter groups which were now taking control of the movement. Josephus mentions these three groups (Zealots, Sicarii and Miracle Workers) as the main parties now causing trouble. The "Jamesian Wing" of the Fourth Philosophy weakened with every passing year and with each death of its original leadership.

2. Suetonius claimed that the Jews in Rome who followed Chrestus were continually causing disturbances. These disturbances may have been the result of Rome's effort to kill off the Jewish Christian leadership in Jerusalem. Note that the sons of Judas the Galilean had been crucified only a few years before.

3. In 62 AD, the last original leader of the Judas/Jesus movement was stoned to death. James, the brother of Jesus, was allegedly 96 years old at his murder. His stoning is very much like the stoning of Stephen in the book of Acts. Like the Stephen episode, Saul was nearby when James died.

4. The Great Fire of Rome occurred during the reign of Nero, in 64 AD. Jewish Christians were blamed for the fire, either because they had set it or to deflect criticism away from Nero. Regardless, Nero used these Christians as a scapegoat. His tortures included being torn apart by wild animals, crucifixions and being set ablaze to illuminate the night sky. Consistent with the Fourth Philosophy, these Christians willingly underwent these horrific tortures rather than deny God.

5. In the beginnings of the Jewish war, Saul was part of the "Peace Party" which desired reconciliation between the Jews and Rome. This desire stood against every faction of the Fourth Philosophy. In 66 AD, Saul escaped with his life from Jerusalem and went to see Agrippa. He petitioned Agrippa for an army to put down the insurgents.

6. After the war broke out, Saul willingly went to meet with Nero in order to excuse himself from the failures in Jerusalem. This was done in 66-67 AD, a few years <u>after</u> Nero had mercilessly slaughtered members of the Jewish Christian movement in Rome. This desire on Saul's part to deal with the devil shows his utter contempt for the Jewish Christian religion of Judas/Jesus, Cephas and James.

7. In 70 AD, Titus led the Roman army into Jerusalem where the Temple was destroyed. The only remaining vestige of the Temple still stands today: the Wailing Wall.

8. When all appeared lost in Jerusalem, a Sicarii band escaped to the fortress at Masada. At first, this must have seemed a prudent move. The Romans encircled the fortress and began a siege which lasted three years. In 73 AD, the Romans broke through the defenses and were about to go on a killing spree. What met the Romans was beyond bizarre. Every last man, woman and child had already been killed, a mass suicide pact. This Sicarii group was led by Eleazar, the grandson of Judas the Galilean. How fitting that the last act by the Fourth Philosophy was led by a descendant of Judas/Jesus.

9. A second failed revolt against Rome was led by Bar Kochba in 132 AD. Remnants of the Fourth Philosophy were still fighting a lost cause. Note that no elements were still clinging to the hope in Jesus' return. If Jesus could not return in 70 AD, then he would never return.

THE PROBLEM OF PAUL

Acts (1)

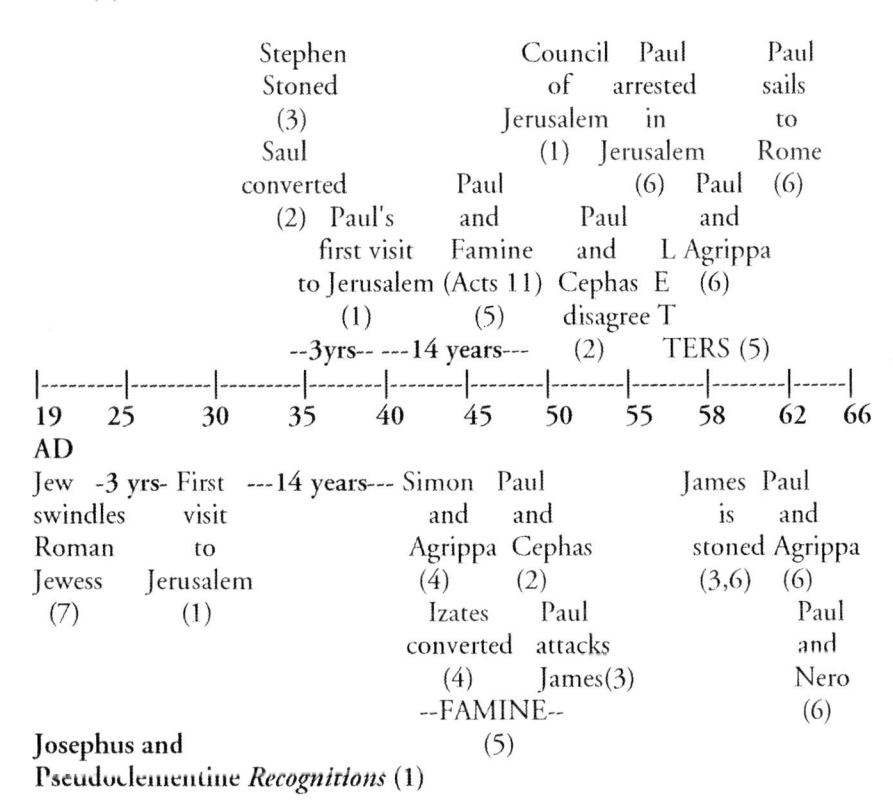

```
              Stephen              Council  Paul        Paul
              Stoned               of       arrested    sails
               (3)                 Jerusalem in         to
              Saul                  (1)     Jerusalem   Rome
              converted             Paul     (6)   Paul  (6)
               (2) Paul's           and              Paul and
                   first visit     Famine    and           L Agrippa
                   to Jerusalem (Acts 11)  Cephas  E      (6)
                    (1)              (5)    disagree T
                   --3yrs-- ---14 years---    (2)    TERS (5)
|---------|---------|---------|---------|---------|---------|---------|---------|------|
19        25        30        35        40        45        50        55        58     62        66
AD
Jew      -3 yrs-  First   ---14 years--- Simon    Paul              James  Paul
swindles          visit                  and      and                is    and
Roman             to                     Agrippa  Cephas             stoned Agrippa
Jewess            Jerusalem              (4)      (2)                (3,6)  (6)
 (7)               (1)                   Izates   Paul                      Paul
                                         converted attacks                  and
                                          (4)      James(3)                 Nero
                                           --FAMINE--                        (6)
Josephus and                                 (5)
Pseudoclementine Recognitions (1)
```

1. Both the New Testament and Josephus timelines incorporate the two meetings in Jerusalem as detailed by Paul in Galatians: 3 years after his conversion and then 14 years later. Note that Paul never mentioned a visit to Jerusalem during the famine. This is due to the fact that the letters to the Corinthians, Galatians and Romans <u>preceded</u> his eventual trip to Jerusalem for the famine relief.

2. Since the actual crucifixion of Jesus occurred 14 years earlier than traditionally thought (19 AD vs. 33 AD), the beginning story of the church would have also been 14 years earlier. Thus, it is possible that Paul persecuted the church in 19 AD and converted to the faith in 20-24 AD. If this scenario is true, then Paul would have been excommunicated by Cephas and James around 40-44 AD.

3. The book of Acts claims that Saul persecuted the early church and approved of Stephen's stoning around 35 AD. In Josephus, Saul persecuted those weaker than himself after the stoning of James, around 62-64 AD. This description of Saul was used by Luke to invent his own version of history. Also, the Pseudoclementine *Recognitions* claims that Paul attacked James in Jerusalem in the 40's. This could not have occurred based upon the chronology of Acts, but it does fit with the earlier positioning of Paul within the movement.

4. The two passages from Josephus concerning Simon and Agrippa as well as King Izates, Ananias and Eleazar, show that a struggle was underway for the hearts and minds of Jewish <u>converts</u>. In the early 40's, Jewish Christians were being sent out from Galilee to ensure converts were accepting full conversion, which included circumcision. This is the exact argument described by Paul in Galatians. This helps prove that Paul's career with the Fourth Philosophy (Jewish Christians) was nearing an end by 40-45 AD.

5. Scholars date 1 and 2 Corinthians, Galatians and Romans at 57 AD, based upon the chronology of Acts (which is absolutely useless in dating events). According to the early placement of Paul within the movement, these letters were written shortly after Paul's excommunication (early 40's). Note that Paul was collecting monies for those in Jerusalem. This effort probably related to the famine which Josephus placed between 44-48 AD. If Paul traveled to Jerusalem at the time of the famine, he may have come in contact with James, and a struggle may have ensued (Ps. *Rec.*). In any event, the monies probably went into the Herodian coffers and not to the Fourth Philosophy (Jewish Christians).

6. The story of Paul's later career in Jerusalem is dated a few years earlier in Acts than in Josephus. This earlier dating of Acts (58-62 AD) helps to distance Paul from the following: the stoning of James in 62 AD; Saul's petition for an army from Agrippa in 66 AD; and Saul's appeal to Nero in 66-67 AD, a few years <u>after</u> Nero massacred Jewish Christians in Rome. In short, Acts sent Paul to Rome before the Saul of Josephus could do his dirty deeds in Jerusalem and beyond. This being the case, the entire ending chronology of Paul's life is bogus. It is therefore possible to shift Paul's career with the Fourth Philosophy to an earlier time.

7. In full circle, the beginnings of Paul's career may be traced back to an unnamed Jew who extorted money from a wealthy Jewess in 19 AD Rome. This

unnamed Jew worked with others, professed to be knowledgeable in the Law and convinced converted Jews to send monies to Jerusalem. All this fits in nicely with Paul's methods as described by himself in Galatians, Corinthians and Romans. Paul's antinomian attitude may have actually preceded his "conversion" to Jewish Christianity. The "conversion" for Paul was the synthesis of antinomian teachings with the death and resurrection of Jesus. It was through this "grace" that Paul could soothe his own conscience.

CONCLUSION

The Fourth Philosophy of Judas the Galilean was an ever-changing movement, based upon the ideals of strict interpretation of the law and a rabid nationalism. Events from as far away as Rome had an impact upon the movement. For example, when Caligula ordered that a statue of himself be placed inside the temple, the Jews were opposed to such an action and would have started the Jewish war in 41 AD instead of 66 AD. Luckily, Caligula was assassinated and the statue idea was shelved. This saved the Jews for a full generation. The Fourth Philosophy would have expected Jesus to return during this statue crisis. If Caligula had lived, then the breakup of the movement would have occurred earlier.

The reason why so many have missed the connection between Jesus and Judas the Galilean has to do with the telescoping of history. Josephus wrote about Judas' life during the census tax (6 AD). Within a few paragraphs, Josephus told us about the dire impacts of Judas' movement. But he did not account for why a tax revolt, led by a charismatic leader, became a movement with no rules (assassinations etc.). We are left with the impression that Judas himself invented the Sicarii and the wild miracle workers that led to the downfall of Israel. Judas preached the Kingdom of Heaven, which relied upon the power of God to change people. His later movement relied upon the work of men, who more often than not lacked good judgment. But this evolution occurs in most organizations, especially ones with nationalistic tendencies.

Jesus was a title for this most formidable of rabbis. Just as Simon was nicknamed Cephas or Peter, which means rock, Judas was titled as Joshua or Jesus, one who would bring his people to the promised land. History proved that this trust was misplaced. Jesus did not return to conquer Rome. Even members of the Fourth Philosophy began to doubt his return. These later members were right in one thing: Jesus was dead, never to return.

17

WHAT WOULD JESUS DO?

The question, "What would Jesus do?," is used to answer many current day problems. The problem is: my Jesus might say and do some things very differently than your Jesus. In fact, your Jesus and my Jesus might not even be recognizable to each other. Therefore, this chapter will focus on the Jewish Messiah, Jesus, not the Jesus of Paul's visions. As has been shown earlier, the Jesus of Paul and of current day Christianity did not actually exist in history. This Jesus was devised by the Gospel writers, taken from the words of a very talented man, Paul.

Without Paul, we are left with a conservative Jewish rabbi who preached adherence to the law and love for God and fellow man. This philosophy was not much different from the Pharisees except that Jesus also preached nationalism. This mixture of religious fanaticism and political aggressiveness led to Jesus' crucifixion. How would this teacher of two thousand years ago answer our pressing questions of the day?

ABORTION

Conservatives universally believe that Jesus would have condemned abortion, and in this they are right! The book of Genesis made clear that man's purpose in life was to reproduce. To Abraham, God provided a son, and promised that his descendents would be like the stars in heaven. Jacob sired twelve sons and numerous daughters by four different women. The wives considered it a sacred duty to produce, produce and produce. In fact, there was an unhealthy competition amongst them. To say the least, in this culture, children were a blessing.

In the time of Jesus, there were four philosophies in Judea: the Sadducees, the Pharisees, the Essenes and the Fourth Philosophy of Judas the Galilean. The Sadducees were few in number, but they did not oppose marriage or children. The Pharisees followed in the footsteps of earlier Biblical heroes such as David and Solomon and gladly practiced marriage and child rearing. There were two groups of Essenes: one practiced chastity but the other married and had children. They reasoned that if they did not reproduce, their movement would die. And the Fourth Philosophy held the same beliefs as the Pharisees. Judas the Galilean had several sons as recorded by Josephus.

The followers of Jesus were members of this Fourth Philosophy. From the writings of Paul, we know that all the apostles had wives.

> Don't we have the right to take a believing wife along with us, as do the other apostles and the Lord's brothers and Cephas? (1 Cor. 9:5)

It is obvious that the Jesus movement practiced marriage, and many of the apostles were brothers or sons of Judas the Galilean/Jesus. It would be ludicrous to even think for a moment that these fanatical followers of the law would ever permit an abortion. But then, their viewpoint of freedom was much different from ours. They had the freedom to follow their religious law, while we have the freedom to live within a democratic society, where majority rules. This majority may not be right about abortion in the eyes of religion, but they have the right under our laws. Like many conservatives today, I believe the true historical Jesus would have fought abortion at every turn.

But what about Paul? Would he have opposed abortion as well? It is hard to imagine that the apostle to the Gentiles would have condoned abortion, but his modus operandi must give us pause. Paul said, "To the Jews I became like a Jew, to win the Jews....To those not under the law I became like one not having the law..., so as to win those not having the law." (1 Cor. 9:20,21) Paul had no moral compass to guide his way. He deftly moved within a group, never alienating himself, in order to impress or deceive.

What if Paul had entered an area where infanticide was regularly practiced? Would he have denounced the practice or would he have ignored it for the greater good, the preaching of his gospel? This is impossible to answer, but Paul's actions in his later career may help in determining his stance.

In 66-67 AD, Paul met with Nero to deflect the blame from his party to that of governor Florus. In 64 AD, Nero had just slaughtered a great many of the Jewish Christians, using them as scapegoats after the Great Fire. Thus, Paul was dealing with the devil, and he showed no remorse for the martyrs of Rome.

It must also be noted that Nero kicked his pregnant wife in the stomach, aborting this unwanted and certainly unloved fetus. This abortion was not enough to stop Paul from wanting Nero's blessing. Would Paul have supported abortion? If there would have been a financial or political advantage to such a stance, then Paul would have taken it. This was the greatest difference between

Jesus and Paul: Jesus had moral standards; Paul changed his standards to meet the situation.

TAXES

Everyone hates to pay taxes, but some taxes are necessary. Without taxes there would be no public schools or libraries, no roads or bridges, no military and no relief for the poor and elderly. In fact, without taxes, the world would be a chaotic mess. This being said, would Jesus have supported taxes?

The charge against Jesus at his trial was sure condemnation: refusal to pay taxes to Rome. This indeed was true. When Jesus said, "Give to Rome what is Rome's and give to God what is God's," he was telling the Romans to take their own money and leave his country. He was refusing to go along with the extortion that Rome demanded through the governors and their henchmen, the Herodians. It should be noted that Judas the Galilean began a tax revolt against Rome at the time of the census. Jesus and Judas were one in the same on this issue.

Jesus opposed paying taxes to Rome, but he did not oppose the temple tax. This tax was necessary to operate the temple. But once again, his view of taxes was not the norm: he understood progressive taxation.

> As he looked up, Jesus saw the rich putting their gifts into the temple treasury. He also saw a poor widow put in two very small copper coins. "I tell you the truth," he said, "this poor widow has put in more than all the others. All these people gave their gifts out of their wealth; but she out of her poverty put in all she had to live on." (Luke 21:1-4)

Unlike conservatives today, Jesus did look upon the taxation of the poor as an unfair burden. Today, Rush Limbaugh says the exact opposite of Jesus. He always defends the rich, saying that they pay the majority of the taxes so they should get the majority of any tax cut. If the rich get richer, then all the better. To Jesus, this was an unfair and tragic situation.

In fact, after the death of Jesus, we get an insight into his movement concerning taxation.

> All the believers were together and had everything in common. Selling their possessions and goods, they gave to anyone as he had need. (Acts 2:44,45)

Jesus and his disciples practiced voluntary communism. This was not unique to Jesus, however. The Essenes also shared everything in common as did the

Fourth Philosophy of Judas the Galilean. This voluntary communism was very attractive to the poor but not so to the rich.

> Now a man came up to Jesus and asked, "Teacher, what good thing must I do to get eternal life?"
> "Why do you ask me about what is good?" Jesus replied. "There is only One who is good. If you want to enter life, obey the commandments."
> "Which ones?" the man inquired.
> Jesus replied, "'Do not murder, do not commit adultery, do not steal, do not give false testimony, honor your father and mother,' and 'love your neighbor as yourself.'"
> "All these I have kept," the young man said. "What do I still lack?"
> Jesus answered, "If you want to be perfect, go, sell your possessions and give to the poor, and you will have treasure in heaven. Then come, follow me."
> When the young man heard this, he went away sad, because he had great wealth.
> Then Jesus said to his disciples, "I tell you the truth, it is hard for a rich man to enter the kingdom of heaven. Again I tell you, it is easier for a camel to go through the eye of a needle than for a rich man to enter the kingdom of God." (Matt. 19:16-24)

This is a very interesting passage about Jesus' core beliefs. Today, most fundamentalist churches teach that faith in Jesus is all that is necessary for salvation. But Jesus asked for much more. The young man told Jesus that he had obeyed the commandments, but still wanted to know if he had done enough. Jesus looked into the man's soul and asked one more question: will you give up your wealth for the kingdom? The man turned away and left, because he could not part with his wealth.

Jesus knew that wealth could easily come between man and God. "No one can serve two masters. Either he will hate the one and love the other, or he will be devoted to the one and despise the other. You cannot serve both God and Money." (Matt. 6:24) This concept of following only God makes it impossible to hoard wealth. Thus, the Pauline notion of faith alone is shown to be alien to Jesus' teachings. Paul's theology is favored today because everyone can follow it without radical changes to one's lifestyle. Jesus called for fundamental changes. We, like the young man, would undoubtedly walk away sad.

The second point of the passage concerns the pure communism of the Jesus movement. By asking the young man to give away all of his wealth to the poor, Jesus was insisting on a new way of life. Instead of keeping things for yourself, share all with your fellow man. As James put it:

> What good is it, my brothers, if a man claims to have faith but has no deeds? Can such a faith save him? Suppose a brother or sister is without clothes and daily food. If one of you says to him, "Go, I wish you well; keep warm and well fed," but does nothing about his physical needs, what good is it? In the same way, faith by itself, if it is not accompanied by action, is dead. (James 2:14-17)

The faith of the young man was not good enough for Jesus. Jesus wanted the young man's heart and soul. His call for his possessions was fundamental in the interpretation of the command to "love thy neighbor as thyself." You cannot love your neighbor if you allow him to starve.

To conclude, Jesus believed in progressive taxes in regards to the temple tax. He totally rejected the tax imposed by Rome. And he favored a communistic community where equality was voluntary: the kingdom of God. In today's society, Jesus would have approved the Social Security tax to help the elderly, the taxes used to help the poor and taxes to help improve the lives of us all, such as for schools and libraries. He would have opposed any taxes which funnel money away from the people into the hands of the wealthy. Two thirds of all federal tax dollars go towards the wealthy. Defense dollars support the military industrial complex. Interest on the debt flows to those who own the government bonds. And one third of Social Security benefits go to the wealthiest Americans.

The teachings of Paul regarding taxes are opposite the concepts of Jesus. Paul himself was an Herodian, that hereditary group who collected taxes for Rome. That he saw nothing wrong in unjust taxes should not surprise us.

> Everyone must submit himself to the governing authorities, for there is no authority except that which God has established. The authorities that exist have been established by God. Consequently, he who rebels against the authority is rebelling against what God has instituted, and those who do so will bring judgment on themselves.... This is also why you pay taxes, for the authorities are God's servants, who give their full time to governing. Give everyone what you owe him; if you owe taxes, pay taxes; if revenue, then revenue; if respect, then respect, if honor, then honor. (Romans 13:1-7)

The letter to the Romans was written anywhere from 40-55 AD. This time period included the reign of Caligula. According to Paul's gospel, God established the reign of Caligula, and it was only proper that you would willingly pay your taxes and show respect for the man. How perverse! Jesus died on the cross protesting the unjust reign of Rome. Paul not only condoned the ruling authorities, he had the gall to say that God wanted you to obey them. Jesus said, "You cannot obey two masters." Paul said that both masters were ordained by God.

Taxes in the ancient world were often unjust and severe. The idea of progressive taxation was not in the cards. Those with power exercised their power and extracted money from the weak. Paul not only condoned this method of taxation, he placed the seal of God upon it. Paul would have been a good Republican.

It should be noted that Paul's view of the governing authorities never wavered. In 66-67 AD, Paul met with Nero, the man who had murdered his mother, his wife and had slaughtered the Jewish Christians only two years earlier. In Paul's theology, Nero had been placed in a leadership role by God and deserved respect and honor. And Jesus wept.

THE RAPTURE

The rapture has been a best seller for some very influential fundamentalists over the past few years. The gist of the rapture is this: at the last days, God's elect will be removed from the earth, leaving the unbelievers to deal with the horrible devastation that Satan will wreak upon them. In cartoon-like style, Christians will be whisked from speeding cars, from dinner tables, from every imaginable situation, leaving the poor unbelievers with the task of explaining their disappearance and ultimately dealing with the devil himself.

To the fundamentalists, this rapture is very important. Believing in this helps them cope with everyday affairs. Why does it matter how you act towards others as long as you will eventually be carted up to heaven? This mentality also disengages the "Christian" from thinking about the environment. Why bother about saving planet earth: God is going to destroy everything after the rapture anyway. In fact, all of fundamentalism is intent on removing personal responsibility. The doctrine of grace excuses one from the problem of sin while this rapture gives hope for the future.

Where did the concept of the rapture originate? It is a fairly recent belief. Surely, Jesus and his disciples did not believe in such an ending to the world. And even Paul would have been amazed at the creativity of the modern preachers. The passage used to support this new doctrine comes from Matthew 24:36-41.

> "No one knows about that day or hour, not even the angels in heaven, nor the Son, but only the Father. As it was in the days of Noah, so it will be at the coming of the Son of Man. For in the days before the flood, people were eating and drinking, marrying and giving in marriage, up to the day Noah entered the ark; and they knew nothing about what would happen until the flood came and took them all away. That is how it will be at the coming of the

Son of Man. <u>Two men will be in the field; one will be taken and the other left. Two women will be grinding with a hand mill; one will be taken and the other left.</u>" (emphasis mine)

First, it should be noted that Jesus himself claimed that he did not know when the final hour would come. Unlike the present day preacher, he left that messy deed to God. We do know that the world will be corrupt at the end. Therefore, he must have meant today or modern society. Yet, the Romans practiced depravity which must marvel even the most licentious modern man. So even though today's society may be corrupt, it is no more corrupt than many ancient cultures.

Believers in the rapture also point to the many natural calamities which are occurring at an alarming rate: earthquakes, hurricanes and floods. Yet these acts of nature have been regularly making an appearance throughout recorded history. The eruption of Vesuvius in 69 AD was as cataclysmic as anything happening today. Yet, many believe that the end is upon us.

The above passage uses Noah as an example of how unexpected the end will be. People will be marrying and given in marriage. This is another way of saying that people were assured of the future. Why marry if the world is coming to an end?

These same people were living their lives as usual when the flood came and took them away. Those that were taken away were the worldly, the enemies of God. This is where the error of the rapture comes to light. The idea that God will remove the Christians comes from the following segment. "Two men will be in the field; one will be taken and the other left." In context of the overall passage, those that were taken were drowned or destroyed. Those left upon the earth were blessed. The fundamentalists have turned this passage upside down. To them, those that will be taken are the raptured Christians.

In addition, this concept of removing the Christians before the final horrible days is not consistent with history. Jesus was crucified and most of his disciples were tortured and killed. Jewish Christians in Rome were torn apart by dogs, crucified and burnt at the stake. When in the history of Christianity have the Christians been allowed to remove themselves from the testing process?

It is obvious why the rapture is so central to fundamentalist thinking. It is an easy way out. Like the concept of grace, the rapture removes the Christian from the end struggles. This is comforting to a group who believe that only faith is necessary for eternal life. They do not listen to Jesus or to James who said, "Show me your faith without deeds, and I will show you my faith by what I do. You believe that there is one God. Good! Even the demons believe that—and shudder." To believe in Jesus or the rapture is meaningless if there is not a good solid life behind the belief.

EVOLUTION OR CREATIONISM?

Unless we can prove or disprove the existence of God, the debate between the evolutionists and the Creationists is futile. If one believes in God, then God is capable of anything. He created the universe and all things in that universe. Is it possible that God also equipped living things with the ability to adapt and evolve over time? If God is all powerful, then he could have created evolution!

If on the other hand, you do not believe in God, then all evolutionary processes prove that we are on our own. The dinosaurs prove that the world is older than 4004 BC, and thus destroying the Creationist myth. This may be true, but it only exposes the simplistic views of those holding the Creationist theory. These Creationists ignore science, afraid that science will destroy their God. If God created the universe, then will not science bring us closer to that God, even if that is not the intention of science?

What would Jesus believe about such a controversy? He would quote Scripture: "Love the Lord thy God with all your heart and with all your soul and with all your mind." To believe in scientific facts is not a sin against God, it is an acknowledgement of Him. Jesus surely would have been a Creationist in that he believed in God and that God created all things. I doubt whether he would have stuck his head in the sand concerning scientific findings. These findings would have been viewed by Jesus as the proof for God.

COMMUNIST OR CAPITALIST?

Would Jesus have supported either economic theory? It is true that Jesus preached a primitive form of communism, as the members of his community shared all their possessions. (Acts 2:44,45) But does that mean that Jesus would have been a card carrying member of the Communist Party? The answer is a resounding no! Jesus' form of pure communism was voluntary. Each member made a lifelong commitment to God and to his fellow man: to share and to help each other. In Jesus' preaching, he made it clear that his disciples must give up everything to follow him. In the story of the rich young ruler, Jesus said to the young man, "If you want to be perfect, go, sell your possessions and give to the poor, and you will have treasure in heaven. Then come, follow me." The young man was driven away for he did not wish to share his possessions. But the point is made clear: fellowship with Jesus is voluntary. Thus, Jesus would oppose any system which takes away the decision-making process.

But what about capitalism? Would Jesus approve of the commercial Christmas season? I have no doubt that Jesus would be the greatest critic of our present system of capitalism. The main tenet of capitalism is the accumulation of wealth in the hands of the few. This is why Jesus was put to death in the days of Rome and Herod. He would have certainly criticized the uneven distribution of wealth today, and would be branded as a left-wing crazy by supporters of the status quo. But this would not bother Jesus. He reveled in the fight against greed and corruption.

Today, the fundamentalist preachers tell their flocks to give in abundance, for God will reward them ten times over. The more you give, the more you will receive. What a con game! Most of these preachers live a very comfortable lifestyle. Did Jesus give of himself? Did Jesus receive worldly rewards? Did Jesus live in a comfortable house with a swimming pool? No! Jesus gave more of himself, and his reward was crucifixion. The same can be said of his early followers. Many of them also gave their very lives in God's service. To be sure, Jesus would not have approved of the capitalists, the consumerism of today or the money grubbing preachers, who peddle the message of the Herodians, the message of Paul.

Jesus' system of government was the Kingdom of God. This is a system resembling a theocracy, except participation is voluntary: thus, the problem. There is no way for such a system to be implemented on a large scale. Those not agreeing with the system would cause endless headaches. In addition, any form of theocracy can be dangerous, as leaders can become corrupt. The combination of God and government should be stopped as Jefferson clearly believed. So in the end, the best that Jesus could expect would be a democracy (voluntary) where everyone worked for a fair wage (pure socialism) with a decided turn to the left in regards to tax policy (progressive taxes). That would be as close to the Kingdom of God as possible today.

DEMOCRAT OR REPUBLICAN?

A great many fundamentalists believe that Jesus would have wholeheartedly supported the Republican Party. Their whole argument revolves around the abortion issue and gay rights. It is true that Jesus would have opposed abortion and gay rights, but is there any other area where Jesus and Republicans would agree upon? Certainly, the Republican stance on taxation would have been repugnant to Jesus. Jesus was a champion of the poor and believed in progressive taxation, if taxation was even necessary. The Republican mantra of a strong defense would have also rankled Jesus' sensibilities. Jesus would have defended his country by reaching out to others through giving. He would have tried to win the hearts and souls of others by kindness, not by the power of the military. The Republican idea that all individuals can compete evenly in society would have also been opposed by Jesus. Remember, Jesus opposed the Herodians and Romans, the wealthiest of his day.

So if Jesus would have butted heads with the Republicans, then he would have supported the Democrats. This, too, is wrong. Obviously, he would have vigorously opposed abortion and gay rights, but he also would have serious problems with entitlements as they stand today. Jesus believed in equality, but the means to the end was quite different. His community was purely communistic, in that all shared their belongings with others. He did not condone supporting a lifestyle of dependency! His communism demanded work and sacrifice from all. There were no free handouts. No doubt that Jesus would have been more comfortable with the Democrats in terms of helping the poor, but his agenda would have been much more radical.

Jesus would have combined some of the views of Republicans and Democrats and would have merged these with his own beliefs. His strict moral code would have been attractive to the Republican fundamentalists, while his pure communistic society would have steered a few ultra liberals in his direction. However, Jesus would not have been a proponent of democracy, the will of the people. Like the extremist Muslims, he would have advocated a theocracy, the rule of God. His Kingdom of God would have been a theocracy, where all believers followed God's word. Of course, this form of government often leads to repression and is open to large scale abuses by unscrupulous leaders. In short, Jesus would not have fit in with the majority of Americans. He would have been a fringe player, one being labeled as a cultist.

CONCLUSION

What would Jesus do? What would Jesus say? This all depends on which Jesus you follow. Throughout this book, I have challenged traditional Christian thinking. The historical Jesus was a pious Jewish rabbi who stayed within the boundaries of Judaism. The mythical Jesus was built upon the revelations of Paul, a man who was so unlike Jesus. This Paul preached against the Jewish Law and rubbed elbows with Agrippa and Nero. So how you view Jesus depends on how you interpret the New Testament.

Nothing could be clearer than the case of taxes. Jesus was crucified for his stance against Roman taxation. Paul, on the other hand, encouraged his followers to pay Caesar, as a duty to God. Which is right? What would Jesus do? Is it any wonder why there is so much confusion.

Just remember this: Jesus was a man of his times and he interpreted life by his cultural standards. If you really want to know what Jesus would do, you must also accept his philosophy of life. If you are rich, Jesus would tell you to sell everything and give to the poor. If you are proud of your faith, Jesus would tell you to put that faith into action. So the real question is this: Do you really want to know what Jesus would do?

18

JESUS IS STILL DEAD

Theologians and historians have studied the life and death of Jesus Christ for nearly two thousand years. In the past two hundred years there has been an effort to find the historical Jesus. However, this effort has been compromised by pre-existing ideas about Jesus. Thus, the search for the historical Jesus has been limited to a lifespan of thirty-three years, beginning in 4 BC and ending around 30 AD. Even though there is no external evidence for Jesus in these later years, historians have looked nowhere else.

    I have attempted to prove that Judas the Galilean and Jesus were one in the same. In Chapter Two, I listed forty similarities between the two, and the odds against them being separate individuals were staggering. Then my case was strengthened by examining critical parts of the Jesus story. Chapter Three detailed the career of Pontius Pilate and proved his stay in Israel began in 18 AD, not 26 AD as commonly believed. This proves that the death of Judas/Jesus was earlier than tradition has it. The birth narratives of Matthew and Luke were dissected in Chapter Four. It was discovered that the discrepancies between the two accounts make it impossible to believe that Jesus was born in either 4 BC or 6 AD. Instead, Jesus would have been born a generation earlier, a year before his brother James, anywhere from 36-25 BC. The forerunner of Jesus, John the Baptist, was examined in Chapter Five. According to the Slavonic Josephus, John began his ministry in 6 AD, right before Judas the Galilean's nationwide tax revolt. John even had the same philosophy as Judas, a nationalism with God as the Jews' only Master.

    The number of Temple cleansings was questioned in Chapter Six. It was reasoned that both Judas the Galilean and Jesus would have cleansed the Temple in the beginning and in the end of their respective careers. Chapter Seven proved that Barabbas (son of the Father) did exist, but this Barabbas was released to the Jewish mob in 4 BC, not 30 AD. And this Barabbas was none other than Judas the Galilean. The greatest villain in history occupied the pages of Chapter Eight.

There it was proved that Judas Iscariot, one of the Twelve, never betrayed Jesus. In fact, the whole story of Judas was merely a way to place blame upon the Jews, and the name Judas in particular. Chapter Nine answered the question of who drank of the same cup as Jesus. Simon and James, the sons of Judas the Galilean, were crucified like Jesus, all three drinking from the same cup. The traditional story of James and John, the sons of Zebedee, was proved false. And in Chapter Ten, I set straight the confusion about Theudas and Judas the Galilean. The author of Acts distorted history to produce a counterfeit church, one where Paul and his ideas held sway.

Not only did I prove that Judas the Galilean and Jesus were the same, but the life of Paul was exposed in all its shame. Chapter Eleven details the two gospels which were circulating in the early church. The Jewish Christians followed the teachings of Jesus, Cephas and James while the Gentile Christians believed in the visions of Paul. Paul was removed from the movement for his refusal to follow the Everlasting Covenant and only a quirk of history saved his message. The Jewish Christians were massacred in the Jewish war with Rome. Only the counterfeit gospel of Paul remained. This examination of Paul's life continued in Chapter Twelve, where Paul's ties to Herod and Rome become apparent. This champion of the Gentiles met with Nero two years after this monster slaughtered the Jewish Christians after the Great Fire of Rome (64 AD). In fact, I proposed that Saul/Paul persecuted the church three times in his career, once before his conversion (20-24 AD) and twice after his expulsion from the movement, in 45-47 AD and in 62 AD. This hypothesis was tested in Chapter Thirteen, and the timelines prove that Paul was a sinister character.

The book of Acts is categorically shown to be a propaganda tool in Chapter Fourteen, where nineteen sections of the story are shown to be patently false. Together with the forty similarities between Judas the Galilean and Jesus, the case for serious reevaluation is beyond question. The last piece of the puzzle was put in place in Chapter Fifteen. James, the brother of Jesus, was shown to be the Sadduc, the second-in-command to Judas the Galilean. Chapter Sixteen pulls all this information together. The movement of Judas the Galilean/Jesus, the Fourth Philosophy, is shown to have had several phases over the seventy years in which it operated in Israel. This explains how the Kingdom of God turned into assassinations and war.

My hypothesis about Judas the Galilean moves the whole search for Jesus back a generation. In this time frame, all the elements of Jesus' life make sense. The Golden Eagle Temple Cleansing of 4 BC was a model for the Gospel story, and the Barabbas story only makes historical sense after the death of Herod the Great in 4 BC, not under Pilate in 30 AD. A whole list of parallels between Judas and Jesus have been enumerated. Each similarity moves Jesus closer to the historical Judas the Galilean.

In addition, the history of the church after Jesus has been shown to be full of contradictions and falsehoods. The book of Acts had one purpose: to elevate Paul at the expense of Jesus' true followers. And if this is true, then this effort to expose the truth has far reaching consequences. No longer will false preachers and messages go unquestioned.

The Christianity of today is Pauline. But this is no different than the preceding two thousand years. Faith and obedience to church leaders are essential for salvation. Although faith alone is a very attractive doctrine, in that no human effort is needed, it does little to improve its followers or society at large. In fact, this emphasis on faith alone can often lead to more sin and unholy living in the name of God.

I challenge ministers, clergy, historians and the common lay members to read and closely examine my arguments. If they can find error, then I will withdraw my hypothesis. However, if they cannot, then it might be time for them to change their thinking. But this may be impossible. Religion is big business, and fundamentalism is blind to opposing arguments. Just remember this: Jesus said to use your heart, mind and soul. To question is not a sin!

◆ ◆ ◆

In Chapter One, it was explained why the Jews turned their backs upon Jesus. With each passing day, month and year, the promise of his powerful return became more and more questionable. If Jesus could not return during the Jewish war, then he would never return. How can we blame the Jews for abandoning this false hope?

Today, Christians throughout the world have a similar hope in the return of Jesus. While the Jews of the first century hoped for a Messiah who would rid their land of Roman occupation, today's Christians long for the return of a man-god. This current conception of Jesus has nothing to do with the historical Jesus but has much in common with pagan hopes throughout the ages.

Will Jesus come back to earth as a conquering Messiah? Will he bring his followers to heaven? If history is any guide, then you should not sell all of your possessions. Jesus did not return then, and he will not return now. Jesus was a man, a great man, but he was not a god. The true Jesus was Judas the Galilean, and his death was no different than the billions who have died since—there have been no <u>provable</u> resurrections!

So, could Judas/Jesus have been resurrected? His first disciples <u>believed</u> he was. Millions throughout history have also <u>believed</u>. Who am I to say that he was not resurrected. That decision is up to you. By knowing that Jesus was really Judas the Galilean, you can still believe as the first disciples believed. In fact, this whole exercise might strengthen your faith. Maybe Jesus will truly be a inspiration in the <u>way he lived</u>. Judas/Jesus was a human being just like you. See the great things he did. See the great things that you might do.

◆   ◆   ◆

One last warning must be given. In today's war on terror, much has been made of the leaders of the terrorist movements. If only we could catch Osama Bin Laden! But what would happen if we did catch him? Would that make us any safer?

Judas the Galilean/Jesus' movement began as a call to the poor. He referred to this phase as the "Kingdom of God." Everyone would share, and the world would be a much better place. But not everyone wanted this "Kingdom of God." The Romans and their hirelings, the Herodians and Chief Priests, liked the power structure as it was. No change was desired. That is why they crucified Jesus. If they just caught the leader, then everything would go back to normal.

Josephus wrote that the movement of Judas grew to an incredible degree after his death. This movement was not led by Jesus alone but was now being fractured, with different tactics used by the splinter groups. Jesus preached the "Kingdom of God," relying on the power of God to change the existing order. Later followers were not so patient. By the 50's and 60's, the Sicarii (assassins) drove the Jews to war with Rome, a war the Jews could not win. By killing the leader of the Fourth Philosophy (Jewish Christianity), the Romans unwittingly created an environment where the rebels could become more and more extreme. In an early manuscript, Josephus said that the murder of James, the brother of Jesus, was the last straw. With James out of the way, there was no one who could tame the hatred of the movement. With the last remnant of the original Jesus movement gone, the stage was set for war.

We should not be comforted if we bring down a few leaders. As long as the ideology exists, there will be men to replace the fallen heroes. And if we make these leaders into martyrs, then the war has just begun. Let us learn a little bit from Rome's attitude towards the bandits. If we do not diffuse their hatred towards us, then things will only get worse, regardless of who leads the insurgency.

◆   ◆   ◆

To help organize all the information presented in this book, I have placed two timelines at the end of this chapter. The first will detail the traditional view of Jesus and reasons why this is illogical. The second timeline will present my Judas the Galilean hypothesis. By comparing these, it may be easier to grasp the gross manipulations of history. It may be easier to see the truth.

TRADITIONAL TIMELINE

35 BC	James, the brother of Jesus is born. (Died at 96 in 62 AD)
9–6 BC	Jesus, the firstborn of Mary and Joseph is born in Bethlehem.
4 BC	Herod the Great dies.
6 AD	Jesus is born at the Census of Cyrenius.
6 AD	Judas the Galilean leads a tax revolt.
7–15 AD	Annas becomes High Priest.
18–37 AD	Caiaphas becomes High Priest.
26–37 AD	Pilate becomes governor of Judea.
28–29 AD	John the Baptist begins his ministry.
30 AD	Jesus begins his ministry at the age of thirty.
30–33 AD	John the Baptist is beheaded.
30–33 AD	Jesus is crucified under Pilate.
35 AD	Stephen is stoned, becoming the first church martyr.
35 AD	Paul converts to Christianity on the road to Damascus.
38 AD	Paul meets with James and Cephas in Jerusalem.
46–48 AD	James is beheaded and Peter escapes prison.
46–48 AD	Paul goes to Jerusalem for famine relief.
52 AD	The Council of Jerusalem decides the circumcision issue.

52–57 AD	Paul writes to the Romans, Corinthians and Galatians.
58 AD	Paul goes to Jerusalem and escapes the Jews at the Temple.
58–60 AD	Paul is the prisoner of Felix (52-60 AD).
60–62 AD	Paul is the prisoner of Festus and meets with Agrippa.
60–62 AD	Paul sails to Rome to meet Caesar.
62 AD	James, the brother of Jesus, is stoned to death (age 96).
64 AD	Nero persecutes the Christians after the Great Fire of Rome.
67 AD?	Paul and Peter are martyred in Rome.

1. The traditional birth scenarios of Jesus do not work with other information provided by the New Testament. If Jesus was thirty-three years old at his death, then he could not have been crucified between 30-33 AD as traditionally claimed. Matthew's birth date would yield a crucifixion date of 23-26 AD and Luke's birth narrative would also be outside the traditional boundaries, being 39-40 AD.

In addition, the most commonly accepted birth date supplied by Matthew would place the ministry and death of Jesus several years before the arrival of John the Baptist, given as 28-29 AD by Luke. And another problem has Jesus, the firstborn of Mary, being born approximately thirty years after his younger brother, James. The name James means "one who follows after." Tradition claims that James was 96 years old at his death in 62 AD. Since these birth narratives do not make historical sense, then why do scholars and church historians trust them as the truth. Should they not look elsewhere for the birth of Jesus? A good hint would be 36-35 BC, a year or so before his younger brother, James.

2. John the Baptist supposedly introduced the earthly Jesus to the world. This he did, but the year was 6 AD. According to the Slavonic Josephus, John had the same philosophy as Judas the Galilean, and promised a Messiah would rescue the Jews. This promise was made right before Judas the Galilean led his nationwide tax revolt against Rome. Unfortunately, Judas the Galilean was arrested and crucified in 19 AD. However, John was still alive and preaching.

John's later message of repentance coincided with the apostles' message of repentance _after_ the crucifixion of Jesus. It is probable that John was preparing the way for Jesus to return. This is consistent with the dating problem noted above In addition, John's description of Jesus is similar to the resurrected Messiah in Revelation, not to an earthly being.

If John was really preparing the way for the earthly Jesus as claimed by the Gospels, then why did he not join the Jesus movement? It would seem that Jesus would have taken away every one of John's disciples. But according to Paul and Acts, John had disciples into the 40's, long after the death of Jesus. The only explanation for this is that John's ministry lasted many years beyond that of Jesus. It is reasonable to assume that if John introduced Jesus in 6 AD, then he was a follower of Judas/Jesus. But since John lived seventeen years beyond the life of Judas/Jesus, he would have developed his own army of followers. This is the only explanation that makes sense concerning John.

3. If Jesus was crucified in 33 AD, then it becomes unlikely that Annas would have interrogated him as reported in the Gospel of John. Annas was High Priest from 7-15 AD. If he were 55 years old in 7 AD, then his age in 33 AD would have been 81. It is possible that he still had an active role in governing, but doubtful. It is more probable that Jesus was crucified much earlier than the traditional dating.

4. The whole history of Paul does not make sense when using Josephus and Paul's own words in Galatians. The traditional story has Paul converting in 35 AD, traveling to Jerusalem three years later to meet Cephas and James (38 AD), and once again making the trip fourteen years later at the Council of Jerusalem (52 AD). Paul then returned a last time to Jerusalem around 58 AD before being imprisoned. Paul appealed his sentence and was supposedly sent to Rome in 62 AD. Tradition has Paul being martyred in 67 AD with Peter in Rome. How convenient that these old enemies should be united at death. Surely, this tradition is more wishful thinking than actual history.

According to Josephus, Paul was in Jerusalem from 62-66 AD and later traveled to meet Nero in Greece. This dating destroys the whole Acts' mythology concerning Paul's later years. In addition, Paul's confrontation with Cephas and James (Galatians) fits in with Josephus' story of King Izates, dated at 44 AD, a good ten years before the traditional dating. The 44 AD exclusion of Paul from the movement also dovetails with the Pseudoclementine *Recognitions* which claim that Paul attacked James in the 40's. This only can be true if Josephus' account is recognized.

JUDAS THE GALILEAN HYPOTHESIS

36–25 BC	Judas is born in Gamala, near Galilee.
35–24 BC	James, the brother of Judas/Jesus, is born.
25 BC	An assassination attempt on Herod the Great fails.
4 BC	Matthias and Judas lead the Golden Eagle Temple Cleansing.
4 BC	Herod burns Matthias but imprisons Judas.
4 BC	Herod the Great dies.
4 BC	Judas is released by Archelaus to the Jewish crowd.
4-2 BC	Judas is proclaimed Messiah in Galilee.
6 AD	John the Baptist preaches the philosophy of Judas the Galilean.
6 AD	Judas the Galilean leads a tax revolt against Rome—the census.
7–15 AD	Annas is named High Priest and is opposed to Judas.
18 AD	Caiaphas is named High Priest.
18–37 AD	Pilate becomes procurator of Judea.
19 AD	Judas/Jesus is crucified under Pilate.
19 AD	An unnamed Jew swindles Jewish converts in Rome—Saul?
22–25 AD	Saul converts and is renamed Paul.
25–28 AD	Paul visits Jerusalem to meet Cephas and James.
6–36 AD	John the Baptist preaches repentance—for the return of Jesus.
36 AD	John is executed by Herod, long after the death of Jesus.
39–42 AD	Paul returns to Jerusalem 14 years later—Council of Jerusalem.
42–44 AD	Paul is removed from fellowship at Antioch.
44–48 AD	The famine grips Israel.
44–48 AD	Paul collects money from his churches.
44–48 AD	Paul returns with money to Jerusalem—shares it with Herodians.
44–48 AD	Paul attacks James and almost kills him.
46–48 AD	The sons of Judas the Galilean are caught and crucified.
50 AD	Jewish Christians in Rome are causing disturbances.

62 AD	James, the brother of Jesus, is stoned.
62–64 AD	Saul persecutes the poor—Jewish Christians.
64 AD	The Great Fire of Rome burns. Nero persecutes the Christians.
66 AD	Menahem, the son of Judas, enters Jerusalem as Messiah.
66 AD	Saul tries to persuade Agrippa to send an army to Jerusalem.
66–67 AD	Saul meets with Nero to lay blame for the war on Florus.
70 AD	Titus destroys the Temple and Jerusalem.
73 AD	The Sicarii, led by the grandson of Judas, commit mass suicide.

The above timeline has none of the problems associated with the traditional timeline. Every event makes sense and is supported by Josephus and Paul's letters to the Romans, Corinthians and Galatians.

BIBLIOGRAPHY

Barclay, William. *The Daily Study Bible.* Philadelphia: The Westminster Press, 1978.

Bettenson, Henry. *Documents of the Christian Church.* New York: Oxford University Press, 1979.

Brandon, S.G.F.. *The Trial of Jesus of Nazareth.* New York: Dorset Press, 1968.

Crossan, John Dominic and Reed, Jonathan L.. *Excavating Jesus.* San Francisco: Harper San Francisco, 2001.

Ehrman, Bart D.. *Lost Scriptures.* New York: Oxford University Press, 2003.

Eisenman, Robert. *James the Brother of Jesus.* New York: Penguin Books, 1997.

Eusebius. *The History of the Church.* Translated by G.A. Williamson. United States: Dorset Press, 1984.

Grant, Michael. *The History of Ancient Israel.* New York: Charles Scribner's Sons, 1984.

Leeming, H. and Leeming, K. *Josephus' Jewish War and its Slavonic Version.* Leiden: Brill, 2003.

Maccoby, Hyam. *Revolution in Judaea.* New York: Taplinger Publishing Company, 1980.

Maccoby, Hyam. *The Mythmaker.* New York: Harper and Row Publishers, 1986.

Robertson, J.M.. *Pagan Christs.* New York: Dorset Press, 1987.

sacred-texts.com. Slavonic Josephus.

Suetonius. *The Twelve Caesars.* London: Penguin Books, 1979. Translated by Robert Graves; Revised by Michael Grant.

Tacitus. *The Annals and The Histories.* Chicago: Encyclopedia Britannica, Inc., 1952. Translated by Alfred John Church and William Jackson Brodribb.

Unterbrink, Daniel. *Judas the Galilean—the Flesh and Blood Jesus.* New York: iUniverse, Inc., 2004.

Whiston, William. *The Works of Josephus.* Mass.: Hendrickson Publishers, 1984.

Williamson, G.A.. *Josephus The Jewish War.* New York: Penguin Books, 1981.

NOTES

INTRODUCTION

1. Hershel Shanks and Ben Witherington III, *The Brother of Jesus*, pg. 40.

CHAPTER ONE

1. Alvar Ellegard, *Jesus One Hundred Years Before Christ*, pg. 82.

2. J. Bruce Burke and James B. Wiggins, *Foundations of Christianity—From the Beginnings to 1650*, pgs. 13-19.

3. S.G.F. Brandon, *The Trial of Jesus of Nazareth*, pg. 31.

4. *Ibid.*, pg. 32.

5. *Ibid.*, pg. 32.

6. Suetonius, *The Twelve Caesars*, Claudius 25.

CHAPTER TWO

1. Daniel T. Unterbrink, *Judas the Galilean—The Flesh and Blood Jesus*, pg. 7.

2. Slavonic Josephus, After *War* 1.650.

3. John Dominic Crossan and Jonathan L. Reed, *Excavating Jesus*, pg. 18.

4. Hyam Maccoby, *Revolution in Judaea*, pg. 19 and pg. 222 (note 3).

5. G.A. Williamson and E. Mary Smallwood, *The Jewish War*, Appendix A, pg. 461.

6. John Dominic Crossan and Jonathan L. Reed, *Excavating Jesus*, pg. 174.

7. Slavonic Josephus, After *War* 2.110.

8. Slavonic Josephus, After *War* 1.400.

9. Robert Eisenman, *James, the Brother of Jesus*, pg 252.

10. Slavonic Josephus, After *War* 1.650.

CHAPTER THREE

1. Tacitus, *The Annals*, ii.85.

2. Suetonius, *The Twelve Caesars*, Tiberius 36.

CHAPTER FOUR

1. William Barclay, *The Daily Study Bible*, Luke pg. 20.

2. Slavonic Josephus, After *War* 1.400.

3. darkstar1.com

4. Robert Eisenman, *James, the Brother of Jesus*, pg. 254.

5. Slavonic Josephus, *War* 6.313.

6. Suetonius, *The Twelve Caesars*, Augustus 94.

7. Slavonic Josephus, After *War* 2.110.

CHAPTER FIVE

1. William Barclay, *The Daily Study Bible*, Mark pg. 16.

2. Slavonic Josephus, after *War* 2.110.

3. Pseudoclementine *Recognitions*, 1.53,54.

4. Slavonic Josephus, after *War* 2.168.

5. *Ibid.*, after *War* 2.168

6. Pseudoclementine *Recognitions*, 1.54.

CHAPTER SIX

1. Slavonic Josephus, After *War* 1.650.

2. John Dominic Crossan and Jonathan L. Reed, *Excavating Jesus*, pg. 200.

CHAPTER SEVEN

1. Hyam Maccoby, *Revolution in Judaea*, pg. 160.

2. *Ibid.*, pg. 160.

3. *Ibid.*, pgs. 164-165.

4. Slavonic Josephus, After *War* 2.174.

CHAPTER EIGHT

1. Daniel T. Unterbrink, *Judas the Galilean*, pgs. 186-187 and Appendix 4, pgs. 219-228.

2. Slavonic Josephus, follows on *War* 2.9.3.

3. Hyam Maccoby, *Revolution in Judaea*, pgs. 143,144.

CHAPTER TEN

1. Slavonic Josephus, follows on *War* 2.222.

CHAPTER TWELVE

1. Robert Eisenman, *James, the Brother of Jesus*, pg. 452.

CHAPTER FOURTEEN

1. Daniel T. Unterbrink, *Judas the Galilean*, pgs. 56-64.

2. William Barclay, *The Daily Study Bible*, Acts pg. 188.

3. Daniel T. Unterbrink, *Judas the Galilean*, Appendix 4, pgs. 219-228.

CHAPTER FIFTEEN

1. *Community Rule* 8.1-4.

2. Slavonic Josephus, after *War* 1.650.

3. *Eusebius*, Tiberius to Nero, Book 2.23.4.

4. *Ibid.*, Book 2.1.3.

5. Robert Eisenman, *James, the Brother of Jesus*, pg.17.

6. *Ibid.*, pg.133.

7. *Ibid.*, pg.135.

8. *Ibid.*, pg.135.

9. Ysmena Pentelow, *Abstract: The Teacher of Righteousness*, from mystae.com.

10. Robert Eisenman, *James, the Brother of Jesus*, pg. 320.

11. Slavonic Josephus, after *War* 1.400.

CHAPTER SIXTEEN

1. Michael Grant, *The History of Ancient Israel*, pg. 210.

2. *Ibid.*, pg. 216.

3. *Ibid.*, pg. 216.

4. *Ibid.*, pg. 218.

978-0-595-39855-3
0-595-39855-3

Printed in the United Kingdom
by Lightning Source UK Ltd.
113076UKS00001B/47